Researching Private Supplementary Tutoring
Methodological Lessons from Diverse Cultures

CERC Studies in Comparative Education

32. Mark Bray, Ora Kwo & Boris Jokić (eds.) (2015): *Research Private Supplementary Tutoring: Methodological Lessons from Diverse Cultures.* ISBN 978-988-14241-3-6. 292pp. HK$250/US$38.

31. Bob Adamson, Jon Nixon, Feng Su (eds.) (2012): *The Reorientation of Higher Education: Challenging the East-West Dichotomy.* ISBN 978-988-1785-27-5. 314pp. HK$250/US$38.

30. Ruth Hayhoe, Jun Li, Jing Lin, Qiang Zha (2011): *Portraits of 21st Century Chinese Universities: In the Move to Mass Higher Education.* ISBN 978-988-1785-23-7. 486pp. HK$300/US$45.

29. Maria Manzon (2011): *Comparative Education: The Construction of a Field.* ISBN 978-988-17852-6-8. 295pp. HK$200/US$32.

28. Kerry J. Kennedy, Wing On Lee & David L. Grossman (eds.) (2010): *Citizenship Pedagogies in Asia and the Pacific.* ISBN 978-988-17852-2-0. 407pp. HK$250/US$38.

27. David Chapman, William K. Cummings & Gerard A. Postiglione (eds.) (2010): *Crossing Borders in East Asian Higher Education.* ISBN 978-962-8093-98-4. 388pp. HK$250/US$38.

26. Ora Kwo (ed.) (2010): *Teachers as Learners: Critical Discourse on Challenges and Opportunities.* ISBN 978-962-8093-55-7. 349pp. HK$250/US$38.

25. Carol K.K. Chan & Nirmala Rao (eds.) (2009): *Revisiting the Chinese Learner: Changing Contexts, Changing Education.* ISBN 978-962-8093-16-8. 360pp. HK$250/US$38.

24. Donald B. Holsinger & W. James Jacob (eds.) (2008): *Inequality in Education: Comparative and International Perspectives.* ISBN 978-962-8093-14-4. 584pp. HK$300/US$45.

23. Nancy Law, Willem J Pelgrum & Tjeerd Plomp (eds.) (2008): *Pedagogy and ICT Use in Schools around the World: Findings from the IEA SITES 2006 Study.* ISBN 978-962-8093-65-6. 296pp. HK$250/US$38.

22. David L. Grossman, Wing On Lee & Kerry J. Kennedy (eds.) (2008): *Citizenship Curriculum in Asia and the Pacific.* ISBN 978-962-8093-69-4. 268pp. HK$200/US$32.

21. Vandra Masemann, Mark Bray & Maria Manzon (eds.) (2007): *Common Interests, Uncommon Goals: Histories of the World Council of Comparative Education Societies and its Members.* ISBN 978-962- 8093-10-6. 384pp. HK$250/US$38.

20. Peter D. Hershock, Mark Mason & John N. Hawkins (eds.) (2007): *Changing Education: Leadership, Innovation and Development in a Globalizing Asia Pacific.* ISBN 978-962-8093-54-0. 348pp. HK$200/US$32.

19. Mark Bray, Bob Adamson & Mark Mason (eds.) (2014): *Comparative Education Research: Approaches and Methods. Second edition.* ISBN 978-988-17852-8-2. 453pp. HK$250/US$38.

18. Aaron Benavot & Cecilia Braslavsky (eds.) (2006): *School Knowledge in Comparative and Historical Perspective: Changing Curricula in Primary and Secondary Education.* ISBN 978-962-8093-52-6. 315pp. HK$200/US$32.

17. Ruth Hayhoe (2006): *Portraits of Influential Chinese Educators.* ISBN 978-962-8093-40-3. 398pp. HK$250/US$38.

16. Peter Ninnes & Meeri Hellstén (eds.) (2005): *Internationalizing Higher Education: Critical Explorations of Pedagogy and Policy.* ISBN 978-962-8093-37-3. 231pp. HK$200/US$32.

15. Alan Rogers (2004): *Non-formal Education: Flexible Schooling or Participatory Education?.* ISBN 978-962-8093-30-4. 306pp. HK$200/US$32.

14. W.O. Lee, David L. Grossman, Kerry J. Kennedy & Gregory P. Fairbrother (eds.) (2004): *Citizenship Education in Asia and the Pacific: Concepts and Issues.* ISBN 978-962-8093-59-5. 313pp. HK$200/US$32.

Earlier titles in the series are listed at the back of the book.

CERC Studies in Comparative Education 32

Researching Private Supplementary Tutoring
Methodological Lessons from Diverse Cultures

Edited by

Mark Bray, Ora Kwo & Boris Jokić

Springer

Comparative Education Research Centre
The University of Hong Kong

SERIES EDITOR
Mark Bray
Director, Comparative Education Research Centre
The University of Hong Kong, China

ASSOCIATE EDITOR
Yang Rui
Comparative Education Research Centre
The University of Hong Kong, China

INTERNATIONAL EDITORIAL ADVISORY BOARD
Robert Arnove, *Indiana University, Bloomington, USA*
Michael Crossley, *University of Bristol, United Kingdom*
Jiang Kai, *Peking University, Beijing, China*
Cristian Pérez Centeno, *Universidad Nacional de Tres de Febrero, Buenos Aires, Argentina*
Gita Steiner-Khamsi, *Teachers College, Columbia University, New York, USA*

Comparative Education Research Centre
Faculty of Education, The University of Hong Kong,
Pokfulam Road, Hong Kong, China

Copyright © Comparative Education Research Centre.
First published 2015
ISBN 978-988-14241-3-6 Paperback

All rights reserved. No part of this publication may be reproduced, stored in a retrieval system or transmitted in any form or by any means, electronic, mechanical, photo-copying, recording or otherwise, without the written permission of the publisher.

Cover: Basque house, French Pyrenees. Painting by Josette Dacosta https://josettedacosta.wordpress.com, and chosen as the cover for this book because it shows an interpretation in construction. Even when researchers claim to find objective 'truth', they are in fact securing only representations of reality according to the ways they approach the object of inquiry, just as artists paint pictures according to their vision and interpretation.

Cover design and layout: Gutsage
Layout: Emily Mang

Printed and bound by The Central Printing Press Ltd. in Hong Kong, China

Contents

Abbreviations and Acronyms	vii
List of Tables	ix
List of Figures	x
List of Boxes	x

Introduction   3
    Mark BRAY, Ora KWO & Boris JOKIĆ

Employing Quantitative Instruments
1. Shadow Education Research through TIMSS and PIRLS: Experiences and Lessons in the Republic of Georgia   23
   Magda Nutsa KOBAKHIDZE

2. Research on Private Tutoring in Malaysia: Methodological Insights from a Quantitative Study   49
   Husaina Banu KENAYATHULLA

3. Relationships between Shadow Education and Examination Scores: Methodological Lessons from a Chinese Study in Senior Secondary Schools   59
   Yu ZHANG

Discerning Qualities
4. A Qualitative Comparison of Private Tutoring in Azerbaijan, Bosnia & Herzegovina, Croatia, Estonia and Georgia: Lessons from Design and Implementation   77
   Boris JOKIĆ

5. Ethical Dilemmas in Shadow Education Research: Lessons from a Qualitative Study of Learners' Experiences in Lecture-type Tutoring in Hong Kong   97
   Kevin W.H. YUNG

6	Classroom Practices and Private Tuition in the Maldives: Methodological Reflections on an Ethnographic Study *Maryam MARIYA*	117
7	Researching Shadow Education in Iran: Methodological Experiences in an Islamic Republic *Abbas MADANDAR ARANI*	133

Expanding Perspectives with Mixed Approaches

8	Designing and Implementing Mixed Approaches to Shadow Education Research: Experiences and Lessons in Hong Kong *Mark BRAY & Ora KWO*	149
9	Constraints and Possibilities in Small-Scale Research: A Mixed-Methods Study in West Bengal, India *Sulata MAHESHWARI*	179
10	A Mixed-Methods Study of Extra Lessons in Jamaica: Methodological Experiences and Reflections *Saran STEWART*	201
11	Researching Private Supplementary Tutoring in Cambodia: Contexts, Instruments and Approaches *Mark BRAY, Wei ZHANG, Magda Nutsa KOBAKHIDZE & Junyan LIU*	219

Learning and Comparing

12	How a Research Instrument Changed in Different Settings: Methodological Lessons from Adaptation and Adjustment *Junyan LIU*	247
13	Organisational and Cross-Cultural Issues: Learning from Research Approaches *Mark BRAY & Ora KWO*	261

Notes on the Authors	289

Abbreviations and Acronyms

ASEAN	Association of Southeast Asian Nations
ATE	Average Treatment Effect
ATNT	Average treatment effect on the non-treated
ATT	Average treatment effect on the treated
BEd	Bachelor of Education
CERC	Comparative Education Research Centre
CRCP	Community Research and Consultancy Program
CXC	Caribbean Examinations Council
DPC	Data Processing Center
DSE	Diploma of Secondary Education
EPRD	Educational Planning and Research Division
ESF	English Schools Foundation
FG	Focus Group
GDP	Gross Domestic Product
GEL	Georgian Lari [currency]
HKU	The University of Hong Kong
HLM	Hierarchical Linear Modelling
HRECNCF	Human Research Ethics Committee for Non-Clinical Faculties
HSSP	Humanities and Social Sciences Panel
IDP	Internally Displaced Person
IDRC	International Development Research Centre
IEA	International Association for the Evaluation of Educational Achievement
IIEP	International Institute for Educational Planning
IGO	Inter-Governmental Organisation
IRB	Institutional Review Board
IRT	Item Response Theory
IV	Instrumental Variable
JSLC	Jamaica Survey on Living Conditions
KOSIS	Korean Statistical Information Service
LATE	Local Average Treatment Effect
MA	Master of Arts

MoES	Ministry of Education and Science [Georgia]
MoEYS	Ministry of Education, Youth and Sport [Cambodia]
NAEC	National Examinations and Assessment Center
NCEE	National College Entrance Examination
NEP	NGO Education Partnership
NGO	Non-Governmental Organisation
NRC	National Research Coordinator
OECD	Organisation for Economic Co-operation and Development
OLS	Ordinary Least Squares
OSI	Open Society Institute
PERI	Privatization of Education Research Initiative
PhD	Doctor of Philosophy
PIRLS	Progress in International Reading Literacy Study
PISA	Programme for International Student Assessment
PSM	Propensity Score Matching
PT3	Pentaksiran Tingkatan 3
QIRT	Questionnaire Item Review Committee
RGC	Research Grants Council
SES	Socioeconomic Status
SIG	Special Interest Group
SPM	Sijil Pelajaran Malaysia
SPSS	Statistical Package for the Social Sciences
STPM	Sijil Tinggi Persekolahan Malaysia
TALIS	Teaching and Learning International Survey
TEDS-M	Teacher Education and Development Study in Mathematics
TIMSS	Trends in International Mathematics and Science Study
TLC	This Life Cambodia
TOEFL	Test of English as a Foreign Language
UPSR	Ujian Pencapaian Sekolah Rendah
UNESCO	United Nations Educational, Scientific and Cultural Organization
UNICEF	United Nations Children's Fund
UK	United Kingdom
US	United States
USA	United States of America

List of Tables

0.1	The Scale of Private Supplementary Tutoring in Selected Countries	8
1.1	Population and Sample Sizes for Georgia TIMSS and PIRLS 2011	29
1.2	Background Questionnaires and Number of Shadow Education Questions in TIMSS & PIRLS 2011, Georgia	32
1.3	Scale of Tutoring in Grades 4 and 8, Georgia	34
1.4	Paid versus Free Tutoring in Grades 4 and 8, Georgia	35
1.5	Popularity of Subjects for Tutoring, Georgia	36
1.6	Intensity of Shadow Education Classes per Week, Georgia	37
1.7	Duration of all Shadow Education Classes per Week, Georgia	37
2.1	Instructions for Distributing the Questionnaires	54
3.1	Instruments Used in the Models for this Study	65
3.2	Class Size of Private Tutoring	69
3.3	Agency Type of Private Tutoring	69
3.4	Effects of Private Tutoring Participation on NCEE Achievements	70
4.1	Interviews and Focus Groups, by Country	87
4.2	Themes, Aims and Suggested Approaches for Interviews	89
8.1	Final Sample of Schools, Students and Teachers in the Hong Kong Study	156
9.1	Distribution of Students with Usable Survey Data, West Bengal	182
9.2	Distribution of Interview Sample, West Bengal	183
9.3	Demographic Profile of Sampled Schools, West Bengal	184
9.4	Administrative/Curricular Profile of Sampled Schools, West Bengal	184
9.5	Percentages of Students Enrolled in Private Tutoring by School	192
9.6	Percentages of Students Receiving Tutoring by Subject	193
9.7	Students' Indications of the Reasons for Receiving Private Tutoring	193
9.8	Proportions of Students Receiving 'All Subjects' Tutoring	196
10.1	Rationale for Selecting Mixed Methods Design	204
10.2	Construct Areas for the Student Questionnaire	205

10.3	Sample of Student and School Populations in Each Region	208
10.4	School Sample in Terms of Gender and Location	208
11.1	Characteristics of Sampled Schools, Siem Reap Province, Cambodia	224
11.2	Sample of Students and Teachers, Siem Reap Province, Cambodia	224
11.3	Providers of Private Tutoring	233
12.1	Summary of Versions Derived from the Hong Kong Questionnaire	249
13.1	Ethical Approval and Consent Requirements from Participants	278

List of Figures

3.1	Relationships between Components in Education Production	61
3.2	The Venn Diagram of IV Estimation	66
3.3	Common Support Check for PSM	71
3.4	Balance Check for PSM	72
4.1	Coding Scheme for the Level 2 Code 'Users and Providers'	91
6.1	Approval Route for the Study of Private Tuition in the Maldives	121
9.1	School Buildings, West Bengal	199
12.1	A Routing Layout in the Hong Kong Questionnaire	256

List of Boxes

9.1	Ineffective Teaching and Learning at School	194
9.2	"Education is the only weapon with which everything can be done"	197
11.1	Flowchart of the Two-phase Project	231
11.2	An Interactive Model of Data Analysis Components	232

Introduction

Introduction

Mark BRAY, Ora KWO & Boris JOKIĆ

Recent years, particularly since the turn of the present century, have brought substantial global growth of private supplementary tutoring. Young people receive such tutoring in parallel to schooling before or after the regular school day, at weekends, on public holidays, and during school vacations. The tutoring demands considerable household resources, consumes the time of the students and their families, provides incomes and jobs for tutors, and shapes dimensions of learning not just for the individuals but also for whole societies.

Research on private supplementary tutoring has lagged behind the expansion and diversification of the phenomenon. The volume and sophistication of the research is improving, but many gaps remain. To support future research, this book focuses on methodology. To some extent the methods for researching private supplementary tutoring resemble those for researching other domains of education and even social sciences more broadly. Nevertheless, researching out-of-school education is in some ways different from researching in-school education, in part because the former is less structured.

The title of this book refers to lessons from diverse cultures. Cultures are here conceived in two major ways. First within the tradition of comparative education, which is a strong thrust of the book, are the variations of cultures that may be found within and across national boundaries. Mason (2014, pp.225-235) highlighted challenges in definition, but followed Hall (1994, p.292) with the description of culture as "a way of

---

Bray, Mark; Kwo, Ora & Jokić, Boris (eds.) (2015): *Researching Private Supplementary Tutoring: Methodological Lessons from Diverse Cultures*. Hong Kong: Comparative Education Research Centre (CERC), The University of Hong Kong, and Dordrecht: Springer. © CERC

constructing meanings which influences and organizes both our actions and our conception of ourselves". This book has chapters on private supplementary tutoring in countries as different as China, Iran and Jamaica, each of which may be said to have distinctive cultures that shape attitudes to schooling and to supplementary tutoring. Within these countries are sub-cultures allied to race, ethnicity, social class and many other factors.

The word culture is also used in a different sense. The book is about research methodology, and the chapters display diversity in the cultures of research approaches. Most obvious are the cultures of quantitative research contrasted with the cultures of qualitative research and, in some chapters, mixed methods. Many textbooks (e.g. Johnson & Christensen 2012; Creswell 2014) highlight the ontological and paradigmatic implications of different approaches, stressing that the nature of the research methods shapes the nature of the findings.

Because private supplementary tutoring is complex and multifaceted, this Introduction commences with vocabularies and parameters. It then sketches the scale of the phenomenon around the world to underline its importance as a focus for research. These remarks set the stage for an outline of a research agenda and the contents of this book.

Vocabularies and Parameters

The vocabularies used to describe private tutoring vary, even in the English language. Thus it is common for example in Bangladesh, India and Sri Lanka to refer to private tuition rather than private tutoring. Coaching is also common vocabulary in these countries. In the Anglophone Caribbean, a common term is extra lessons; in Ireland supplementary tutoring is called grinds; in the USA the common term is supplemental education; and in The Gambia it is studies. Other languages bring their own nuances. In French, for example, *soutien scolaire* would usually be translated as school support; and in Greek *parapedia* literally means parallel education.

A further common term, used in several chapters of this book, is shadow education. This vocabulary is used because much supplementary tutoring mimics the curriculum of regular schooling – as the content of the curriculum changes in regular schooling, so it changes in the shadow; and as the regular school system expands or contracts, so does the shadow system (Stevenson & Baker 1992; Bray 1999, 2009). Like many metaphors, however, the metaphor of the shadow is imperfect. Private supplementary tutoring is not always a precise mimic, and students may study content in the supplementary sector before rather than after their classes in regular schooling. Moreover, as noted by Paviot (2015, pp.168-169), private tutoring appears "to have evolved in such a way that we can no longer consider it a 'parallel' form of practice but instead as a crucial element in most pupils' daily school life".

Private supplementary tutoring may take many different forms. In some societies the most common is one-to-one or small-group tutoring, but in other societies large classes are widespread. In Hong Kong, for example, major tutoring companies offer classes in lecture theatres with overflow rooms served by video links (Kwo & Bray 2011; Yung 2011; Koh 2014). These companies also offer pre-recorded lessons, which are shown in classrooms or viewed on computers on the company premises. These types of lessons require physical space, but tutoring can also be offered in virtual space. The internet provides an expanding array of offerings both in recorded form and in real time with tutors and students who may be located in different countries. The chapters that follow are more concerned with live face-to-face provision than with recordings and internet use, but these other forms are of growing significance and should certainly be part of research agendas.

Concerning the content of private supplementary tutoring, the chief focus of this book is on academic subjects such as languages, mathematics and sciences. Families commonly invest in such tutoring either for remedial purposes, i.e. helping their children to keep up with peers, or for enrichment, i.e. helping their children to excel and keep ahead of their peers. Tutoring in academic subjects is especially important in education systems dominated by high-stakes examinations (Dawson 2010; Bray & Lykins 2012; Jokić 2013). These examinations are particularly prominent at the end of secondary schooling, but some education systems also have high-stakes examinations at the end of primary schooling. In addition, school-level examinations are commonly used to classify students within institutions.

Tutoring may also be provided in other domains including music, dance, religious studies, etc.. Families may invest in such tutoring in order to promote more rounded development and/or to develop social capital for advancement. Chua's (2011) book about 'tiger mothers' in the USA (and elsewhere) presented an extreme example of this phenomenon. On a related note, Aurini and Davies (2013, p.162) highlighted the proliferation in parts of Canada of 'learning centres' that promise to develop children's general learning capacities and enhance self-esteem. Such enterprises are related to the focus of this book, but are not at its core.

In terms of levels, the book is mainly about primary and secondary education. Private supplementary tutoring certainly exists at pre-primary and post-secondary levels (see e.g. Khuwaileh & Al-Shoumali 2001; Ong 2012; Suleiman 2012), but has rather different dynamics. At the pre-primary level, tutoring commonly has a child-minding function in addition to rounded development and a desire to secure a place in a good primary school. The child-minding function is also relevant at primary school, but reduces in importance at secondary level and has ceased to exist by the post-secondary stage. Tutoring in post-secondary education is more focused on helping learners to pass examinations set by the institutions, though may also of course have an extra-curricular dimension. The nature and implications of private supplementary tutoring at pre-primary and post-secondary levels certainly deserve more research attention; but meanwhile the focus of this book on primary and secondary schooling is already a large topic.

The Scale of Private Supplementary Tutoring

Private supplementary tutoring is not a new phenomenon. Indeed it has probably existed for as long as schooling has existed, albeit until recent times in small amounts and mostly confined to prosperous social strata.

To highlight the longstanding existence of private supplementary tutoring, remarks in the literature may be noted in settings as different as Mauritius, Greece and Ceylon (present-day Sri Lanka) during the first half of the 20th century.

- *Mauritius*. Foondun (2002, p.488) quoted a 1901 statement by a school principal who identified negative dimensions of tutoring but "felt helpless" to prevent it. A decade later the head of Mauritius' Royal College (quoted in Mauritius 1994, pp.1-2) complained that 12 of his staff were giving 13 to 33 hours of private tutoring per week but did not see how he could stop them. Again, this principal focused on negative dimensions though presumably others – such as the teachers who gained extra incomes and the students who gained extra knowledge – saw the situation more positively.

- *Greece*. Kassotakis and Verdis (2013, p.94) highlighted two forces underlying the expansion of shadow education during the first half of the 20th century. The first was pressure on limited places in higher education which promoted demand for shadow education to assist students to compete with their peers. The second force was political. With the ascendancy of a right-wing government, teachers with left-wing sympathies were prevented from working in schools. Some of them provided tutoring as an alternative way to make a living (see also Tsiloglu 2005). Many of these teachers were talented and committed, so presumably their students benefitted from the tutoring.
- *Ceylon*. In 1943, a Special Committee on Education commented on the coaching centres that operated alongside schools. The report (quoted by Suraweera 2011, p.9) lamented "the practice too frequently adopted by many parents of supplementing the school work by private coaching", arguing that the coaching focused on rote learning and ultimately destroyed its objective "by making the student incapable of originality and initiative". This perspective, like the views recorded in Mauritius, was negative towards tutoring.

Yet although tutoring in these countries was highlighted, the scale was modest during the first half of the 20th century compared to what it subsequently became (Foondun 2002; Hagitegas 2008; Suraweera 2011; Pallegedara 2012; Kassotakis & Verdis 2013).

Moreover, expansion in these countries was paralleled by expansion in most other parts of the world. Table 0.1 presents snapshots of the scale of private supplementary tutoring in countries of diverse income levels, cultures and locations. The tutoring had greater magnitudes in some countries than others, but in all cases it had become a significant phenomenon.

Table 0.1 lists countries in alphabetical order, but a clearer picture may emerge from consideration of regional patterns.

- *Africa* has growing incidence of private tutoring across the continent. In addition to the countries mentioned in Table 0.1, the incidence is exemplified by reports in Benin (Napporn & Baba-Moussa 2013), Nigeria (Oyewusi & Orelade 2014), and Rwanda (Williams et al. 2015). Much of the tutoring is provided by teachers seeking extra incomes rather than by commercial companies.

Table 0.1: The Scale of Private Supplementary Tutoring in Selected Countries

Country	Scale
Australia	Dillon (2011) reported that parents were spending up to Aus$6 billion a year on private tutoring, with the industry having grown by almost 40% over the previous five years.
Brazil	Surveying 423 secondary school students in three municipalities, Mariuci et al. (2012, p.68) found that 27.7% were receiving private tutoring.
Canada	Aurini and Davies (2013, p.157) reported that 21% of nine-year-old children had received some kind of private tutoring. Eckler (2015) described tutoring as the "new normal".
Egypt	An official study noted by Sobhy (2012, p.49) indicated that 81% of households had children who received private tutoring at the secondary stage, and that the proportion was 50% at the primary stage.
England & Wales	A 2014 survey of 2,700 young people asked whether they had ever received private or home tutoring. In London, 37% of respondents replied affirmatively, and 20% in the rest of the country did so (Sutton Trust 2014, p.2).
Ghana	A 2008 survey of 1,020 households found that 48% were paying additional fees for tutoring in primary education (Antonowicz et al. 2010, p.21).
India	A nationwide rural survey showed rates of private tutoring received by children aged 6-14 ranging from 2.8% in Chhattisgarh to 73.9% in West Bengal (Pratham 2014, p.73).
Japan	A 2007 survey found that tutoring institutions (*juku*) served 16% of Grade 1 children, that this proportion rose steadily in later grades, and that it reached 65% in Grade 9. In addition, 7% of Grade 9 pupils received tutoring at home, and 15% followed correspondence courses (Japan 2008, p.13).
Kazakhstan	Kalikova and Rakhimzhanova (2009) asked 1,004 first year university students about their experiences in the last year of secondary schooling. They found that 59.9% of students had received tutoring (private lessons, preparatory courses, or both).
Kenya	A 2007 representative sample of 4,436 Grade 6 pupils indicated that 44.3% were receiving paid tutoring (Paviot 2015, p.111).
Korea, Republic of	In 2014, 81.1% of elementary school pupils were estimated to be receiving tutoring. In middle school the proportion was 69.1%; and in general high school it was 56.2% (KOSIS 2015).
Malta	Statistics cited by Buhagiar and Chetcuti (2013, p.136) indicated a range between 37.6% and 51.9% at primary level, and up to 82.9% in secondary.
Pakistan	A 2013 survey found that in 13 urban centres, 44.8% of Grade 1 students in private schools received private supplementary tutoring, with the proportion rising to 49.7% in Grade 10. In government schools, respective proportions were 19.5% and 31.1% (ASER-Pakistan 2014, pp.68, 77).
Poland	Data from a 2006 national sample of students aged 15 indicated that 19% were receiving individual or small group tutoring, 25% were receiving supplementary courses in mathematics, and 20% were receiving supplementary courses in humanities (Safarzyńska 2013, p.144)
Trinidad & Tobago	A sample of 801 children in primary schools found that 5.7% in Standard 1 received tutoring. Proportions rose in subsequent grades to 7.4%, 25.4%, 68.4% and then 88.2% in Standard 5 (Barrow & Lochan 2012, p.411).

- Among the *Arab States*, Egypt has long had high rates of tutoring (Abd-al-Aaty 1994; Hartmann 2013). Other countries with significant rates include Jordan (Al Farra 2009; Ali 2013), and United Arab Emirates (Farah 2011; Naismith 2014). Again, much tutoring has been provided by teachers, especially in Egypt.
- *Asia* may be divided into several sub-categories.
  - Shadow education has long been a major phenomenon in parts of East Asia, including Japan, the Republic of Korea and Taiwan (Rohlen 1980; Tseng 1998; Dawson 2010; Lee et al. 2010; Sato 2012), and now China is catching up (Xue & Ding 2008; Zhang 2014). These are relatively high-income countries, and most tutoring is provided by the commercial sector rather than by teachers.
  - South Asia has also long had much tutoring. This is exemplified by Sri Lanka, as noted above (see also Hemachandra 1982; de Silva 1994), and by Bangladesh (Barman 1964). In contemporary times, tutoring is also evident in India and Pakistan (Sujatha & Rani 2011; Aslam & Atherton 2014). Much tutoring is provided by teachers, but coaching centres also operate.
  - Central and Northern Asia had almost no tutoring during the Soviet era, but it emerged in the period following the collapse of the Soviet Union as these countries shifted to a market economy (Silova 2009, 2010; Kozar 2013; Kobakhidze 2014).
- *Europe* also has diversity.
  - In Southern Europe, including Malta, Cyprus and Greece, supplementary tutoring has been accepted for several decades as a normal fact of family life, especially for students at the secondary level (Falzon & Busuttil 1988; Lamprianou & Afantiti Lamprianou 2013; Kassotakis & Verdis 2013).
  - Eastern Europe had limited private tutoring before the political and economic transitions of the late 1980s and early 1990s but, as in Central and Northern Asia, has witnessed great expansion of shadow education since that period. When the purchasing power of teachers' salaries collapsed as part of the economic restructuring, many teachers turned to tutoring as a way to secure supplementary incomes. The practice of students receiving tutoring, and of teachers providing it, has remained widespread even in countries where teachers' salaries subsequently improved (see e.g. Jokić & Ristić Dedić 2007; Kirss 2011).

- Western Europe has also had long traditions of private tutoring on a small scale. Since the turn of the century the scale of tutoring has greatly increased (see e.g. Oller & Glasman 2013; Ireson & Rushforth 2014). Trends are shaped by increasing competitiveness of societies in the context of greater mobility of labour and skills, and are part of the marketisation of education that has become more socially acceptable.
  - Northern Europe is least affected by the rise of private tutoring. Scandinavia seems to maintain stronger traditions of schools adequately meeting their students' needs. Certainly students in Scandinavia receive extra lessons, both to help slow learners keep up with their peers and to stretch the learning of high achievers; but much of this work is provided within the framework of public schooling rather than through a parallel system (Bray 2011; Sahlberg 2011; OECD 2011).
- *Australia, Canada and the USA* can in some respects be treated as a group. Private supplementary tutoring has not reached the scale of Asia and Southern Europe, but has become increasingly visible (Buchmann et al. 2010; Aurini & Davies 2013; Davis 2013; Mori 2013).
- *Latin America* also has less private tutoring, but such countries as Argentina (Cámara et al. 2014) and Brazil (Mattos 2007; Mariuci et al. 2012; de Castro 2013) are showing significant signs of the phenomenon. Thus it appears to be growing in Latin America as well as in other world regions.

Underlying the geography in the above patterns are various cultural and economic factors which may be depicted with broad brush strokes. Among examples of cultural factors are the Confucian values of East Asia which emphasise diligence and effort (Salili 2005) and which may also be found among Chinese and Korean diaspora in such places as the USA (Zhou & Kim 2008; Chua 2011) and Australia (Sriprakash et al. 2015). Broader forces include cultures of competition which are fuelled by globalisation as families become increasingly aware that in the labour market they are competing not just with similar families in their immediate neighbourhoods but with millions of others across national boundaries. In turn this makes a link to economics. Families see investment in education as a way to get ahead, and this perspective shapes the actions of poor and middle-income families as well as rich ones.

The Research Agenda and the Contents of this Book

The considerable – and growing – scale of tutoring has many implications that require documentation and consideration. Data are uncertain even on basic descriptive matters. Thus Table 0.1 presents a collection of studies which do not have standardised criteria. Extensive descriptive data are available on schooling, commonly presented in tables on a cross-national basis (e.g. OECD 2014; UNESCO 2015). Comparable data are not available on private supplementary tutoring, in part because of challenges in defining the phenomenon and then securing data in a consistent format across national boundaries. Such challenges have been noted, for example, in the Programme for International Student Assessment (PISA) operated under the auspices of the Organisation for Economic Co-operation and Development (OECD) and the Trends in International Mathematics and Science Study (TIMSS) operated under the auspices of the International Association for the Evaluation of Educational Achievement (IEA) (Bray & Kobakhidze 2014).

Beyond basic description, the range of research topics for shadow education resembles that for regular schooling. Much research is needed, for example, on the curriculum of shadow education, approaches to teaching and learning, assessment, financing, management, and sociology; and all this work can be undertaken either with narrow geographic foci in specific cities, provinces or countries or with a wider lens in an international comparative framework at macro, meso and micro levels.

At the macro level, a particular concern is with social inequalities since it is obvious that high-income families can purchase greater quantities and better qualities of private supplementary tutoring than can low-income families. Macro-level foci also include aspects of economic development through investment in human capital and employment of tutors; and educators may be concerned with the backwash of tutoring on national education systems. Such factors may also be pertinent at the meso level of institutions when some students receive private tutoring and some teachers provide private tutoring but others do not; and at the micro level of individuals, much more research is needed into what sorts of students benefit (or do not benefit) from what sorts of students in what sorts of circumstances. Private supplementary tutoring is a multifaceted and evolving phenomenon in which a huge number of dimensions need investigation (Manzon & Areepattamannil 2014).

These remarks lead to the present book, the origins of which were in a 2014 Colloquium hosted by the Comparative Education Research Centre (CERC) at the University of Hong Kong (HKU). The Colloquium was funded by the Prestigious Fellowship Scheme of the Humanities and Social Sciences Panel (HSSP) of Hong Kong's Research Grants Council (RGC). The Fellowship had been granted to Mark Bray to build on his work on shadow education, which had origins in the 1990s (Bray 1996, 1999) but which had expanded in more recent times with a team of PhD students focusing on Bangladesh, Cambodia, China, Eritrea, Hong Kong, and Georgia; with postdoctoral fellows focusing on China, Hong Kong, Thailand and Taiwan; and with colleagues in the professoriate collaborating in various local and cross-national studies (e.g. Bray & Lykins 2012; Bray & Kwo 2013, 2014; Zhan et al. 2013).

The starting point for the Colloquium, in line with the funding provided by the HSSP, was RGC-funded work in Hong Kong that had developed instruments subsequently used in adapted form in a number of other locations. Information on the Hong Kong project and its instruments is presented in Chapter 8 of the present book. Adaptations of the instruments had been undertaken in China, Dubai, India, Iran, Jamaica and Malaysia (see Chapter 12), and researchers from five of these locations (i.e. with the exception of Dubai) presented their work during the Colloquium.

Among other partners invited to the Colloquium was Boris Jokić, from the Institute for Social Research in Zagreb, Croatia. Jokić had contributed to a pair of books co-edited by Mark Bray (Ristić Dedić et al. 2006; Jokić et al. 2013), and as such was also part of the CERC professional network. The organisers of the Colloquium were very pleased when Jokić indicated availability to join the event and then to help shape the products that have led to this book. They were equally pleased with the contributions from other authors based both in HKU and in other institutions.

The final set of contents, therefore, is a collection of chapters that were originally presented in the 2014 Colloquium plus additional chapters that were solicited because they brought further valuable insights. The resulting collection cannot claim to be comprehensive in either a geographical or a methodological sense. Many parts of the world have not been touched upon by these chapters, and research in those locations would bring further insights from their own cultural contexts. Moreover, while the chapters cover a spectrum from highly quantitative to highly qualitative, many other methodological approaches could be employed (and, the editors hope, will be employed) to investigate themes. Similarly, the sets of research questions addressed by the chapters only represents a small part of the possible agenda.

Nevertheless, the set of chapters can claim originality as the first to be gathered on this theme. Each chapter has its own contribution, and together the collection has even greater impact. The nature of this impact, and suggestions for the future, will be considered in the final chapter of the book.

References

Abd-al-Aaty, Fatma (1994): *Private Tutoring: Analysis and Foundation*. Taata, Egypt: Dar Al-kotob. [in Arabic]

Al Farra, Samia (2009): *Private Tuition Phenomenon in Mathematics in Greater Amman-Jordan: Does Private Tuition Improve Achievement in Mathematics?*. Saarbrücken: Verlag Dr Müller.

Ali, Yahya A. (2013): 'Private Tutoring in Jordan: Underpinning Factors and Impacts'. *International Journal of Humanities and Social Science*, Vol.3, No.13, pp.109-114.

Antonowicz, Laetitia; Lesné, Frédéric; Stassen, Stéphane & Wood, John (2010): *Africa Education Watch: Good Governance Lessons for Primary Education*. Berlin: Transparency International.

ASER-Pakistan (2014): *Annual Status of Education Report 2013: National*. Islamabad: South Asian Forum for Education Development (SAFED). http://www.aserpakistan.org/document/aser/2013/reports/national/ASER_National_Report_ 2013.pdf.

Aslam, Monazza & Atherton, Paul (2014): 'The Shadow Education Sector in India and Pakistan: Opening Pandora's Box', in Macpherson, Ian; Robertson, Susan & Walford, Geoffrey (eds.), *Education, Privatisation and Social Justice: Case Studies from Africa, South Asia and South East Asia*. Oxford: Symposium Books, pp.137-158.

Aurini, Janice & Davies, Scott (2013): 'Supplementary Education in a Changing Organizational Field: The Canadian Case', in Aurini, Janice; Davies, Scott & Dierkes, Julian (eds.), *Out of the Shadows: The Global Intensification of Supplementary Education*. Bingley: Emerald, pp.155-170.

Barman, Santosh Gopal (1964): *The Reasons of Private Tutoring by the Teachers of Non-Government High Schools of East Pakistan and its Effects on Teachers*. MEd thesis, University of Dacca.

Barrow, Dorian A. & Lochan, Samuel N. (2012): 'Supplementary Tutoring in Trinidad and Tobago: Some Implications for Policy Making'. *International Review of Education*, Vol.58, No.3, pp.405-422.

Bray, Mark (1996): *Counting the Full Cost: Household and Community Financing of Education in East Asia*. Washington DC: The World Bank in collaboration with UNICEF.

Bray, Mark (1999): *The Shadow Education System: Private Tutoring and its Implications for Planners*. Fundamentals of Educational Planning 61, Paris: UNESCO International Institute for Educational Planning (IIEP).

Bray, Mark (2009): *Confronting the Shadow Education System: What Government Policies for What Private Tutoring?*. Paris: UNESCO International Institute for Educational Planning (IIEP).

Bray, Mark (2011): *The Challenge of Shadow Education: Private Tutoring and its Implications for Policy Makers in the European Union*. Brussels: European Commission.

Bray, Mark & Kobakhidze, Magda Nutsa (2014): 'Measurement Issues in Research on Shadow Education: Challenges and Pitfalls Encountered in TIMSS and PISA'. *Comparative Education Review*, Vol.58, No.4, pp.590-620.

Bray, Mark & Kwo, Ora (2013): 'Behind the Façade of Fee-Free Education: Shadow Education and its Implications for Social Justice'. *Oxford Review of Education*, Vol.39, No.4, pp.480-497.

Bray, Mark & Kwo, Ora (2014): *Regulating Private Tutoring for Public Good: Policy Options for Supplementary Education in Asia*. Hong Kong: Comparative Education Research Centre, The University of Hong Kong, and Bangkok: UNESCO, 98 pp.

Bray, Mark & Lykins, Chad (2012): *Shadow Education: Private Supplementary Tutoring and Its Implications for Policy Makers in Asia*. Hong Kong: Comparative Education Research Centre, The University of Hong Kong, and Mandaluyong City: Asian Development Bank.

Buchmann, Claudia; Condron, Dennis J. & Rosigno, Vincent J. (2010): 'Shadow Education, American Style: Test Preparation, the SAT and College Enrollment'. *Social Forces*, Vol.89, No.2, pp.435-461.

Buhagiar, Michael & Chetcuti, Deborah A. (2013): 'The Private Tuition Phenomenon in Malta: Moving Toward a Fairer Education System, in Bray, Mark; Mazawi, André E. & Sultana, Ronald G. (eds.), *Private Tutoring Across the Mediterranean: Power Dynamics and Implications for Learning and Equity*. Rotterdam: Sense, pp.129-149.

Cámara, Florencia; Coseiani, Guillermo & Gertel, Héctor R. (2014): 'Private Tutoring: a necessary supplement to admission in Higher Education?'. Paper presented to the XXIII Meeting of the Economics of Education Association, 2-4 July, Valencia, Spain.

Chua, Amy (2011): *Battle Hymn of the Tiger Mother*. New York: Penguin.

Creswell, John W. (2014): *Research Design: Qualitative, Quantitative, and Mixed Methods Approaches*. 4th edition, Thousand Oaks: Sage.

Davis, Jenny (2013): *Educational Legitimation and Parental Aspiration: Private Tutoring in Perth, Western Australia*. PhD thesis, University of Western Australia.

Dawson, Walter (2010): 'Private Tutoring and Mass Schooling in East Asia: Reflections of Inequality in Japan, South Korea, and Cambodia'. *Asia Pacific Education Review*, Vol.11, No.1, pp.14-24.
de Castro, Nadia Studzinski Estima (2013): *Investigação sobre as Formas de Preparação para o Ingresso no Ensino Superior: Uma Educação na Sombra ou uma Sombra na Educação?*. Mestrado em Educação, Pontifícia Universidade Católica do Rio Grande do Sul, Porto Alegre.
de Silva, W.A. (1994): *Extra-School Tutoring in the Asian Context with Special Reference to Sri Lanka*. Mahargama: National Institute of Education.
Dillon, Jenny (2011): '$200 an Hour buys a Better Education with Private Tutoring'. *The Daily Telegraph* [Sydney], 22 August.
Eckler, Rebecca (2015): 'The New Tutor Dynasty'. *Macleans*, 12 April. http://www.macleans.ca/education/the-new-tutor-dynasty
Falzon, Paul A. & Busuttil, John (1988): *Private Tuition in Malta: A Hidden Educational Phenomenon Revealed*. BEd (Hons) dissertation, University of Malta.
Farah, Samer (2011): *Private Tutoring Trends in the UAE*. Policy Brief 26, Dubai: Dubai School of Government.
Foondun, A. Raffick (2002): 'The Issue of Private Tuition: An Analysis of the Practice in Mauritius and Selected South-East Asian Countries'. *International Review of Education*, Vol.48, No.6, pp.485-515.
Hagitegas, George (2008): *The End of the Greek Myth*. Athens: Livanis. [in Greek]
Hall, Stuart (1994): 'The Question of Cultural Identity', in Hall, Stuart; Held, David & McGrew, Tony (eds.), *Modernity and its Futures*. Cambridge: Polity Press, pp.273-325.
Hartmann, Sarah (2013): 'Education "Home Delivery" in Egypt: Private Tutoring and Social Stratification', in Bray, Mark; Mazawi, André E. & Sultana, Ronald G. (eds.), *Private Tutoring Across the Mediterranean: Power Dynamics and Implications for Learning and Equity*. Rotterdam: Sense, pp.57-75.
Hemachandra, H.L. (1982): 'The Growing Phenomena of Tuition Classes: The Perceived Reasons and Some Latent Social Factors'. *Sri Lanka Journal of Social Sciences*, Vol.5, No.2, pp.39-69.
Ireson, Judith & Rushforth, Katie (2014): 'Why do parents employ private tutors for their children? Exploring psychological factors that influence demand in England'. *Journal of Educational Research Online*, Vol.6, No.1, pp.12-33.
Japan, Ministry of Education and Training (2008). *Report on the situation of academic learning activities of children*. Tokyo: Monbukagakusho Hokokusho. [in Japanese]
Johnson, Burke & Christensen, Larry (2012): *Educational Research: Quantitative, Qualitative, and Mixed Approaches*. Los Angeles: Sage.
Jokić, Boris (ed.) (2013): *Emerging from the Shadow: A Comparative Qualitative Exploration of Private Tutoring in Eurasia*. Zagreb: Network of Education Policy Centers.

Jokić, Boris & Ristić Dedić, Zrinka (2007): *U sjeni: Privatne instrukcije u obravzovanju Hrvatske*. Zagreb: Institute for Social Research.

Jokić, Boris; Soldo, Andrea & Ristić Dedić, Zrinka (2013): 'Private Tutoring and Social Equity in Croatia and Bosnia & Herzegovina: A Comparative Qualitative Study', in Bray, Mark; Mazawi, André E. & Sultana, Ronald G. (eds.), *Private Tutoring Across the Mediterranean: Power Dynamics and Implications for Learning and Equity*. Rotterdam: Sense, pp.11-27.

Kalikova, Saule and Zhanar Rakhimzhanova (2009): 'Private Tutoring in Kazakhstan', in Silova, Iveta (ed.), *Private Supplementary Tutoring in Central Asia: New Opportunities and Burdens*. Paris: UNESCO International Institute for Educational Planning (IIEP), pp.93-118.

Kassotakis, Michael & Verdis, Athanasios (2013): 'Shadow Education in Greece: Characteristics, Consequences and Eradication Efforts', in Bray, Mark; Mazawi, André E. & Sultana, Ronald G. (eds.), *Private Tutoring Across the Mediterranean: Power Dynamics and Implications for Learning and Equity*. Rotterdam: Sense, pp.93-113.

Khuwaileh, Abdullah A. & Al-Shoumali, Ali (2001): 'Private Tuition in English: The Case of Two Universities in Jordan'. *English Today*, Vol.17, No.1, pp.31-35.

Kirss, Laura (2011): 'Education in the Shadows: The Case of Estonia'. *Praxis*, No.8. http://www.edupolicy.net/images/pubs/reports/pt_ee.pdf

Kobakhidze, Magda Nutsa (2014): 'Corruption Risks of Private Tutoring: Case of Georgia'. *Asia Pacific Journal of Education*, Vol.34, No.4, pp.455-475.

Koh, Aaron (2014): 'The "Magic" of Tutorial Centres in Hong Kong: An Analysis of Media Marketing and Pedagogy in a Tutorial Centre'. *International Review of Education*, Vol.60, No.6, pp.803-819.

KOSIS [Korean Statistical Information Service] (2015): 'Private Education Participation Rate by School Level'. http://kosis.kr/eng/statisticsList/statisticsList_01List.jsp?vwcd=MT_ETITLE&parentId=C#SubCont, accessed 30 May 2015.

Kozar, Olga (2013): 'The Face of Private Tutoring in Russia: Evidence from Online Marketing by Private Tutors'. *Research in Comparative and International Education*, Vol.8, No.1, pp.74-86.

Kwo, Ora & Bray, Mark (2011): 'Facing the Shadow Education System in Hong Kong'. Newsletter of the International Institute for Asian Studies (IIAS), University of Leiden, No.56, p.20.

Lamprianou, Iasonas & Afantiti Lamprianou, Thekla (2013): 'Charting Private Tutoring in Cyprus: A Socio-Demographic Perspective', in Bray, Mark; Mazawi, André E. & Sultana, Ronald G. (eds.), *Private Tutoring Across the Mediterranean: Power Dynamics and Implications for Learning and Equity*. Rotterdam: Sense, pp.29-56.

Lee, Chong Jae; Lee, Heesook & Jang, Hyo-Min (2010): 'The History of Policy Responses to Shadow Education in South Korea: Implications for the Next Cycle of Policy Responses'. *Asia Pacific Education Review*, Vol.11, No.1, pp.97-108.

Manzon, Maria & Areepattamannil, Shaljan (2014): 'Shadow Educations: Mapping the Global Discourse'. *Asia Pacific Journal of Education*, Vol.34, No.4, pp.389-412.

Mariuci, Sergio; Ferri, Maricia Da Silva & Felicetti, Vera Lucia (2012): 'Uma Sombra na Educação Brasileira: Do Ensino Regular ao Paralelo'. *Revista Latinoamericana de Educación Comparada*, Vol.3, No.3, pp.85-96.

Mason, Mark (2014): 'Comparing Cultures', in Bray, Mark; Adamson, Bob & Mason, Mark (eds.), *Comparative Education Research: Approaches and Methods*. CERC Studies in Comparative Education 19, 2nd edition. Hong Kong: Comparative Education Research Centre, The University of Hong Kong and Dordrecht: Springer, pp.221-257.

Mattos, Luiz Otavio Neves (2007): 'Explicadores do Rio de Janeiro: Encontros e Desencontros em Trajetóroas Profissionais Singulares'. *Revista Brasileira de Estudos Pedagógicos*, Vol.88, No.218, pp.140-156.

Mauritius, Ministry of Education and Science (1994): *Use and Abuse of Private Tuition*. Port Louis: Ministry of Education and Science.

Mori, Izumi (2013): 'Supplementary Education in the United States: Policy Context, Characteristics, and Challenges', in Aurini, Janice; Davies, Scott & Dierkes, Julian (eds.), *Out of the Shadows: The Global Intensification of Supplementary Education*. Bingley: Emerald, pp.191-207.

Naismith, Luke (2014): 'Supplementary Private Tutoring in Dubai'. Unpublished report, Dubai: Knowledge and Human Development Authority.

Napporn, Clarisse & Baba-Moussa, Abdel Rahaman (2013): 'Accompagnement et soutien scolaires : L'expérience béninoise'. *Revue international d'éducation de Sèvres*, No.62, pp.1-10.

OECD (2011): *Quality Time for Students: Learning in and out of School*. Paris: Organisation for Economic Co-operation and Development (OECD).

OECD (2014): *Education at a Glance 2014: OECD Indicators*. Paris: Organisation for Economic Co-operation and Development (OECD).

Oller, Anne-Claudine & Glasman, Dominique (2013): 'Education as a Market in France: Forms and Stakes of Private Tutoring', in Bray, Mark; Mazawi, André E. & Sultana, Ronald G. (eds.), *Private Tutoring Across the Mediterranean: Power Dynamics and Implications for Learning and Equity*. Rotterdam: Sense, pp.77-91.

Ong, Wan Roe (2012): *Private Supplementary Tutoring for Preschoolers in Hong Kong: A Case Study of the Determinants of Demand in Tsuen Wan New Town*. MEd dissertation, The University of Hong Kong.

Oyewusi, Lawunmi Molara & Orelade, Kayode Stephen (2014): 'Private Tutoring Boom in Nigeria: An Investigation into the Emerging but Controversial Learning Space'. *Journal of Educational and Social Research*, Vol.4, No.6, pp.271-274.

Pallegedara, Asankha (2012): 'Demand for Private Tutoring in a Free Education Country: The Case of Sri Lanka'. *International Journal of Education Economics and Development*, Vol.3, No.4, pp.375-393.

Paviot, Laura Ciero (2015): *Private Tuition in Kenya and Mauritius: Policies, Practices and Parents' Perceptions Examined from an Ecological Systems Perspective*. EdD thesis, University College London (UCL) Institute of Education.

Pratham (2014): *Annual Status of Education Report 2013*. Mumbai: Pratham. http://img.asercentre.org/docs/Publications/ASER%20Reports/ASER_2013/ASER20 13_ report%20sections/aser2013fullreportenglish.pdf

Ristić Dedić, Zrinka; Jokić, Boris & Jurko, Lana (2006): 'Croatia', in Silova, Iveta; Būdienė, Virginija & Bray, Mark (eds.), *Education in a Hidden Marketplace: Monitoring of Private Tutoring*. New York: Open Society Institute, pp.169-190.

Rohlen, Thomas P. (1980): 'The *Juku* Phenomenon: An Exploratory Essay'. *Journal of Japanese Studies*, Vol.6, No.2, pp.207-242.

Safarzyńska, K. (2013). Socio-economic determinants of demand for private tutoring, *European Sociological Review*, 29 (2), 139-154.

Sahlberg, Pasi (2011): *Finnish Lessons: What can the World Learn from Educational Change in Finland?*. New York: Teachers College Press.

Salili, Farideh (2005): 'Accepting Personal Responsibility for Learning', in Watkins, David A. & Biggs, John B. (eds.), *The Chinese Learner: Cultural, Psychological and Contextual Influences*. Hong Kong: Comparative Education Research Centre, The University of Hong Kong, pp.85-105.

Sato, Yuji (ed.) (2012): *100 Years of Juku and 50 Years of Juku Associations*. Tokyo: Private Tutoring Federation. [in Japanese]

Silova, Iveta (2009): *Private Supplementary Tutoring in Central Asia: New Opportunities and Burdens*. Paris: UNESCO International Institute for Educational Planning (IIEP).

Silova, Iveta (2010): 'Private Tutoring in Eastern Europe and Central Asia: Policy Choices and Implications'. *Compare: A Journal of Comparative and International Education*, Vol.40, No.3, pp.327-344.

Sobhy, Hania (2012): 'The De-facto Privatization of Secondary Education in Egypt: A Study of Private Tutoring in Technical and General Schools'. *Compare: A Journal of Comparative and International Education*, Vol.42, No.1, pp.47-67

Sriprakash, Arathi; Proctor, Helen & Hu, Betty (2015): 'Visible Pedagogic Work: Parenting, Private Tutoring and Educational Advantage in Australia'. *Discourse: Studies in the Cultural Politics of Education*, DOI 10.1080/01596306. 2015.1061976.

Stevenson, David L. & Baker, David P. (1992): 'Shadow Education and Allocation in Formal Schooling: Transition to University in Japan.' *American Journal of Sociology*, Vol.97, No.6, pp.1639-1657.

Sujatha, K. & Rani, P. Geetha (2011): *Management of Secondary Education in India*. New Delhi: Shipra and National University of Educational Planning & Administration (NUEPA).

Suleiman, Hana (2012): 'Shadow Learning in Undergraduate Mathematics: An Exploratory Study'. *International Journal of Modern Education*, Vo.1, No.2, pp.58-63.

Suraweera, A.V. (2011): *Dr. Kannangara's Free Education Proposals in Relation to the Subsequent Expansion of the Tuition Industry*. Dr. C.W.W. Kannangara Memorial Lecture. Maharagama: National Institute of Education.

Sutton Trust (2014): *Research Brief: Extra-curricular Inequality*. London: The Sutton Trust. http://www.suttontrust.com/wp-content/uploads/2014/09/Extracurricular-inequality.pdf.

Tseng, Li-chen Jackie (1998): *Private Supplementary Tutoring at the Senior Secondary level in Taiwan and Hong Kong*. MEd Dissertation, The University of Hong Kong.

Tsiloglu, Lefteris (2005): *Frontistiria in Greece: Their History and People*. Athens: Kedros. [in Greek]

UNESCO (2015): *Education for All 2000-2015: Achievements and Challenges Report*. EFA Global Monitoring Report, Paris: UNESCO.

Williams, Timothy P.; Abbott, Pamela & Mupenzi, Alfred (2015): '"Education at our School is not Free": The Hidden Costs of Fee-free Schooling in Rwanda'. *Compare: A Journal of Comparative and International Education*, Vol.45, DOI 10.1080/03057925.2014.938611

Yung, Kevin Wai-Ho (2011): *Shadow Education in Hong Kong: The Experience of Learners of English*. Master of Arts in Applied Linguistics dissertation, The University of Hong Kong.

Xue, Haiping & Ding, Xiaohao (2008): 'An Empirical Study on Private Tutoring for Students in Urban China'. *Economics of Education Research*, Vol.6, No.1, pp.1-14. [in Chinese].

Zhan, Shengli; Bray, Mark; Wang, Dan; Lykins, Chad & Kwo, Ora (2013): 'The Effectiveness of Private Tutoring: Students' Perceptions in Comparison with Mainstream Schooling in Hong Kong', *Asia Pacific Education Review*, Vol.14, No.4, pp.495-509.

Zhang, Wei (2014): 'The Demand for Shadow Education in China: Mainstream Teachers and Power Relations'. *Asia Pacific Journal of Education*, Vol.34, No.4, pp.436-454.

Zhou, Min & Kim, Susan S. (2008): 'Community Forces, Social Capital, and Educational Achievement: The Case of Supplementary Education in the Chinese and Korean Immigrant Communities'. *Harvard Educational Review*, Vol.76, No.1, pp.1-29.

Employing
Quantitative Instruments

1

Shadow Education Research through TIMSS and PIRLS: Experiences and Lessons in the Republic of Georgia

Magda Nutsa KOBAKHIDZE

Introduction

Shadow education has long been clearly visible in the Republic of Georgia. Increasing numbers of students from different socio-economic backgrounds receive private tutoring from *repetitors*, the term used colloquially in Georgia for individual tutoring providers. According to a 2011 study, the majority (69%) of *repetitors* were schoolteachers while others were university professors, students and graduates (EPPM 2011). Profit-driven tutoring companies are rare in Georgia.

Despite its widespread existence, private tutoring as a parallel education system has attracted little academic and policy interest in Georgia. A few studies shed some light on the matter, but much work remains to be done. The existing studies primarily examined demand from students and families rather than the supply by teachers and other providers. Further, the studies were small-scale, and none was based on a nationally representative sample. Moreover, no studies explore methodological aspects of collecting and interpreting data on private tutoring in Georgia.

This chapter reflects on methodological aspects of data obtained through the Trends in International Mathematics and Science Study (TIMSS) and Progress in International Reading Literacy Study (PIRLS). It

---

Bray, Mark; Kwo, Ora & Jokić, Boris (eds.) (2015): *Researching Private Supplementary Tutoring: Methodological Lessons from Diverse Cultures*. Hong Kong: Comparative Education Research Centre (CERC), The University of Hong Kong, and Dordrecht: Springer. © CERC

discusses questions related to the ethics of research, questionnaire construction, characteristics of children as respondents in survey research, and validity and reliability of data obtained through international assessments. The chapter draws on data from a nationally representative sample of 9,362 students obtained through the national component of TIMSS and PIRLS in 2011. The quantitative findings reflect Grade 4 and Grade 8 students' perspectives on shadow education, and provide information about the scope, nature, intensity, duration and seasonal variations of the phenomenon. The chapter also summarises numerical findings from 4,744 parents of Grade 4 students. Comparison of data from Grade 4 students and their parents provides methodological insights on how to interpret responses from 10-year-old children, raising the questions:

- How much weight should be placed on children's responses?
- How can researchers interpret what children are saying?
- What should be the rules for constructing questionnaires for different age groups?

Noting some inconsistencies in data obtained through TIMSS and PIRLS in 2011 and building on a wider paper by Bray and Kobakhidze (2014), the paper remarks on ways in which methodological nuances may affect the quality of data.

Background

Shadow education is firmly embedded in Georgian daily life, and its origins go back to the pre-1991 Soviet era. Patterns exemplify the processes of marketisation of education in a post-Soviet transitional state, and reflect neo-liberal reforms in education policy. Tutoring provided by teachers (often the teachers who are already responsible for their tutees in regular classes) is considered a norm, but the government prefers silence on the matter and does not acknowledge it in any official educational strategy plans. Thus, the government not only tries to ignore private tutoring as a supplement to the mainstream education but also closes its eyes to a serious challenge for the education system – low teacher salaries. Since commercial forms of private tutoring are not (yet) developed, teachers are the main, unconstrained actors in the marketplace. In some cases this involves corruption-related practices. While Georgian students and teachers can have some benefit from private supplementary tutoring, it can have serious backwash effects on teaching and learning in mainstream schools.

Increasing demand for private tutoring has many causes, including perceived low quality in mainstream education, depleted teacher salaries, introduction of high stakes examinations, and inadequate content learned at schools (EPPM 2011; Bregvadze 2012). After the collapse of the Soviet Union, private tutoring became widespread in the former Soviet countries, serving as a complementary strategy when public schools failed to offer quality education to students or ambitious parents desired better education for their children (Silova et al. 2006; Silova 2009; Jokić 2013). Thus in the post-Socialist transformations period, as Silova and Bray (2006, p.45) put it, private tutoring became "a long-awaited opportunity for educational choice that was never available during the socialist period". With increasing decentralisation and mercerisation of state education in the early 1990s, private tutoring became a highly-demanded service.

Immediately after the demise of the Soviet Union, salaries in schools and universities dropped dramatically as a result of curtailed public expenditure. For example, in 2002 the average monthly salary of a university professor in Georgia was 60 GEL (US$34), which at that time was less than a half of subsistence level (World Bank 2012, p.75). Corruption in higher education was widespread and mainly related to private tutoring as a means to enter the higher education institutions (World Bank 2012; Gabedava 2013).

The role of private tutoring in higher education is widely considered negative due to frequent cases of corruption in university entrance examinations. However, some scholars have also noted positive roles. For example, in the context of post-Soviet countries in Central and Eastern Europe and Mongolia, Silova and Bray (2006, p.19) observed that:

> Tutoring has been viewed as an effective way for children and young adults to adapt to the new reality and cope with system changes. Responding to students' needs in a more efficient, flexible, and prompt manner, private tutoring has been perceived as an important supplement to the rigid mainstream education system, which has been slow to embrace changes.

Thus in parallel to mainstream education, which lost credibility after painful socio-political and economic transitions, tutoring has attained the competitive advantage of being flexible and tailored to students' needs.

From a supply side, a positive aspect of private tutoring is related to teacher remuneration. During the transformation period, tutoring helped teachers in Georgia to survive economic hardships, and it reduced teachers' migration from schools (Matiashvili & Kutateladze 2006, p.196). On the negative side, proliferation of private tutoring was linked to exacerbating social inequalities and distorted curricula, and deprived the state of tax revenues (Silova et al. 2006).

Georgia launched a new university entrance examination policy in 2005 with financial support from a World Bank project. The major aim was to free university entrance examinations from corruption, ensure transparency, and raise the quality of higher education (World Bank 2012). The introduction of Unified National Examinations (UNE) marked a new era for both supply and demand of tutoring. University professors lost their control over entrance examinations, and consequently demand for university professors as major suppliers dropped significantly. In contrast, schoolteachers became major providers of tutoring as cheaper and more convenient options. The reported mismatch between the school curriculum and the programmes required in university entrance examinations has been a major driver of private tutoring (Matiashvili & Kutateladze 2006; EPPM 2011; Bregvadze 2012). Other drivers include perceptions of overcrowded classes and overloaded curriculum in the context of inadequate teaching hours in school.

The 2011 EPPM study, with a sample 1,200 parents, showed that although majority of parents felt that the quality of education in mainstream schools had improved over the previous two years, over 90 per cent considered that "it was necessary" for students to take private tutoring in school subjects as well as in the General Ability Test (EPPM 2011, p.23). The combined statistics of the capital and villages showed that one in four students had received some kind of tutoring during the previous 12 months (p.22). The EPPM study showed that, as in other countries, private tutoring is closely linked to high-stakes examinations.

Regardless of its negative or positive implications, private tutoring has been a demanded educational service by Georgian families during and since the transformation period. In addition to economic and educational drivers of demand, such as low teacher salaries and the perceived poor education in mainstream schools, socio-cultural drivers have to be mentioned. Education has always been a valuable asset in Georgia. Families have invested in education in the hope of getting access to higher education and thus moving up the social ladder. Investing in private tutoring was seen as a means for that access, but sometimes to the extent of what Dore (1997) called "the diploma disease" when attaining educational credentials became more important than the education itself. More empirical research is needed to understand what the growth of shadow education tells about the characteristics and overall profile of mainstream education in Georgia; who benefits and who loses in this process, and to what extent; how various types and qualities of tutoring impact education processes in schools; and what lessons can be drawn from research to facilitate education policy decisions.

Methodology

The periodic TIMSS and PIRLS surveys have been administered under the umbrella of the International Association for the Evaluation of Educational Achievement (IEA). Located in Amsterdam, the IEA has overseen overall policy and financial planning of the studies, while Boston College's TIMSS & PIRLS International Study Center has supervised international project activities. The IEA's Data Processing and Research Center (DPC) located in Hamburg, Germany has been responsible for the data management and software development of international studies, and assists participating countries with data analysis and reporting. Another international organisation, Statistics Canada located in Ottawa, has performed sampling and weighting procedures for TIMSS and PIRLS.

TIMSS started in 1995, at that time known as the Third International Mathematics and Science Study, and has since been administered every four years. PIRLS was launched in 2001, and has since been administered every five years. Thus in 2011 TIMSS was in its fifth iteration and PIRLS was in its third iteration. The fact that the cycles coincided in this year gave participating countries the opportunity to evaluate the same students at Grade 4.

TIMSS assesses students' performance in sciences and mathematics at Grades 4 and 8. PIRLS focuses only on Grade 4, and evaluates students' reading comprehension skills. TIMSS 2011 assessed students' achievements in 63 countries and 14 states or regions, while PIRLS 2011 assessed students' achievements in 49 countries and nine states or regions (Boston College 2013). Georgia joined TIMSS in 2007 and again in 2011; and joined PIRLS in 2006 and again in 2011. This participation over time permitted some analysis of trends.

Sampling

TIMSS and PIRLS employ a two-stage stratified random sampling design. In the first stage, schools are sampled on a probability proportional to size; and in the second stage one or two classes are chosen at random from the selected schools. For field operations this means that large schools are selected for higher probability than smaller schools (Rutkowski et al. 2010; Joncas & Foy 2012). The IEA requests national research teams to provide lists of schools for the first sampling stage, and for the second stage schools provide lists of Grade 4 and 8 classrooms. TIMSS and PIRLS do not use simple random sampling, according to which each individual in the population is given an equal chance to be surveyed. For this reason, the standard variation estimation formula is irrelevant for analysing the data and creates a constraint in analysis (Rutkowski et al. 2010, p.144).

Based on the information gathered from schools, Statistics Canada designs national samples for participating countries. The IEA Data Processing and Research Center has developed the Within-school Sampling Software (WinW3S), which has been used for data entry, class and student sampling, random assignment of booklets to students, student-teacher linkage forms, and production of labels for test booklets and questionnaires (IEA 2014).

The international design in 2011 included both explicit stratification of schools by region and implicit stratification by highland, town and village (Joncas & Foy 2012, p.9). Coverage in Georgia was restricted to students whose medium of instruction was the Georgian language, so the study excluded a small portion of ethnic minority students, mainly Armenians and Azeris living in the south of the country. The sampling frame also excluded very small schools as well as specialised schools for students with special needs (Martin & Mullis 2012). Although schools from the Russian-occupied Abkhazia and South Ossetia were excluded from the sample due to lack of access, the survey did include schools for internally displaced persons (IDPs) from Abkhazia that were situated in various parts of the country. The sample also included private as well as public schools. PIRLS and TIMSS sampled the same Grade 4 students, and TIMSS also sampled Grade 8 students.

In total, in both grades 180 schools were sampled among which 172 schools participated in the study at Grade 8 and 173 schools at Grade 4. The average age of students at Grade 8 was 14.2 years, while at Grade 4 the average age was 10.0 years (Joncas 2012). The student population size for Grade 8 was 49,618, from which 4,563 students were selected as the TIMSS national sample. The TIMSS and PIRLS Grade 4 national sample was 4,799 students from a population size of 41,194 (Table 1.1).

Table 1.1: Population and Sample Sizes for Georgia TIMSS and PIRLS 2011

Size	Grade 4	Grade 8
Population size	41,191	49,618
Sample size	4,799	4,563

Source: TIMSS & PIRLS International Study Center, Boston College.

The within-school student participation rates (weighted percentage) in TIMSS and PIRLS 2011 reached 99 per cent in Grade 4 and 98 per cent in Grade 8. The number of students who did not come to school on the test day at Grade 4 was 80 and at Grade 8 it was 99. Compared to other countries, student absenteeism during the TIMSS and PIRLS tests was low. For example, in Australia 1,118 students (sample size 7,556) were absent from Grade 8 on the day of the test, and in England 448 students (sample size 3,842) were absent (Martin & Mullis 2012, p.441).

TIMSS and PIRLS administration
The TIMSS and PIRLS surveys were administered in May and June 2011 by a trained team from the National Assessment and Examinations Center (NAEC), a legal entity under the Ministry of Education and Science. The pen-and-pencil tests and background questionnaires were administered in the Georgian language, and the NAEC team provided training for school coordinators according to the international guidelines. The TIMSS and PIRLS National Research Coordinators (NRCs) were responsible for management of overall process, including instrument translation, adaptation, training of test administrators and school coordinators, test preparation and administration, scoring, and coding of data. The NRCs also monitored compliance with the standardised procedures. The IEA provided manuals which detailed each procedure to support the adherence to international standards.

Most school coordinators were nominated by the school principals, but sometimes the roles were undertaken by the principals. The school coordinator positions were remunerated with a one-time compensation of 50 GEL (US$29), and required the coordinators to provide information from the schools, participate in the training, and keep test booklets and questionnaires in secure places. The test administrators, most of whom were class teachers, distributed tests and questionnaires in class, instructed students on how to complete the tests, and monitored time taken. Test materials were collected by the school coordinators and test administrators and delivered to regional locations from which the NAEC staff transported them to the NAEC office in Tbilisi. During the test administration, a number of national and international quality control monitors observed the process. The international procedures stipulated that international quality control monitors should visit a random sample of at least 10 per cent of the participating schools (Johanson & Neuschmidt 2007).

Data preparation, scoring and processing
After retrieving the national data, the processes of entry and scoring started immediately. Data from the questionnaires and booklets were entered in special software, the Data Entry Manager for Windows (WinDEM). Data files in a specified format were sent to the IEA DPC for processing in August 2011. Data went through extensive cleaning and checking. Data scaling included estimation of students' performance scores using an item response theory (IRT) model. TIMSS and PIRLS sampling design characteristics generated missing data, because students did not respond to all items in the tests. For this reason, the scaling process involved plausible values estimation. Plausible values represented imputed values rather than real test scores obtained from students. Further data processing included weighting of students' responses to accommodate the complex nature of the TIMSS and PIRLS sampling frame (Rutkowski et al. 2010, p.143). All problems arising during the data preparation process were addressed by national research teams and DPC staff to ensure that data were consistent within and across countries.

The IEA DPC processed the international data of TIMSS and PIRLS 2011 together with the Georgian national component, i.e. questions on shadow education. After the release of the international TIMSS and PIRLS database in February 2013, the author of this chapter obtained the dataset from the DPC on tutoring in SPSS format. The dataset was later merged with the international database using the IEA-developed software.

Instruments for TIMSS and PIRLS

The instruments for TIMSS and PIRLS 2011 included test booklets and background questionnaires. In addition to taking standardised tests in mathematics, science and reading, students answered questions on attitudes toward schooling, habits, homework, involvement of parents, assessments of teachers' qualifications, and time for extra-curricular activities. TIMSS and PIRLS at Grade 4 included a questionnaire for parents or guardians on home environment. At the teacher and school level, TIMSS and PIRLS questionnaires solicited information about school climate and resources, teachers' pedagogical approaches, and related topics.

Like the test booklets, the background questionnaires were prepared in English by the IEA and translated by participating countries, sometimes with adaptation to fit national contexts. The Georgian versions of the background questionnaires underwent careful translation and back-translation. The TIMSS and PIRLS 2011 questionnaires were revised versions of the 2007 TIMSS and 2006 PIRLS background questionnaires. The Questionnaire Item Review Committee (QIRC) within the IEA and the NRCs extensively reviewed background questionnaires before the field test in 2010.

As the PIRLS NRC, the author of this chapter designed national questions on tutoring and included them in the TIMSS and PIRLS instruments as a national component. Adding national components to the international study was permitted by the IEA. A few countries had already used this opportunity to obtain national data on tutoring within the international framework (see e.g. Safarzyńska 2013; Hof 2014; Tse 2014). After negotiating with the top management of the NAEC and consulting with an international scholar, the questions were finalised and placed at the end of both students' and parents' background questionnaires for Grades 4 and 8.

Table 1.2 indicates that several background questionnaires accompanied TIMSS and PIRLS 2011 at both grades. It also shows the questionnaires to which questions of shadow education were added. The shadow education questions were placed in the same layout as the other TIMSS and PIRLS questions, formatted with Adobe®InDesign® software. Since it was important to maintain the international format, the completed questionnaires were sent to the TIMSS and PIRLS International Study Center for layout verification and final review. Because Georgia administered TIMSS and PIRLS at Grade 4 with the same sampled students, there was only one combined student background questionnaire for

Grade 4. As shown in Table 1.2, nine questions on shadow education were asked in the Grade 8 and Grade 4 students' questionnaires, and eight questions were asked in the parents' questionnaire. Appendices 1.1 and 1.2 show the student and parent questionnaires for Grade 4.

Table 1.2: Background Questionnaires and Number of Shadow Education Questions in TIMSS & PIRLS 2011, Georgia

	Student questionnaire	Curriculum questionnaire	School questionnaire	Teacher questionnaire	Parent questionnaire*
Number of shadow education questions	*Grade 4*				
	9	-	-	-	8
	Grade 8				
	9	-	-	-	-

* The parents' questionnaire was originally called Learning to Read Survey, and was only administered at Grade 4.

Shadow Education Questions in TIMSS and PIRLS 2011 Student and Parent Questionnaires

The nine shadow education questions were placed on pages 32 and 33 of the Grade 4 and Grade 8 students' questionnaires. Given the small format of the parents' questionnaire, the shadow education questions occupied three pages (pages 20 to 22). The questions covered:

- whether or not students received private tutoring during the given academic year;
- subjects in which they received tutoring (mathematics, Georgian Language, English, etc.);
- different providers of tutoring (own teacher, teacher from another school, student/graduate, etc.);
- information about paid or free tutoring;
- tutoring expenditure per month;
- length of tutoring practice;
- intensity of tutoring;
- perceived effectiveness of tutoring (only in parents' questionnaire); and
- reasons for receiving tutoring (only Grade 8 students and parents' questionnaire).

Placing the same shadow education questions in the student questionnaires of both grades permitted comparison of data across grades. Similarly, use of the same questions in Grade 4 student and parent questionnaires permitted triangulation of data and crosschecking of validity of responses.

Findings

Scale of tutoring in Grades 4 and 8

The TIMSS data showed that 38.6 per cent of Grade 8 students had received some sort of tutoring within the academic year (Table 1.3). Given that there were no examinations at the end of Grade 8, the scale of tutoring was considered high. Similar remarks applied to Grade 4, where the scale of tutoring reached 33.4 per cent as reported by the students.[1]

It is interesting to compare the scale of tutoring reported by the parents (27.2%) and by Grade 4 students (33.4%). The same question – "In this school year, have you [your child] received private lessons (tutoring) in any school subject?" – was asked to students and their parents, but responses differed by 6.2 percentage points. Some analysts might consider these numbers close enough, but others might look more deeply e.g. to ask whether question was clearly formulated for 10-year-old students to comprehend. Further, what students consider as private tutoring may differ from parents' understanding. Moreover, while the question asked about "tutoring in school subjects", some students might not have paid proper attention to the phrase "in school subjects" and might have included tutoring in non-academic subjects such as piano, ballet or chess. This could lead to overestimation of the shadow education phenomenon by Grade 4 students. Scholars who specialise in surveying argue that in middle childhood (7-12 years) children's memory capacity and speed are still developing and that such children may not pay proper attention to the details (Leeuw et al. 2004, pp.411-412). Children of this age can answer survey questions that are well-designed with some consistency, but

---

[1] This finding contrasts with data provided by EPPM, according to which 15 per cent of primary school students received tutoring in 2011 (EPPM 2011, p.25). The difference may be explained by the sample sizes and target populations. EPPM targeted parents rather than students, and the 15 per cent was a combined statistic for all elementary school grades (1 through 6). By contrast, TIMSS and PIRLS targeted only Grade 4 students.

their understanding of the words should be carefully examined and tested. For this age group, yes/no questions might be preferable.

The data gathered from parents also need scrutiny. It is likely that parents paid more attention than children to the phrase "tutoring in school subjects", but some parents may not have wished to report the real numbers. Discussing problems related to obtaining precise data, Bray (2009, p.16) noted that:

> Parents may not welcome attention. They may also fear that it [shadow education] would be perceived as purchasing an unfair advantage and/or indicating the distrust of the mainstream system or fear that their children would be perceived as stupid.

Thus it is possible that some parents purposely hid information regarding tutoring, and avoided further questions about costs, providers of tutoring, effectiveness and reasons. Given that TIMSS and PIRLS 2011 were administered by the MoES, parents might have felt that the information they provided would be reviewed by teachers and school principals, and could affect their children's schooling. Owing to the large scale and quantitative nature of the study, it is not possible to check the validity of the above-mentioned possibilities.

Table 1.3: Scale of Tutoring in Grades 4 and 8, Georgia

In this school year, have you [your child] received private lessons (tutoring) in any school subject?		
	Yes (%)	No (%)
Grade 4 students	33.4	66.6
Grade 8 students	38.6	61.4
Parents of Grade 4 students	27.2	72.8

Table 1.3 generates findings about the scale of shadow education in general, which, given the nature of the questions, can include both paid and free tutoring. Table 1.4 elaborates on this issue and shows percentages of paid tutoring in both grades. Students and parents were asked if they paid money for the tutoring classes. The reported scale of unpaid tutoring was high at Grade 4, reaching 38.1 per cent, while at Grade 8 it was much lower at 16.3 per cent. This may be explained by the widespread practice of elementary school students receiving extra free help from their teachers and/or relatives. Given the complexity of the Grade 8

curriculum, it is less likely that free help could have been obtained easily, which can explain the lower numbers reported by the Grade 8 students. The third option "I do not know" (9.9% for Grade 4 and 3.4% for Grade 8) also seems logical since many 10-year-olds may not be aware of financial transactions related to tutoring compared with 14-15 year-olds. Because the TIMSS and PIRLS studies were administered at the end of the school year, asking students "in this school year" was an appropriate question to cover the whole year.

Table 1.4: Paid versus Free Tutoring in Grades 4 and 8, Georgia

Do your parents pay money for your supplementary private lessons?			
	Yes (%)	No (%)	I do not know (%)
Grade 4	52.0	38.1	9.9
Grade 8	80.3	16.3	3.4

Popularity of subjects
In line with previous studies (e.g. Matiashvili & Kutateladze 2006; Bregvadze 2012), mathematics and English were the most popular subjects as reported by Grade 4 and Grade 8 students (Table 1.5). The data were consistent with parents' responses regarding two subjects – mathematics and English. However, parents reported quite different numbers from their children regarding reading literacy and science. Thus 36.9 per cent of Grade 4 students reported that they received tutoring in reading literacy and 36.2 per cent indicated that they received private classes in science. In contrast, only 17.0 per cent of parents reported the use of tutoring in reading literacy and 16.2 per cent indicated tutoring in science. The difference between students' and parents' reports raises the question of reliability. Which data are more reliable, and on what grounds might either data set be believed?

For Grade 4, the explanation behind the gap can be found in the school curriculum. Like Malta, Qatar, Russia, United Arab Emirates and other countries, there was no separate curriculum for reading in Georgian primary education (Grades 1–6). The reading curriculum was part of the Georgian language curriculum. In primary school, teaching and learning of the Georgian language is a foundation to the development of all essential linguistic skills for self-expression: listening, speaking, reading, and writing (Kobakhidze 2012, p.246). Some primary school children received private tutoring in the Georgian language, while others gained extra training only in reading literacy. The question about tutoring in different subjects included both options: tutoring in reading literacy and tutoring in the Georgian language. These two options may overlap and have caused inconsistency in responses. Moreover, Grade 4 students may not understand why these two options were provided side by side. However, the reported numbers by students and parents in science cannot be explained with similar arguments, and the divergence remains unexplained.

Table 1.5: Popularity of Subjects for Tutoring, Georgia

In which of the following school subject(s) have you taken private tutoring in this school year?			
Subjects	Grade 4	Parents of Grade 4 students	Grade 8
English	54.4	67.1	68.3
Math	48.1	46.5	58.4
Reading literacy	36.8	17.0	N/A
Georgian language	35.9	31.5	16.7
Foreign languages [other than English]	26.0	32.9	31.9
History	N/A	N/A	10.3
Geography	N/A	N/A	9.9
Biology	N/A	N/A	9.6
Physics	N/A	N/A	17.0
Chemistry	N/A	N/A	2.7
Sciences	36.2	16.2	N/A
Other subjects	26.3	9.4	6.5

Note: The table shows percentages of students among those who indicated that they received tutoring in any subject.

N/A = Not Applicable

As noted earlier, scholars maintain that children's memory capacity is forming in this age, which has implications for the number and order of response options in questionnaire design. Leeuw et al. (2004, p.412) recommended limiting response options to three to five for children in middle childhood. The question about tutoring in school subjects in TIMSS and PIRLS 2011 had seven option categories, which may have been too cognitively demanding.

Duration and intensity of private tutoring

Most students stated that they received tutoring twice a week in both grades (Table 1.6). These data were consistent with parents' responses. It is puzzling that more Grade 4 students (22.3%) stated that they received tutoring "more than three times a week" than Grade 8 students (15.6%), because previous studies had shown that the demand for tutoring increases by levels of education (see e.g. EPPM 2011). Since the Grade 8 students were in early adolescence (12-16 years) and with well-developed cognitive functioning (Leeuw 2011, p.8), it is reasonable to assume that they produced more reliable responses than Grade 4 students. This is consistent with the hypothesis that reliability of responses increases with cognitive level (Borgers et al. 2004, p.19). The data on seasonal variations were collected only at Grade 8 through TIMSS 2011. They showed that the majority of students received private tutoring during the school year (63%), but some indicated that they also took tutoring during summer holidays (30%).

Table 1.6: Intensity of Shadow Education Classes per Week, Georgia

How many times do you visit a private tutor in a regular week during term time?				
	Once a week (%)	Twice a week (%)	Three times a week (%)	More than three times a week (%)
Grade 4	20.4	34.2	23.0	22.3
Grade 8	5.2	45.5	33.6	15.6
Parents of Grade 4 students	5.3	43.7	32.6	18.4

Table 1.7 demonstrates the average duration of all private tutoring classes per week as reported by the students. The majority of students in both grades indicated that they received shadow education up to two hours per week.

Table 1.7: Duration of all Shadow Education Classes per Week, Georgia

What is a total average duration of all your private classes per week?				
	Up to 2 hours	2.5 hours	3 hours	4 hours or more
Grade 4	71.0	10.9	9.7	8.3
Grade 8	70.8	7.6	8.8	12.7

The data from Table 1.7 are problematic for the following reasons:

- They seem inconsistent with data about intensity of tutoring (Table 1.6) on both grades. It is likely that some students indicated duration of one tutoring class instead of average duration of all tutoring classes combined.
- Grade 4 students may have found it difficult to answer this question. Ten-year-olds were expected to calculate hours of spending on tutoring and then average them per week.
- Some Grade 8 students could also have found this question demanding, and may not have answered it consistently.

For these reasons, the data from this question cannot be used for statistical analysis because they may mislead readers. The remarks show that a complicated and age-inappropriate question may have reduced the reliability of responses of students. It would have been more appropriate to have asked more simple questions such as "How long does your normal tutoring class last?". Students could have been given options to indicate duration of tutoring classes in different subjects, and such a question would not have required respondents to make specific calculations. Thus, different wording of the same question might have produced different data.

These observations indicate that data quality is related to respondents' ages, and special care is needed when designing instruments for young children (Knäuper et al. 1997). Borgers et al. (2004, p.18) indicated three main factors that affect answers to questions: motivation in answering, difficulty of the task, and cognitive ability to perform the task. Concerning the question presented in Table 1.7, the last two factors were problematic at least at Grade 4.

Ethics and politics of TIMSS and PIRLS assessments
Managers of international large-scale assessments, such as TIMSS, PIRLS and the Programme for International Student Assessment (PISA) operated by the Organisation for Economic Co-operation and Development (OECD) usually enjoy easy access to schools because the organisers co-operate with government bodies. For example in England and the USA, Departments of Education are responsible for TIMSS and PIRLS, while in Hong Kong and Finland public universities oversee the studies in cooperation with the government bodies. In Georgia, the NAEC under the Ministry of Education and Science (MoES) has conducted not only TIMSS

and PIRLS but also PISA, the Teaching and Learning International Survey (TALIS), and the Teacher Education and Development Study in Mathematics (TEDS-M).

According to the international protocol, schools are invited to join studies before the fieldwork begins. The Georgian MoES issues a letter to each school and provides information about upcoming international studies followed by the information packet. The TIMSS and PIRLS International Study Center provides sample notification letters for schools and parental permission consent forms, if needed. For the 2011 survey, Georgia had no official regulation for ethical research compliance and parental consent forms were not sent to families. No parents protested or complained about the issue. Part of the explanation could be that they were not informed that such consent forms existed elsewhere, and considered participation of their children in the international studies as a part of the 'mandatory' activities of schools. As reported by many school coordinators in personal communications, parents in general felt privileged that their children participated in the international study but never requested individual results of the assessment. For example, in the USA, where regulations require parental consent, in TIMSS 2011 nearly 400 schools used passive consent and 50 schools used active consent (US Department of Education 2013, p.116).

In general, schools in Georgia have the right to reject participation in the study given the formal school decentralisation policy. However, usually schools obey almost all instructions from the MoES. This indicates that the Soviet-style centralisation is still deeply ingrained, and schools seldom enjoy the autonomy given by new legislation.

Collecting shadow education data through TIMSS and PIRLS studies was a great opportunity for the author of this chapter to reach a large sample in all regions. Moreover, there were no additional financial costs for the researcher, and the authority of the MoES guaranteed high response rates. Absence of requirement for parental permission further facilitated the research process and minimised student non-participation. Yet although involving governmental authority assures high interest and participation in international studies, it may lead some respondents to hide information on sensitive topics such as shadow education which is not regulated or monitored by the government. This was the primary reason why the author did not include shadow education questions in the teacher questionnaire of TIMSS and PIRLS 2011.

Going further, the absence of ethical compliance requirements in Georgia allows the IEA and other international organisations such as the OECD to conduct research with minors without parental permission. This creates two problems: first, it gives unfair advantage to the IEA and OECD compared to other international researchers who have to undergo lengthy ethical compliance procedures. Second, it raises ethical questions about the IEA's research in Georgia and other countries where ethical requirements for research do not exist. One can argue that a lack of national regulations is not an excuse for an international organisation to forego ethical requirements.

Conclusions

The TIMSS and PIRLS 2011 study suggested that the use of shadow education in Georgia by students at Grade 4 (33.3%) and Grade 8 (38.6%) was quite high taking into consideration that there were no public examinations at the end of either grade. Many issues arise from this picture, both nationally and internationally. The purpose of the present chapter was to examine methodological issues related to studying the phenomenon through large-scale international assessments.

Concerning questionnaire design, the chapter has highlighted reasons for formatting the additional questions in the same way as the international questions. It has also noted limitations arising from the structure of the questions. A broader lesson is that these additional questions should have been carefully piloted before implementation.

Overall, the advantages and disadvantages related to collecting data on shadow education in Georgia through TIMSS and PIRLS 2011 may be summarised as follows:

Advantages:
- It was the first study of shadow education based on nationally representative samples.
- Large sample size strengthened statistical power and permitted generalisation over the population.
- It provided subject- and grade-specific data on private tutoring, which had been missing in previous studies.
- Surveying students from two different education levels permitted comparability across grades.
- Additional surveying of parents permitted triangulation with

student data.
- The governmental authority and machinery generated high student response rates.

Disadvantages:
- Data from some questions are problematic due to the construction and wording of those questions.
- Some questions were not age-specific and may not have been clear enough for some students. Those questions did not take sufficient account of cognitive development, and contributed to inconsistencies and ambiguities.
- Bypassing the compliance requirements for research ethics and exercise of strong political power provides unfair advantage to IEA compared to other international studies, and raises questions whether ethics of research are universal or subject to the regulations of individual countries.

These observations suggest that investigating shadow education through large-scale quantitative research requires extra care in designing instruments and interpreting results, especially when research deals with children. The insights from this chapter may caution readers about accepting at face value similar datasets from other countries. IEA and other studies appear authoritative, but may contain hidden flaws. Thus, the chapter provides methodological insights that may have wider relevance.

References

Boston College, PIRLS and TIMSS International Study Center (2013): *Press Release: Achievement Results for IEA's 2011 Trends in International Mathematics and Science Study (TIMSS) and Progress in International Reading Literacy Study*. http://timssandpirls.bc.edu/data-release-2011/pdf/TIMSS-PIRLS-2011-International-Press-Release.pdf. Accessed 12 June 2015

Borgers, Natacha; Hox, Joop & Sikkel, Dirk (2004): 'Response Effects in Surveys on Children and Adolescents: The Effect of Number of Response Options, Negative Wording, and Neutral Mid-Point'. *Quality & Quantity*, Vol.38, No.1, pp.17-33.

Bray, Mark (2009): *Confronting the Shadow Education System: What Government Policies for What Private Tutoring?* Paris: UNESCO International Institute for Educational Planning (IIEP).

Bray, Mark & Kobakhidze, Magda Nutsa (2014): 'Measurement Issues in Research on Shadow Education: Challenges and Pitfalls Encountered in TIMSS and PISA'. *Comparative Education Review*, Vol.58, No.4, pp.590-620.

Bregvadze, Tamar (2012): 'Analyzing the Shadows: Private Tutoring as a Descriptor of the Education System in Georgia'. *International Education Studies*, Vol.5, No.6, pp.80-89.

Dore, Ronald (1997): *The Diploma Disease: Education, Qualification and Development*. London: Institute of Education, University of London.

EPPM [International Institute of Education Policy, Planning and Management] (2011): *Study of Private Tutoring in Georgia*. Tbilisi: EPPM. [In Georgian]

Gabedava, Mariam (2013): 'Reforming the University Admission System in Georgia', in *Global Corruption Report: Education*. London and Berlin: Transparency International, Earthscan and Routledge, pp. 155-160.

Hof, Stefanie (2014): 'Does Private Tutoring Work? The Effectiveness of Private Tutoring: A Nonparametric Bounds Analysis'. *Education Economics*, Vol.22, No.4, pp.347-366.

IEA [International Association for the Evaluation of Educational Achievement] (2014): *Data Processing and Research Center*. http://www.iea.nl/dpc.html, Accessed 29 May 2014

Johanson, Ieva & Neuschmidt, Oliver (2007): 'Chapter 6' in *TIMSS 2007 Survey Operations Procedures Units and Manuals*. Chestnut Hill, MA: Boston College. http://timss.bc.edu/timss2007/PDF/T07_TR_Chapter6.pdf.

Jokić, Boris (ed.) (2013): *Emerging from the Shadow: A Comparative Qualitative Exploration of Private Tutoring in Eurasia*. Zagreb: Network of Education Policy Centers.

Joncas, Mark (2012): 'TIMSS 2011 Target Population Sizes', in Martin, Michael O. & Mullis, Ina V.S. (eds.), *Methods and Procedures in TIMSS and PIRLS 2011*. Chestnut Hill, MA: TIMSS & PIRLS International Study Center, Boston College.

Joncas, Mark & Foy, Pierre (2012): 'Sampling Design in PIRLS and TIMSS', in Martin, Michael O. & Mullis, Ina V.S. (eds.), *Methods and Procedures in TIMSS and PIRLS 2011*. Chestnut Hill, MA: TIMSS & PIRLS International Study Center, Boston College, pp.1-21.

Kobakhidze, Magda Nutsa (2012): 'PIRLS 2011 Encyclopedia: Education Policy and Curriculum in Reading: Georgia', in Mullis, Ina V.S.; Martin, Michael O.; Minnich, Chad A.; Drucker, Kathleen T. & Ragan, Moira A. (eds.), *Georgia*. Chestnut Hill, MA: TIMSS & PIRLS International Study Center, Boston College, pp.243-251.

Knäuper, Bärbel; Belli, Robert F.; Hill, Daniel H. & Herzog, A. Regula (1997): 'Question Difficulty and Respondents' Cognitive Ability: The Impact on Data Quality'. *Journal of Official Statistics*, Vol.13, No.2, pp.181-199.

Leeuw, Edith; Borgers, Natacha & Smits, Astrid (2004): 'Pretesting Questionnaires for Children and Adolescents', in Presser, Stanley; Rothgeb, Jennifer

M.; Couper, Mick P.; Lessler, Judith; Martin, Elizabeth; Martin, Jean & Singer, Eleanor (eds.), *Methods for Testing and Evaluating Survey Questionnaires*. New Jersey: Wiley-Inter-science, pp.409-429.

Leeuw, Edith (2011): *Improving Data Quality when Surveying Children and Adolescence: Cognitive and Social Development and Its Role in Questionnaire Construction and Pretesting*. Naantali, Finland: The Academy of Finland: Research Programs, Public Health Challenges and Health and Welfare of Children and Young People. http://www.aka.fi/Tiedostot/Tiedostot/LAPSET/Presentations%20of%20the%20annual%20seminar%202010-12%20May%202011/Surveying%20Children%20and%20adolescents_de%20Leeuw.pdf.

Matiashvili, Anna & Kutateladze, Nino (2006): 'Georgia', in Silova, Iveta; Būdienė, Virginija & Bray, Mark (eds.), *Education in a Hidden Marketplace: Monitoring of Private Tutoring*. New York: Open Society Institute, pp.191-210.

Martin, Michael O. & Mullis, Ina V.S. (eds.) (2012): *Methods and Procedures in TIMSS and PIRLS 2011*. Chestnut Hill, MA: TIMSS & PIRLS International Study Center, Boston College.

Rutkowski, Leslie; Gonzalez, Eugenio; Joncas, Mark & von Davier, Matthias (2010): 'International Large-scale Assessment Data: Issues in Secondary Analysis and Reporting'. *Educational Researcher*, Vol.39, No.2, pp.142-151.

Tse, Shek Kam (2014): 'To What Extent Does Hong Kong Primary School Students' Chinese Reading Comprehension Benefit from After-school Private Tuition?'. *Asia Pacific Education Review*. Vol.15, No.2, pp.283-297.

Safarzyńska, Karolina (2013): 'Socio-economic Determinants of Demand for Private Tutoring'. *European Sociological Review*, Vol.29, No.2, pp.139-154.

Silova, Iveta (ed.) (2009): *Private Supplementary Tutoring in Central Asia: New Opportunities and Burdens*. Paris: UNESCO International Institute for Educational Planning (IIEP).

Silova, Iveta; Būdienė, Virginija & Bray, Mark (eds.) (2006): *Education in a Hidden Marketplace: Monitoring of Private Tutoring*. New York: Open Society Institute.

Silova, Iveta & Bray, Mark (2006): 'The Context: Societies and Education in the post-Socialist Transformation', in Silova, Iveta; Budiene, Virginija & Bray, Mark (eds.), *Education in a Hidden Marketplace: Monitoring of Private Tutoring*. New York: Open Society Institute, pp.41-61.

US Department of Education (2013): *U.S. TIMSS and PIRLS 2011 Technical Report and User's Guide*. Washington, DC: National Center for Education Statistics.

World Bank, The (2012): *Fighting Corruption in Public Services: Chronicling Georgia's Reforms*. Washington DC: The World Bank.

Appendix 1.1: Shadow Education Questions in the TIMSS and PIRLS Grade 4 Student Questionnaire

PT 1

In this school year, have you received private lessons with a private tutor in any school subject?

Fill one circle only

Yes ------- O
No -------- O

If your answer is "Yes", then proceed to question # 2.
If your answer is "No", then you may stop here.

PT 2

In which of the following school subject(s) have you taken the private lessons in this school year?

Fill one circle for each line

	Yes	No
Georgian language and literature	O	O
Mathematics	O	O
English	O	O
Foreign language (other than English)	O	O
Sciences	O	O
Reading (basic reading literacy, reading comprehension)	O	O
Other (please, specify)	O	O

PT3

Who is the private tutor that gives you private lessons?

You may select more than one circle

Schoolteacher, who teaches me at school as well	O
A teacher in my school who teaches other students but does not teach me at school	O
Teacher from other school	O
A university student/recent graduate	O
Famous tutor	O
Don't know exactly	O
Other (please specify)	O

PT4

Do your parents pay money for your supplementary lessons with a private tutor?

*Fill **one** circle only*

Yes -------------------- ○
No --------------------- ○
I do not know ------ ○

If your answer is "Yes", then proceed to question # 5.
If your answer is "No", then go to question # 6.

PT5

What is a total expenditure in Laris your parents pay during <u>one month</u> for <u>all</u> your private lessons?

*Fill **one** circle only*

Up to 50 Lari --- ○
51-90 Lari -- ○
91-130 Lari --- ○
131-170 Lari --- ○
171-210 Lari --- ○
211-250 Lari --- ○
251 Lari and more ----------------------------------- ○
We do not pay money. Private tutor is our family's
    close friend/colleague/neighbor/relative ----- ○
I do not know --- ○

PT6

a) Which period of a year do you usually take private lessons?

*Fill **one** circle for each line*

                                                    Yes No
                                                    ↓   ↓

During a school year ---------------------- ○ ○
In the beginning of a school year -------- ○ ○
In the end of a school year --------------- ○ ○
On vacations ------------------------------ ○ ○

b) How many times do you visit a private tutor in a regular week during term time?

*Fill **one** circle only*

Once a week ---------------------- ○
Twice a week --------------------- ○
Three times a week --------------- ○
More than three times a week --- ○

c) **What is a total average duration of <u>all your private lessons per week</u>?**
*Fill **one** circle only*

Up to two hours -------------------- ○
Two and a half hours -------------- ○
Three hours ------------------------ ○
More than four hours -------------- ○

d) **For how many years have you been taking supplementary private tutoring?**

Answer: _____ Years

Write in numbers

Appendix 1.2: Shadow Education Questions in the Parent Questionnaire, Grade 4

PT 1

In this school year, has your child received private lessons in any school subject with a private tutor?
*Fill **one** circle only*

Yes ---- ○
No ----- ○

If your answer is "Yes", then proceed to question # 2.
If your answer is "No", then you may stop here.

PT 2

In which of the following school subject(s) has your child taken the private lessons in this school year?

*Fill **one** circle for each line*

	Yes	No
Georgian language and literature	○	○
Mathematics	○	○
English	○	○
Foreign language (other than English)	○	○
Sciences	○	○
Reading (basic reading literacy, reading reading comprehension)	○	○
Other (please, specify)	○	○

PT 3

Who is the private tutor that gives your child private lessons?
*You may fill **more than one** circle*

Schoolteacher, who teaches my child at school as well ---- ○
A teacher in my child's school who teaches other students
    but does not teach my child at school ---------------------- ○
Teacher from other school ------------------------------------ ○
A university student/recent graduate ------------------------ ○
Famous tutor --- ○
Don't know exactly -- ○
Other (please specify) -- ○

PT4

What is a total expenditure in Laris you pay during <u>one month</u> for your child's <u>all</u> private lessons?
*Fill **one** circle only*

Up till 50 Lari --- ○
51-90 Lari --- ○
91-130 Lari --- ○
131-170 Lari -- ○
171-210 Lari -- ○
211-250 Lari -- ○
251 Lari and more -- ○
I do not pay money. Private tutor is my close friend/colleague/
    neighbor/relative --------------------------------------- ○
I do not know --- ○

PT5

a) **During the school year, how many times does your child usually take private lessons?**
*Fill **one** circle only*

Once a week --------------------- ○
Twice a week -------------------- ○
Three times a week -------------- ○
More than three times a week ---- ○

b) **For how many years have you been sending your child to a private tutor?**

Answer: _____ Years

Write in numbers

PT6

Do you think additional preparation with a private tutor helps your child to improve his/her academic achievements?
*Circle only **one** circle*

It is very helpful -------------------------------- O
It is partially helpful -------------------------- O
It is no help at all ------------------------------ O
Don't know --------------------------------------- O

From the list below what are the reason(s) for hiring private tutor for your child?
*Fill **one** circle for each line*

	Agree a lot	Agree a little	Disagree a little	Disagree a lot
a) My child doesn't study well enough at school and I would like him/her to study a school programme very well.	O	O	O	O
b) It is impossible to achieve success at school without private tutoring.	O	O	O	O
c) It is prestigious to send a child to a private tutor.	O	O	O	O
d) Everyone around my child takes private classes and I do not want my child to fall behind.	O	O	O	O
e) I think that school does not provide quality education to my child.	O	O	O	O
f) School textbooks are difficult for my child to understand individually. I need extra help from a private tutor.	O	O	O	O
g) Information given in school textbooks is difficult for child to understand. Time allocated in lesson is not enough to explain all study material.	O	O	O	O
h) In order my child to have a better reading comprehension skills, he/she needs extra help from a private tutor.	O	O	O	O
i) I think that a private tutor has a better professional qualification.	O	O	O	O
j) I do not have a clear idea.	O	O	O	O

2

Research on Private Tutoring in Malaysia: Methodological Insights from a Quantitative Study

Husaina Banu KENAYATHULLA

Introduction

In Malaysia, private tutoring is widely perceived as a household necessity. A 2004/05 household expenditure survey recorded that 20.1 per cent of households with at least one child aged seven to 19 indicated expenditures on private tutoring (Kenayathulla 2013, p.634). In a smaller sample of urban students, Tan (2011) surveyed 1,600 Year 7 (lower secondary) students from eight schools in Selangor and Kuala Lumpur, and found that 88.0 per cent had received tutoring during their primary schooling.

The marketplace has various forms of tutoring: individualized, small-group, large-group and online tutoring. Fees differ according to the types and places of tutoring. If the tutoring is conducted in the students' homes, the fees are usually higher because they cover the tutors' travelling costs. According to the Ministry of Education, in January 2013 the country had 3,107 registered private tutoring centres, with 3.2 per cent of the total number of primary and secondary students enrolled and 11,967 tutors (Malaysia, Ministry of Education 2013). No data are available on the scale of informally-provided tutoring and online tutoring.

Bray, Mark; Kwo, Ora & Jokić, Boris (eds.) (2015): *Researching Private Supplementary Tutoring: Methodological Lessons from Diverse Cultures*. Hong Kong: Comparative Education Research Centre (CERC), The University of Hong Kong, and Dordrecht: Springer. © CERC

This chapter presents methodological dimensions of a quantitative study that sought to investigate students' perceptions of tutoring. It includes remarks on challenges that were encountered by the researcher in Malaysia when adapting a questionnaire from Hong Kong.

Mainstream Schooling and Private Tutoring in Malaysia

Formal education in Malaysia follows a 6+3+2+2+4 model, i.e. six years of primary (Standards 1-6), three years of lower secondary (Forms 1-3), two years of middle secondary (Forms 4-5), two years of upper secondary (Lower 6 and Upper 6), and four years for a standard university degree. The medium of instruction in National Schools is Malay, and National-Type Schools use Tamil or Chinese. Malay is the national language, and the use of the other languages reflects the presence of Chinese and Indians alongside Malays in the population (Joseph 2008). At the secondary level, the system only has National Secondary Schools since the government desires to promote loyalty to Malaysia among children of the various cultures and languages.

Each stage of the education system has national examinations. After six years of primary education, students take the Ujian Pencapaian Sekolah Rendah (UPSR – Primary School Achievement Test). All children who have completed primary school are eligible to continue to lower secondary education. Since 2014, Form 3 students have been evaluated through school-based assessments and an examination called Pentaksiran Tingkatan 3 (PT3 – Form 3 Assessment). Different sets of PT3 questions are prepared by the Examinations Syndicate of Ministry of Education but are chosen by the head teachers of each school. The examinations are conducted and marked by the teachers of the respective schools, but scores are moderated and verified by appraisers from the Examinations Syndicate and state Departments of Education.

After completing Form 5, students have to pass the examination for the Sijil Pelajaran Malaysia (SPM – Malaysian Certificate of Education) in order to continue to Form 6 or matriculation centres. At the end of two years of upper secondary, the students sit the examination for the Sijil Tinggi Persekolahan Malaysia (STPM – Malaysian Higher School Certificate). In addition, the matriculation programmes have decentralised examinations to meet the admission requirements of universities. Matriculation programs are offered based on an ethnic quota: 90 per cent of spaces are reserved for Bumiputeras, and the other 10 per cent are reserved for non-Bumiputeras. Thus, much emphasis is given to both centralised and decentralised examinations. Competition among students to gain entry into the best secondary schools and top-ranking universities becomes the main driving force for private tutoring (Arshad 2004).

Much tutoring is provided by active and retired teachers. The Ministry of Education permits school teachers to tutor outside school hours provided they have secured a permit from the Ministry at least two months in advance (Malaysia, Ministry of Education 2006). Teachers are limited to four hours of tutoring per week, but there are no restrictions on the types of students they can tutor. This means that they can tutor students who attend their regular classes, though the policy prohibits teachers from distributing promotional materials to their students in school. Teachers are only permitted to undertake private tutoring if their annual performance scores are 80 per cent or more for the previous year. In addition, they should ensure that tutoring does not interfere with their duties as teachers.

Teachers are also allowed to tutor in private tuition centres, each of which must be registered with the Department of Education of the state in which it is located. The registration procedure requires permits from the Health Department, the Fire Department and the Local Authority. The administrative system allows for government inspections in response to complaints from the public.

Although enrolment rates in private tutoring are high and demand considerable household expenditures (Kenayathulla 2012), evidence on the effectiveness of tutoring is scarce. With that in mind, the researcher designed a quantitative study to examine perceptions of effectiveness and related factors. The following sections focus on the methods employed in the study.

Methodology in an Empirical Study

The author solicited data from a stratified sample of 4,200 secondary students in Selangor State. Questionnaires were distributed to two secondary schools in each of the 10 districts. The research covered three classes of Forms 3 and 5 in each school. The normal class size in Malaysia is about 30-40 students, so an average class size of 35 was used to design the sample. The target sample was 4,200 students (35 students x three classes x two forms x 20 schools). The questions addressed the scale, focus and types of tutoring received, and the reasons for seeking it.

Approval to conduct the survey was obtained from the Educational Planning and Research Division (EPRD) of the Ministry of Education, and from the Selangor Department of Education. The EPRD approval required the proposal and questionnaires plus an approval letter from the researcher's university. Applications can be made online, and normally approval is given within five working days provided the research is not related to sensitive issues. Sensitive issues include the implementation of government policies associated with economic development, education and social affairs; research that questions religious freedom, Malay as a national language, citizenship and related matters; and research that questions the power or ability of certain ethnic groups (Malaysia, Ministry of Education 2014). For the research on which his chapter focuses, approval was granted promptly.

The EPRD does not require researchers to secure consent from parents for school-aged children to participate in surveys, but parental consent is required for interview and video-recording of school-aged children (Malaysia, Ministry of Education 2014). This policy differs from that in other countries. For instance in the USA, approval must usually be sought from an Institutional Review Board (IRB) for research that involves living individuals through interaction, intervention or identifiable private information (see e.g. Indiana University 2014). The process generally requires informed consent, in which researchers should ensure that the research subjects (or their parents in the case of minors) are aware of the purpose of the research and of risks and benefits of participation.

In the research reported in this chapter, questionnaires were handed to the Selangor Department of Education, which then distributed them to the District Education Offices. Two of the government officers who agreed to help the researcher to distribute the questionnaires to principals were doctoral students at the researcher's institution. In this case, relationships helped to get the research done. Even if these officers had not been not doctoral students, the existence of personal connections would probably have assisted the process. In this case the officers were staff of the Ministry of Education, and schools are expected to adhere to instructions given by a higher authority.

The principals were given the questionnaires when they attended meetings at the District Education Offices. These questionnaires had been adapted from the research conducted by Bray and colleagues in Hong Kong (see Chapter 8 in this book; Bray 2013; Zhan et al. 2013). However, some questions had been modified to suit the local context. For instance, the term 'tutorial king' is not used in Malaysia so 'famous tutor' was used instead. The questions on the subjects in which tutoring was received were also modified to fit Malaysian syllabuses.

In addition, for questions on the comparison between teachers and tutors, the question was rephrased to "To what extent do you agree with the following comparison about your school teachers and your tutors?" [*Sejauh manakah anda bersetuju mengenai perbandingan di antara guru sekolah dan guru tuisyen?*]. However, this question was poorly phrased for the Malaysian setting because teachers are legally allowed to tutor and thus the same school teacher can also be a tutor. This question was suitable in Hong Kong since teachers there do not provide paid supplementary tutoring to their own students, but was not suitable for Malaysia. The adapted questionnaire had been piloted, but the issue was not picked up at that time.

The piloting was undertaken with 30 students in an urban secondary school in Selangor. The questionnaires were distributed through a teacher in that school who was also the researcher's doctoral student. In this case, the researcher used relationships to negotiate access. The teacher distributed questionnaire to students in an average class, and reported that the students had no problem understanding the questions and completing the work in about half an hour. One approach to measure reliability of a questionnaire identifies internal consistency and evaluates the degree to which each item consistently measures the same underlying construct (Santos 1999). Cronbach alpha is the method most commonly used by researchers to measure internal consistency. The value of Cronbach alpha for the questions ranged between 0.771 and 0.849. Thus, the questions were considered to be within the acceptable range of reliability.

Nevertheless, another problem arose from omission of a question. This was about race and ethnicity, which is important in Malaysia but not Hong Kong. The researcher overlooked this matter, and it was not identified during piloting because all students in this urban school were from the Malay community. This experience underlines the need for researchers to select representative samples if possible when conducting pilot studies (Salant & Dillman 1994). In this study, the pilot should have been conducted in two schools with students of multiple ethnicities, preferably one urban and one rural, so that terms such as 'internet tutoring' which might not be common for rural students could be scrutinised.

The researcher only realized that the variable 'ethnicity' had been omitted after the questionnaire had been photocopied and was ready for distribution. The researcher then decided to include ethnicity in the instruction sheet prepared for teachers. The sheet requested teachers to ask students to add a question on race in the questionnaires and then to answer the question. However, many students did not do this. It seems likely that many teachers did not ask the students to add the question on race, and 81.3 per cent of the returned questionnaires had missing values on that item. An important methodological lesson is not to add questions when the questionnaire has already been finalised and reproduced.

Procedures for Distribution of Questionnaires

Instructions on the distribution of questionnaires were given to each level in the education system as indicated in Table 2.1. The instructions were

Table 2.1: Instructions for Distributing the Questionnaires

Selangor Department of Education	District Education Offices	Principals	Class Teachers
1. Distribute questionnaires to 10 District Education Offices. 2. Each district will be given three bundles of white questionnaires for Form 3 and three bundles of blue questionnaires for Form 5. 3. All questionnaires will be collected back from the District Education Office. 4. Contact the researcher to return the completed questionnaire.	1. Choose two schools in your district. 2. Distribute the questionnaires to those schools. Each school will receive a bundle of white questionnaires for Form 3 and of blue questionnaires for Form 5. Each bundle has 105 questionnaires (for three classes). 3. Request the principal to distribute the questionnaires to class teachers of Forms 3 and 5. 4. Collect and send the questionnaires to the quality assurance sector of the State Education Department.	1. Distribute the questionnaires to three class teachers of Form 3 (white forms) and three class teachers of Form 5 (blue forms). 2. Collect back the questionnaires from the class teachers. 3. Send the questionnaires back to the District Education Office.	1. Distribute the questionnaires, and ask the students to complete them. 2. Ask the students to add a question on race to the questionnaire. 3. Ask the students to write the race as follows: M = Malay, C = Chinese, I = Indian, O = Other. 4. Collect the questionnaires and hand them to the principal.

pasted on 10 boxes, each of which contained questionnaires for schools in one district. In each box were two small boxes. Each smaller box contained the questionnaires needed for one school.

Nevertheless, while this experience shows the importance of the researcher administering the questionnaires herself, in Malaysian schools it would be an unusual arrangement. The common practice is to pass questionnaires to the school office, from which the researcher to collects back the questionnaires after one or two weeks. If the researcher knows a principal personally, it might be easier for the researcher to enter the school to distribute the questionnaires. In rural areas, it is commonly easier for researchers to negotiate access since permission to enter the school in rural areas will be given as long as approval letters are obtained from the EPRD of the Ministry of Education and from the state Department of Education. However, principals in urban schools do not always permit distribution of the questionnaires since these schools are approached by many researchers from different institutions and the research can disrupt teaching and learning processes.

A further question in research design for this particular study was whether the government involvement would affect the results of the study. Certainly this issue must be recognised, but the researcher stated clearly that all the information would be kept confidential and that the identities of students would not be revealed. Further, the questionnaires address students' perceptions on tutoring and were about their daily activities. If the questionnaires had been about teachers' perceptions, then the distribution through the government might have led to more bias since teachers who were not paying tax on their tutoring incomes might have concealed their tutoring work.

Although the distribution of questionnaires through government personnel has advantages, the approach has several drawbacks. First, the researcher was not there to clarify any ambiguities that students might have regarding the questionnaires. For instance, lecture style by tutors (video) might not be something familiar to students in Malaysia. In addition, the researcher was not there to assure respondents on the confidentiality of the information that they provided in the questionnaire. In this context, if the researcher had been present clear instructions would have been given to those who did not attend private tutoring, and proper guidance would have been given on answering questions related to reasons for not taking tutoring. Thus, students would have understood that the questionnaires need to be filled up by those who were taking and not taking tutoring classes.

Findings

The survey responses indicated that 58.7 per cent were female students and 41.3 per cent were male. Among them, 47.7 per cent were in Form 3 and 52.3 per cent were in Form 5. Most students reported that they had received small-group tutoring during the previous 12 months, but 17.1 per cent indicated that they had received one-to-one and 17.8 per cent received lecture-style tutoring. Additionally, 8.4 per cent of the students reported that they received online tutoring. Such tutoring is increasingly popular, and the Malaysian Government approves programmes such as Score A (Kenayathulla et al. 2013). Lecture-style tutoring through video recording is not common in Malaysia.

Just over half of the students described themselves as good or excellent performers compared with all students of their grade in their schools. In addition, 40.8 per cent of the students described their performance as fair. Only 6.8 per cent of the students described their performance as weak. However, in this analysis, reporting of percentages does not take into consideration the number of unfilled questionnaires. Thus, no conclusion can be reached on whether tutoring is mostly taken by both high performing and weak students or dominated by high achievers.

Students were also asked about the subjects in which they received tutoring. Most students received tutoring in Malay, English, Mathematics, Science and History. International literature commonly shows that English and Mathematics are popular subjects, but Malaysian students need to pass both Malay and History to be eligible for a high school certificate.

Conclusions

International comparisons involving large numbers of countries have commonly been undertaken to analyse educational spending, educational achievement and other aspects. While these international comparisons are useful, they always face challenges in obtaining systematically comparable and equivalent data due to diversities across and within countries (Manzon 2014). Such challenges may be especially evident in the domain of shadow education, which is not easy to define and measure (Bray 2010; Bray & Kobakhidze 2014).

International comparisons are typically derived from common administration of instruments devised externally. Such instruments may require adaptation, which creates further challenges. This chapter has provided an example of the challenges that researchers might encounter when adapting questionnaires from a previous study in another context. Socio-cultural factors that shape norms and practices in one country might be different from those in another country, and context-specific variables may need to be incorporated when adapting questionnaires. For instance, ethnicity is an important variable in Malaysia since it is a multi-ethnic society and perceptions about tutoring might differ by ethnicity.

In this research, some of the questions in the Hong Kong questionnaire were deemed unsuitable for respondents in Malaysia. For instance, 'tutorial king' is not a common term in Malaysia. Additionally, Malaysia has an overlap in the identity of teachers and tutors because teachers can tutor their own students. Another methodological challenge encountered in this research is when questionnaires were routed through government personnel. Since the researcher was not directly involved in questionnaire administration and distribution, it is unclear whether the students who did not fill up the questionnaires were not taking tutoring or were reluctant to participate in the survey. In addition, the researcher was not present to address ambiguities and clarify terms.

References

Arshad, Mahzan (2004): 'Amalan Tuisyen Dalam Sistem Pendidikan'. *Portal Pendidikan Utusan*. http://www.geocities.com/pendidikmy/berita/berita012004.html
Bray, Mark (2010): 'Researching Shadow Education: Methodological Challenges and Directions'. *Asia Pacific Education Review*, Vol.11, No.1, pp.3-13.
Bray, Mark (2013): 'Benefits and Tensions of Shadow Education: Comparative Perspectives on the Roles and Impact of Private Supplementary Tutoring in the Lives of Hong Kong Students'. *Journal of International and Comparative Education*, Vol.2, No.1, pp.18-30.
Bray, Mark & Kobakhidze, Magda Nutsa (2014): 'Measurement Issues in Research on Shadow Education: Challenges and Pitfalls Encountered in TIMSS and PISA'. *Comparative Education Review*, Vol.58, No.4, pp.590-620.
Indiana University (2014) Human Subject New Studies. Office of Research Compliance, Indiana University. http://researchcompliance.iu.edu/hso/hs_submission.html

Joseph, Cynthia (2008): 'Ethnicities and Education in Malaysia: Difference, Inclusions and Exclusions', in Wan, Guofang (ed.), *The Education of Diverse Student Populations: A Global Perspective*. Dordrecht: Springer, pp.183-208.

Kenayathulla, Husaina Banu (2012): *An Economic Analysis of Household Educational Decisions in Malaysia*. PhD Dissertation, Indiana University.

Kenayathulla, Husaina Banu (2013): 'Household Expenditures on Private Tutoring: Emerging Evidence from Malaysia'. *Asia Pacific Education Review*, Vol.14, No.4, pp.629-644.

Kenayathulla, Husaina Banu; Afshari, Mojgan; Alias Norlidah; Ghani, Muhammad Faizal A. & Ibrahim, Mohammed Sani Bin (2013): '"Score A" – Online Tutoring Programme in Malaysia'. *The Online Journal of Science and Technology*, Vol.3, No.1, pp.1-11.

Malaysia, Ministry of Education (2006): Bil. No. 1 Year 2006. *Garis Panduan Kelulusan Melakukan Pekerjaan Luar Sebagai Guru Tuisyen atau Tenaga Pengajar Sambilan*. Putrajaya: Ministry of Education.

Malaysia, Ministry of Education (2013): *Private Institution Statistics*. Putrajaya: Ministry of Education. http://www.moe.gov.my/v/IPS-di-Malaysia

Malaysia, Ministry of Education (2014): *Educational Research Application System*. Education Planning and Research Department, Putrajaya: Ministry of Education. http://eras.moe.gov.my/eras/Index2.aspx

Manzon, Maria (2014): 'Comparing Places', in Bray, Mark; Adamson, Bob & Mason, Mark (eds.) *Comparative Education Research: Approaches and Methods*. 2nd edition, Hong Kong: Comparative Education Research Centre, The University of Hong Kong, and Dordrecht: Springer, pp.97-137.

Salant, Priscilla & Dillman, Don A. (1994): *How to Conduct your own Survey*. New York: John Wiley.

Santos, J. Reynaldo A. (1999): 'Cronbach's Alpha: A Tool for Assessing the Reliability of Scales'. *Journal of Extension*, Vol.37, No.2, pp.1-5.

Tan, Peck Leong (2011): *The Economic Impacts of Migrant Maids in Malaysia*. PhD thesis, University of Waikato.

Zhan, Shengli; Bray, Mark; Wang, Dan; Lykins, Chad & Kwo, Ora (2013): 'The Effectiveness of Private Tutoring: Students' Perceptions in Comparison with Mainstream Schooling in Hong Kong'. *Asia Pacific Education Review*, Vol.14, No.4, pp.495-509.

3

Relationships between Shadow Education and Examination Scores: Methodological Lessons from a Chinese Study in Senior Secondary Schools

Yu ZHANG

Introduction

Shadow education has been expanding for decades in China and in other Asian countries. One of the most important reasons for taking shadow education is to improve test scores, especially in contexts where such scores are crucial for access to better institutions and subsequent employment (Bray & Lykins 2012, pp.23-25).

The author's PhD dissertation (Zhang 2011), focused on relationships between shadow education and students' scores in the National College Entrance Examination (NCEE) in Jinan city. This chapter draws on methodological dimensions of the study. It interprets quantitative approaches to identification of the effects of shadow education on students' academic performance, and discusses lessons from these quantitative approaches.

The chapter has five sections. First it identifies the key research question and theoretical framework. Second, it discusses quantitative issues in this investigation and empirical models that attempt to address these issues. Third, it reports on data collection methods in the study. Fourth, it presents empirical findings on the relationships between private tutoring

---

Bray, Mark; Kwo, Ora & Jokić, Boris (eds.) (2015): *Researching Private Supplementary Tutoring: Methodological Lessons from Diverse Cultures.* Hong Kong: Comparative Education Research Centre (CERC), The University of Hong Kong, and Dordrecht: Springer. © CERC

and test scores; and finally it discusses methodological lessons from this study.

Research Question and Theoretical Framework

The key research question sought to identify the causal effect of private tutoring on students' academic performance. Of course, even if private tutoring helps to improve academic performance, it might have negative dimensions such as corrupting influence and/or increased social inequalities (see e.g. Bray 2009; Aurini et al. 2013). Nevertheless, parents and students need to know whether or not private tutoring can deliver what it promises, because they commonly spend much time and money on it.

The education production function helps to explore this question. This is a mathematical relation showing the maximum education outputs that can be produced with given educational resources under a specific education technology (Cohn & Geske 1990, p.168). The generalised education production function is given by:

$$f(Q, X/S) = 0$$

where

> Q is the vector of educational outputs: $Q: q_1, q_2, \ldots q_n$
> X is the vector of educational inputs: $X: x_1, x_2, \ldots x_k$
> f is the functional operator.

As Cohn and Geske (1990, p.167) pointed out, within a certain range of data, a linear relationship between the X inputs and the Q outputs would be empirically valid to the extent that the curvature of this part of output function is only mildly violated by employing a linear approximation. However, if the range of the data is wide, linear assumption might be invalid. In addition, any conclusion derived from linear analysis should not be applied to input levels beyond the range of the data sample.

For a linear model, the general form of the ith production function is:

$$q_i = a_0 + \sum_{k=1}^{k} a_k x_k + \varepsilon_i$$

where a_0 is the intercept, and a_k are the coefficients to be estimated. The coefficient in a linear function means a constant marginal productivity of the corresponding input, and ε_i is a stochastic error term.

Education inputs possess a hierarchical structure (Raudenbush & Bryk 2002). Figure 3.1 illustrates relationships between inputs at five hierarchical levels: society, community, school, classroom, and student. The society provides the broad environment including culture, institutional features of the education system, and education policies. The community provides neighbourhood inputs including safety, peer effects, economic conditions, and social capital. The school-level inputs could be classified as institutional and physical. Institutional inputs include principal leadership, school culture, student composition with regard to socioeconomic status (SES), and study ability. Physical inputs refer to school-level resources such as equipment, facilities, and buildings. Classroom level inputs include teacher experience, teacher expectations, and peer effects from the perspectives of gender, study ability and SES. Student level inputs could be divided into student input and family input. Student inputs include gender, study ability, motivation and expectation, test skills, and health. Family inputs include family SES, parental education, private cost of education (including expenditure on tutoring), and parenting styles.

Figure 3.1: Relationships between Components in Education Production

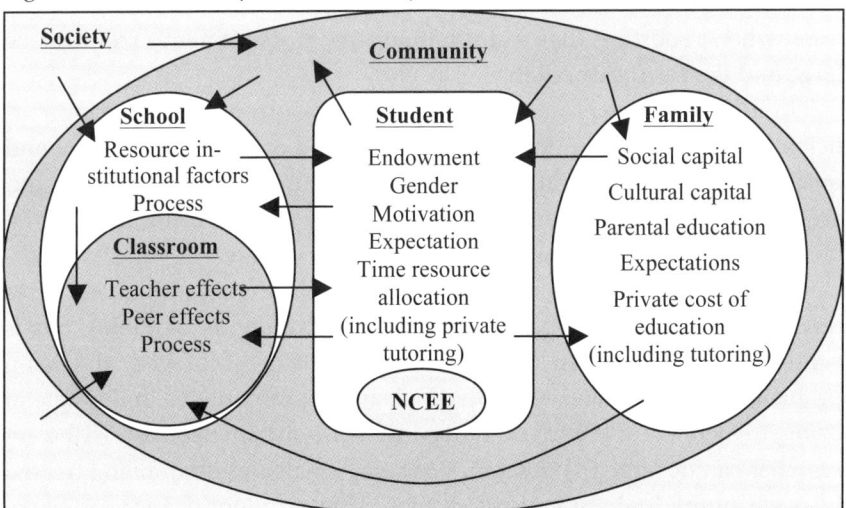

A key objective of the econometric estimation of an educational production function is identification of causal relationships. However, the education production process is complex and selective, and inputs may be difficult to identify and quantify (Cohn & Geske 1990, p.170). Sometimes researchers only capture a small part of the real causal relationships or even wrong causal relationships. Various research methods have been devised to handle this challenge.

Quantitative Issues and Empirical Models
Quantitative issues
The first challenge encountered by private tutoring researchers is how to measure private tutoring participation. The most straightforward way uses a dummy variable to document private tutoring participation status, with 'private tutoring = 1' meaning that students received private tutoring, and 'private tutoring = 0' meaning that students did not receive. However, since the definition of private tutoring is complex, students who report their participation status might have different understandings from the researchers. For example, one kind of English tutoring aims to improve scores in the NCEE, while another concentrates on helping students to prepare for the Test of English as a Foreign Language (TOEFL), or just for improving oral English. Only the first kind of tutoring is the focus of this study, but it is not easy to specify all kinds of English tutoring in surveys. If students have vague and inconsistent definitions when reporting their information, the measurement error will be large and the results unreliable.

In addition, it may not be enough to measure private tutoring participation using a dummy variable alone while omitting the quality and quantity of private tutoring. The duration of tutoring, fees per hour, etc. are introduced to address this issue. These are usually continuous variables, but are difficult to measure, especially for quality.

The next quantitative challenge varies with respect to the two types of measurements (i.e. binary variable and continuous variable), but is similar in nature. When the dummy variable is employed, the main problem is missing data. An individual student can only be in the state of being treated or not, and cannot be in both simultaneously. If the researcher can observe the outcomes of being treated and not being treated for each individual student, there would be no identification problem. Constructing this counterfactual in a convincing way is the main purpose of any identification strategy.

Several approaches may be used to identify causal effects (Angrist & Pischke 2009; Blundell & Costa-Dias 2009), including:

- random experiment methods,
- natural experiment methods (i.e. differences-in-differences),
- discontinuity regression methods,
- propensity score matching (PSM) methods,
- instrumental variable (IV) methods,
- control function methods, and
- quantile regression.

Among them, discontinuity regression and propensity score matching attempt to mimic the randomised assignment of the experimental setting with non-experimental data. The adaption of these identification strategies heavily depends on whether the model hypotheses are valid on specific data structure. Instrumental variable and control function methods deal with the same issue using structured two-step regression. Since it is very difficult to conduct a random experiment in the field of private tutoring, and observations are usually the only available data for researchers, quasi-experimental design and regression models are the most frequently used approaches.

When the measurement of private tutoring participation is a dummy variable, the problem to be addressed is called self-selection. This means that students self-select themselves into the treatment (i.e. private tutoring participation) or not according to their own characteristics, which may also influence the academic achievement. From this perspective, PSM can be used to construct a quasi-experimental approach based on second-hand data.

When the measurement of private tutoring includes continuous variables such as time or financial cost, the endogeneity of private tutoring quality and/or quantity must be addressed. Some variables may have effects on both student achievement and private tutoring participation, but are omitted in the regression function and thus are in the residual term. The frequently-omitted variables include study motivation, parents' education philosophy, and students' psychological conditions facing test competition. In this situation, the key variable of interest (i.e. private tutoring) and the residual are correlated, which violates the classical assumption of the ordinary least squares (OLS) model, and the OLS estimation of the effect of private tutoring effect would be biased. The instrumental variable (IV) model should be used to address this problem. However, it is usually difficult to find a valid IV, especially when using second-hand databases. With these matters in mind, the rest of this section will first discuss the IV approach and then introduce the PSM design.

Instrumental variable model

The basic model attempts to control for endogeneity of private tutoring and selection bias generated by non-random private tutoring assignment by a two-stage regression. If there is no selection issue and endogeneity problem, the latent education production function should be:

$$NCEE^*_{ijk} = \alpha_0 + \alpha X_{ijk} + \rho T_{ijk} + \beta C_{jk} + \gamma S_k + u_{ijk} \quad (1)$$

where

- the dependent variable $NCEE^*_{ijk}$ is the NCEE score of student i in class j in school k;[1]
- X_{ijk} is a vector of individual level educational inputs including age, gender, pre-test score, socioeconomic status (SES), and parenting styles;
- T is the measurement of private tutoring inputs;
- C_{jk} is a vector of class level inputs, including peer effects and class type;
- S_k is a vector of school level inputs including average teacher quality, physical school inputs, school culture, etc.; and
- u_{ijk} is the error term.

Table 3.1 provides more detailed information on the instruments used for the present study. Most instruments were selected following previous studies, and the other variables were designed according to the pilot studies. The measurement of parenting style was constructed from students' evaluations of their parents' parenting behaviours using principal component analysis.

According to the literature and common knowledge, students' decisions on private tutoring participation are affected by variables that also influence their academic performance, such as study ability, family background, and school level inputs. If variables such as teaching quality in the classroom and aspects of education policy influencing both the

---

[1] The study reported later in this chapter only considers the selection problem at school level, not at class level.

Table 3.1: Instruments Used in the Models for this Study

Category	Instruments	Measurement or Comments
Student level characteristics	Gender	Dummy variable: female = 1, male = 0
	Academic track	Dummy variable: science track = 1, humanity track = 0
	Registered residence	Dummy variable: rural = 1, urban = 0
	Student ability	HSEE score as pre-existing difference in academic ability
	Socioeconomic status	Socioeconomic status index calculated from individual variables including parental education level and parents' professions.
	Parenting styles	Four indices calculated from a series of instruments measuring parents' style of involvement in child's education.
Private tutoring inputs	Participation status	Dummy variable indicating whether or not participated in private tutoring
	Money spent on private tutoring	Total money spent on private tutoring
	Time spent on private tutoring	Index calculated from hours spent on private tutoring for Chinese, mathematics and English during weekdays, weekends, and summer
Class level inputs	Peer effects	Average SES index of the class
	Class Type	Dummy variable: key class = 1, non-key class = 0
School level inputs	School selectivity	The HSEE admission line
	School size	Number of students
	Average teacher quality	1) Percentage of teachers with certain professional ranks 2) Percentage of teachers at certain education levels
	Physical school inputs	1) Student teacher ratio index 2) Index calculated from the scale and condition of laboratories 3) Computer index calculated from per student computers, and per student computer used in instruction.

NCEE score and private tutoring participation are not included in the model and thus left into the residual, the variable T will be correlated with the error term which violates the basic assumption of OLS.

The proposed way to solve this problem argues that the variation of T includes both endogenous variation and exogenous variation, and that if researchers can cut the endogenous part and keep the exogenous part, then they can still use the exogenous variation of T to estimate the treatment effect. If researchers can find valid IVs (named Z), which have an impact on T but are not correlated with the residual u_{ijk}, they can distinguish the exogenous variation with the endogenous variation by first regressing T on Z and then calculating the fitted value $\hat{T}$ which only contains the exogenous variation.

Figure 3.2: The Venn Diagram of IV Estimation

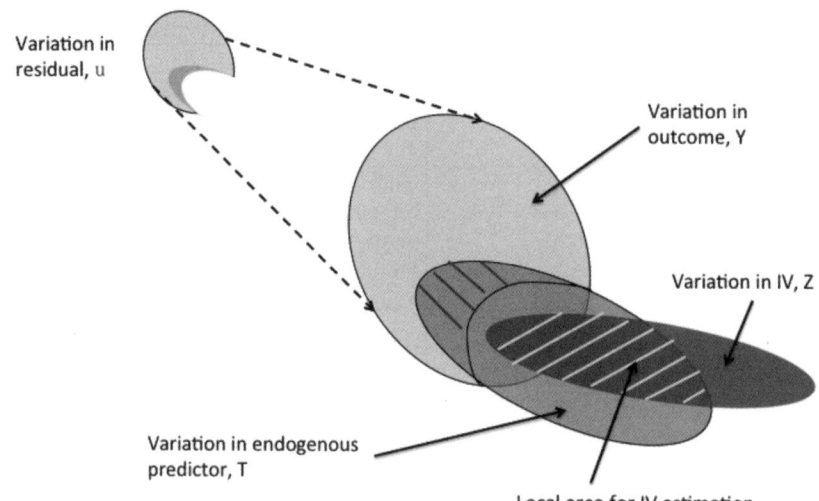

Source: Murnane & Willett (2010), p.231

Figure 3.2 gives the interpretation of IV estimation through a Venn Diagram. The central ellipse is the variation of Y, the overlapping ellipse is the variation of T, and T is correlated with the residual u, with their overlap being highlighted by the area with dark stripes. The dark ellipse in the bottom right is the variation of Z, which has overlap with X but not with u. Therefore, the predicted variation of the fitted value $\hat{T}$ is the shaded area with light stripes and is exogenous (because there is no overlap between this area and the residual).

IV analysis has two key assumptions. First, the IV must be related to the potentially endogenous predictor, i.e. $\sigma_{TZ} \neq 0$. Second, the IV cannot be related to the unobserved effects (i.e. the original residuals) that rendered the question predictor endogenous in the first place, i.e. $\sigma_{uz} = 0$.

In line with these assumptions, two IVs were proposed in this study. First, as indicated in the literature (e.g. Baker & LeTendre 2005; Bray 2009; Zhang et al. 2015), students may be influenced by their peers in making decisions about private tutoring participation. The more friends participate in private tutoring, the more likely that a specific student will participate in private tutoring. Thus, the number of private tutoring participants among one's five closest friends could be a valid IV.

Second, if the supply of private tutoring in certain districts or neighbourhoods is higher, the probability of students' participation in private tutoring would be higher. The measurement of private tutoring supply could be measured by the distance between the nearest private tutoring agency and home.

The Sargan test of over-identifying restrictions can check the exogeneity of these instrumental variables. There are different ways of IV estimation. This study adopts the two-stage least square (2SLS) because of the desire to combine the IV estimation with other approaches. The reduced form of 2SLS regression is:

$$NCEE^*_{ijk} = \alpha_0 + \alpha X_{ijk} + \pi_2 Z_{ijk} + \beta C_{jk} + \gamma S_k + u_{ijk} \quad (2)$$

where $E\left(u_{ijk} \middle| X_{ijk}, Z_{ijk}, C_{jk}, S_k\right) = 0$,

and $V\left(u_{ijk} \middle| X_{ijk}, Z_{ijk}, C_{jk}, S_k\right) = \sigma^2$.

The IV estimation is not the average treatment effect (ATE) but the local average treatment effect (LATE). The IV estimation is within a new region defined by the exogenous variation in the instrument. The interpretations of the IV estimator are therefore limited by the localisation of the analytic attention to only the light and medium-shaded variation that falls within the newly defined dark ellipse. It is only the variation in private tutoring participation that is affected by the peers and the distance to the nearest private tutoring centre upon which the study has capitalised in estimating the effect of private tutoring on student achievement. The IV estimation does not provide any information about the impact of private tutoring on student achievement for individuals whose private tutoring participation decision was not influenced by peers or distance.

Propensity score matching

The IV model discussed above takes the endogeneity of private tutoring participation into account. When the measurement of private tutoring participation is a binary variable, the problem becomes one of self-selection: students self-select themselves into the treatment or not. PSM is an appropriate approach to address this selection bias. Through estimating the students' decision-making process of private tutoring participation, PSM enables the researcher to construct an unbiased counterfactual group for the treatment group from observational data.

There are two assumptions for PSM to work:

- *Conditional independence*: there exists a set of observable covariates X such that after controlling for X, the potential outcome NCEE score is independent of treatment status:

$$(NCEE_1, NCEE_0) \perp T|X,$$

where $NCEE_1$ is the score when T = 1 (i.e. participate in private tutoring), and $NCEE_0$ is the score when T = 0 (i.e. not participate in private tutoring).

- *Common support*: for each value of X, there is a positive possibility of being both treated and untreated.

The first step of PSM is to run a Probit (or Logit) model to estimate the propensity score of participating in private tutoring for each individual student:

$$Pr(T_{ijk} = 1|X, C, S) = \varphi(a_0 + aX_{ijk} + bC_{ijk} + rS_{ijk})$$

where φ is the cumulative distribution function of the standard normal distribution.

The second step of PSM is to choose a matching algorithm that will use the estimated propensity score to match untreated students with treated students. Matching algorithms include nearest-neighbour matching, radius matching, kernel matching, and local-linear method.

The third step of PSM is to calculate the impact of private tutoring participation on NCEE score with the matched sample. Therefore, PSM derives the average treatment effect on the treated (ATT), instead of the average treatment effect on the whole population (ATE). It is possible that the ATT is different from the average treatment effect on the non-treated (ATNT), which is the average achievement effect on those who did not participate in private tutoring.

Data in the Chinese Study

The data used in this study were collected from Jinan city in Eastern China. For feasibility, a non-proportional stratified clustered sampling strategy was employed. Twenty-five out of 34 regular public high schools were randomly sampled, with the sample proportionally covering schools with different quality in different regions and districts. Within each sampled school three to five classes were randomly sampled, and all students in these sampled classes were invited to answer the questionnaire. The total sample size was 6,474 students. The non-response rate was below 5 per cent, and sampling weights were calculated and used in analyses.

Table 3.2 reports the shares of students participating in different types of private tutoring classes. For each school subject (i.e. mathematics, Chinese and English), one-to-one tutoring, middle-sized classes (6-25 students) and large classes (above 26 students) were much more popular than small groups. In mathematics, a larger share of students chose one-to-one tutoring, compared to the same share in Chinese and English.

Table 3.2: Class Size of Private Tutoring

Class size	Mathematics		Chinese		English	
	N	%	N	%	N	%
One-to-one	556	36.3	142	29.8	370	29.5
2-5 students	141	9.2	48	10.1	117	9.3
6-25 students	390	25.5	124	26.1	338	27.0
Above 25 students	443	29.0	162	34.0	429	34.2
Total	1,530	100.0	476	00.0	1,254	100.0

Table 3.3 shows the shares of student participation in private tutoring by agency types. For all the three subjects, personal tutors and private tutoring institutions accounted for the majority share. In English, a larger share of students chose private tutoring institutions, compared to the same share in Chinese and mathematics. This might be due to parents' hypotheses on the effectiveness of pedagogies provided by different kinds of tutors.

Table 3.3: Agency Type of Private Tutoring

	Mathematics		Chinese		English	
	N	%	N	%	N	%
Personal	696	52.5	191	50.0	517	47.4
Private institution	561	42.3	166	43.5	509	46.7
Higher education institute	61	4.6	19	5.0	52	4.8
Internet	6	0.5	5	1.3	11	1.0
Total	1,325	100.0	382	100.0	1,090	100.0

Key Empirical Findings

The estimates of the first step in the IV model[2] are the main findings on the determinants of private tutoring participation by subject and by the measurement of private tutoring. In general, the results are consistent across subjects. SES, parents who regulate students, parents who do too much for their children,[3] and percentage of private tutoring participants in school were significantly positive predictors of private tutoring participation for all three subjects. Females were significantly more likely than males to receive mathematics tutoring, and less likely to receive Chinese tutoring. Students with lower HSEE mathematics scores were more likely to receive mathematics tutoring, and those with lower HSEE total scores were more likely to receive tutoring in at least one subject. Students from non-key classes were significantly more likely to receive tutoring in at least one subject. The two IVs were significant predictors for all three subjects.

Table 3.4: Effects of Private Tutoring Participation on NCEE Achievements

	private tutoring measurement	T-test	OLS	IV	PSM
		(1)	(2)	(3)	(4)
Maths	*Dummy variable*	-0.018	0.010	0.149	-0.006
		(0.031)	(0.023)	(0.138)	(0.045)
Chinese	*Dummy variable*	0.023	-0.051	-0.722	-0.015
		(0.053)	(0.043)	(0.470)	(0.075)
English	*Dummy variable*	-0.021	-0.051*	0.470*	-0.081
		(0.034)	(0.023)	(0.202)	(0.050)
Total score	*Dummy variable*	-0.118**	-0.109**	-0.393**	-0.180**
		(0.026)	(0.018)	(0.107)	(0.041)
	Expenditure		-0.014	-0.310**	
			(0.009)	(0.111)	
	Time index		-0.053**	-0.115**	
			(0.007)	(0.038)	

Notes: Standard errors in parentheses. ** $p<0.01$, * $p<0.05$
Source: Zhang (2013, p.15).

---

[2] Please refer to Zhang (2013) for details.

[3] These are parenting style indices constructed from questionnaire items using principal component analysis. See Zhang (2013), p.23, Table A3.

Table 3.4 presents the effects of private tutoring participation on NCEE scores using various methods discussed above. Column (1) reports the simple mean comparison using t-test. Column (2) lists the results from OLS regression. Column (3) presents the IV estimations; and Column (4) reports the average treatment effect on the treated by PSM. In general, private tutoring appeared to have no effect on NCEE performance, except that the IV model identified a significantly positive effect of English private tutoring on NCEE English score. Concerning the private tutoring effect on NCEE total score, most models implied a negative effect. This might be due to the measurement error of private tutoring participation, which is not as accurate as for single subjects.

Figure 3.3 shows the common support assumption check for PSM by subjects. It is clear that for each value interval of propensity score, there are enough students to be either treated or untreated. Figure 3.4 reports the balance check for PSM after matching. Before matching, the covariates were significantly different between the private tutoring participants and non-participants. After matching, the gaps became not significant for all covariates. The table for this t-test is not presented here.

Figure 3.3: Common Support Check for PSM

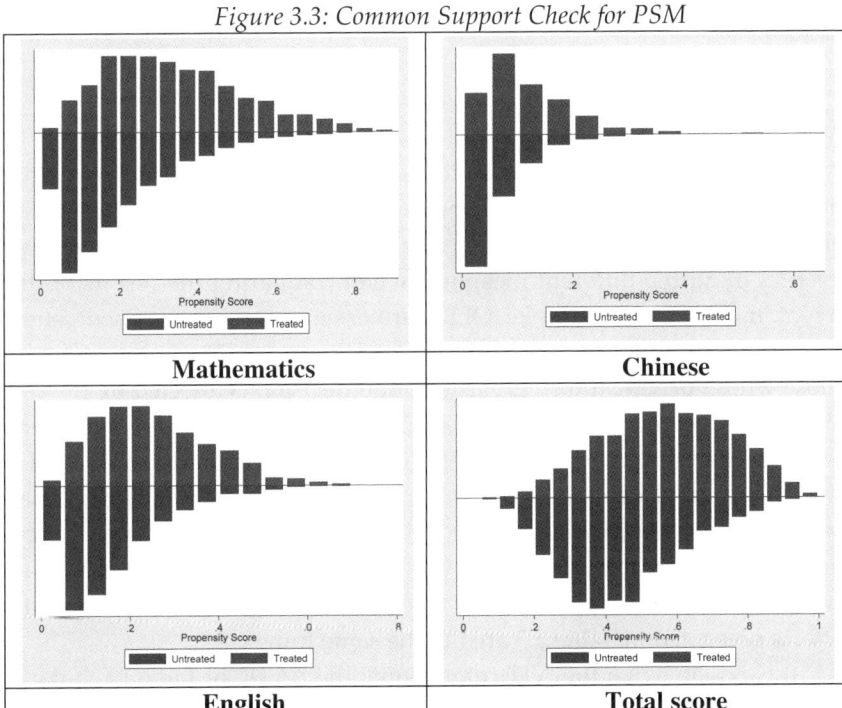

Figure 3.4: Balance Check for PSM

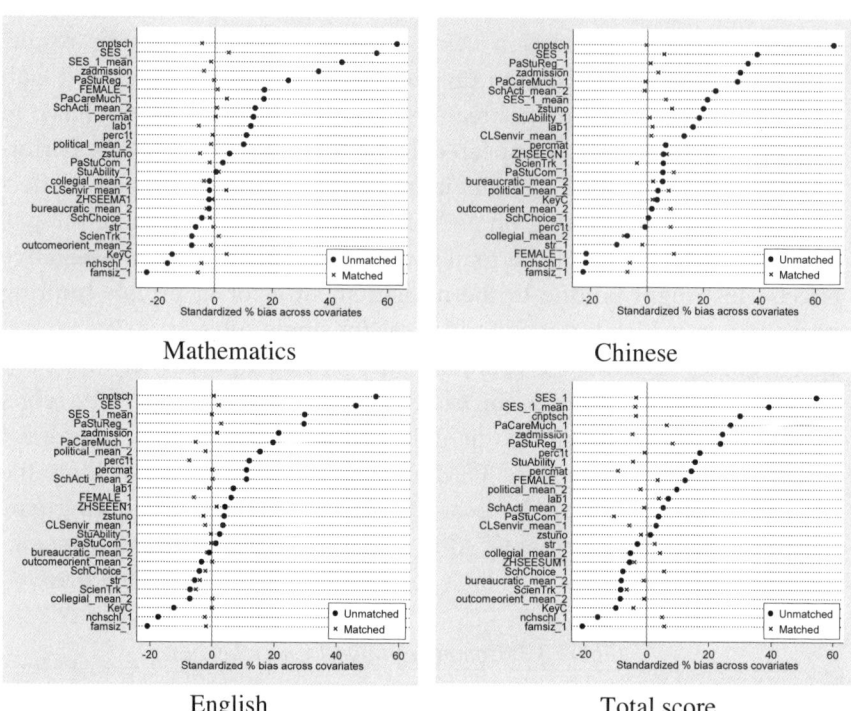

Mathematics

Chinese

English

Total score

Methodological Lessons

After addressing the issue of endogeneity in private tutoring participation, quantitative methods can derive unbiased estimation of the causal effect of private tutoring on academic achievement. However, one must keep in mind the different meanings when comparing the results of different models. For example, OLS derives an average treatment effect (ATE, although it is biased here); IV provides a LATE, i.e. the effect on those whose private tutoring participation decision is affected by the two IVs (for those whose decision is not influenced by the distance and peers, the IV results cannot be generalised to them); and PSM gives an ATT, i.e. the achievement gap of the private tutoring participants between being treated (i.e. if they participated in private tutoring, which is the reality) and not being treated (i.e. if they did not participate in private tutoring, which is estimated from the constructed control group). Therefore, the effects presented in Table 3.5 are not the same thing.

It is possible that the ATE might equal the LATE, or the ATT, but it is not necessary. For example, according to columns (3) and (4) in Table 3.5, the effect of English private tutoring is high, positive, and significant (effect size 0.47) in the IV model, but is not significant (and the size of the coefficient is very small: -0.081) in PSM. This indicates that for those whose decisions on English private tutoring participation are affected by the two IVs, English private tutoring has a positive effect. However, this effect may not exist on those whose decision-making is not affected by the two IVs. Yet when evaluating the ATT, it is not significant – meaning that for those who have already taken English private tutoring, if they did not take English private tutoring, the achievement gap between the two statuses is not significant. Therefore, scholars and policy makers should be aware of the conditions required by different empirical results, and should only rely on specific models according to their group of interest.

In addition to distinguishing the meanings of effects estimated by various models, some other issues should be considered. The matter of definition has already been mentioned: respondents may not always have the same definitions in mind as the researchers. Second, the sampling strategies and corresponding sampling weights of the data should be examined to see if the results from the sample could be reasonably generalised to the population. Third, the significant differences in culture, economic development level, and educational development level should be recognised when making comparisons across regions and countries. Some comparisons might not be appropriate, and results might be misleading if these are not carefully evaluated.

To summarise, although large datasets and sophisticated quantitative approaches provide the potential to examine the causal effects of private tutoring on students' academic achievement, many issues must be addressed in order to get valid and reliable results. Further research demands theories that are constructed specifically for private tutoring analysis and that can guide the empirical model design.

References

Angrist, Joshua D. & Pischke, Jorn-Steffen (2009): *Mostly Harmless Economics: An Empiricist's Companion*. Princeton: Princeton University Press.
Aurini, Janice; Davies, Scott & Dierkes, Julian (eds.) (2013): *Out of the Shadows: The Global Intensification of Supplementary Education*. Bingley: Emerald.
Baker, David. P. & LeTendre, Gerald K. (2005): *National Differences, Global Similarities: World Culture and the Future of Schooling*. Stanford: Stanford University

Press.

Blundell, Richard & Dias, Monica C. (2009): 'Alternative Approaches to Evaluation in Empirical Microeconomics'. *Journal of Human Resources*, Vol.44, No.3, pp.565-640.

Bray, Mark (2009): *Confronting the Shadow Education System: What Government Policies for What Private Tutoring?* Paris: UNESCO International Institute for Educational Planning (IIEP).

Bray, Mark & Lykins, Chad (2012). *Shadow Education: Private Supplementary Tutoring and its Implications for Policy Makers in Asia.* Hong Kong: Comparative Education Research Centre, The University of Hong Kong, and Mandaluyong City: Asian Development Bank.

Cohn, Elchanan & Geske, Terry G. (1990): *Economics of Education*. 3rd edition, Oxford: Pergamon Press.

Murnane, Richard J. & Willett, John B. (2010): *Methods Matter: Improving Causal Inference in Educational and Social Science Research.* Oxford: Oxford University Press.

Raudenbush, Stephen W. & Bryk, Anthony S. (2002): *Hierarchical Linear Models: Applications and Data Analysis Methods*. 2nd edition, Newbury Park: Sage.

Zhang, Yu (2011): *The Determinants of National College Entrance Exam Performance in China – with an Analysis of Private Tutoring*. PhD dissertation, Columbia University.

Zhang, Yu (2013): 'Does Private Tutoring Improve Students' National College Entrance Exam Performance? A Case Study from Jinan, China'. *Economics of Education Review*, Vol.32, No.1, pp.1-28.

Zhang, Yu; Liu, Juanjuan & Li, Manli (2015): 'Survival Analysis of Private Tutoring Participation among Primary Education Students in Beijing', *Exploring Education Development*, No.4, pp.31-37. [in Chinese]

Discerning Qualities

4
A Qualitative Comparison of Private Tutoring in Azerbaijan, Bosnia & Herzegovina, Croatia, Estonia and Georgia: Lessons from Design and Implementation

Boris JOKIĆ

Introduction

This chapter focuses on methodological decisions and challenges during the design and implementation of a comparative qualitative study over a period of 18 months in Azerbaijan, Bosnia & Herzegovina, Croatia, Estonia, and Georgia. The findings from the research, reported in Jokić (2013), confirmed that private tutoring was an all-encompassing phenomenon in all five countries, endorsing the view that it transcends national and class boundaries (Mazawi et al. 2013).

The study built on a quantitative project covering nine countries (Silova et al. 2006), among which four were in the group of five that participated in the research on which this chapter is based (Husremović & Trbić 2006; Matiashvili & Kutateladze 2006; Ristić Dedić et al. 2006; Silova & Kazimzade 2006). The research aimed to move beyond the 'diagnostic' picture of private tutoring in individual countries towards an in-depth

---

Bray, Mark; Kwo, Ora & Jokić, Boris (eds.) (2015): *Researching Private Supplementary Tutoring: Methodological Lessons from Diverse Cultures*. Hong Kong: Comparative Education Research Centre (CERC), The University of Hong Kong, and Dordrecht: Springer. © CERC

exploration of the foundations and implications of this complex phenomenon.

The research focused on the demand side of private tutoring, placing the decision to use (or not use) private tutoring at the centre of the conceptual framework. While the word 'decision' might imply a position, opinion or judgement reached after consideration at a specific moment, in the research it was used in a more general sense as a tendency towards reaching a certain conclusion.

Two core assumptions underpinned placing the decision to use private tutoring at the centre of the conceptual framework. First was that the decision is made almost exclusively by pupils and/or their parents. Second was that it is always intrinsically associated with *their perspectives on the formal system* of education and *their educational aspirations*. These elements were contextualised within a system broadly based on Bronfenbrenner's ecological paradigm and resulting models (Bronfenbrenner 1979). This ecological system consisted of five socially organised subsystems, representing a set of nested and interconnected structures that all had potential to influence the decision and upon which this decision could have a reciprocal effect. These structures included the individual characteristics of the pupil, parental sphere, school, educational policy, and the larger society.

Data were collected through semi-structured interviews and focus group discussions. Individuals and organisations from varied contexts were identified through criterion and purposive sampling. In order to assure comparability, interview schedules, focus group protocols and data-collection procedures were agreed by the research teams in all countries. The project included two rounds of interviews. In total, 105 individual interviews and 18 focus group discussions were conducted. A coding scheme was developed for analysis in which some codes were pre-determined based on the project's conceptual framework, interview schedules and focus group protocols, while other codes emerged and were established in response to the collected data. The coding scheme was applied consistently to the data from all five contexts.

The findings (Jokić 2013) indicated that in all contexts the probability of opting for private tutoring was increased by various curricular issues. These included excessive curricular breadth, large numbers of subjects, content that had low relevance or was poorly adjusted to the assigned number of teaching hours, a lack of horizontal and vertical consistency, and assessment arrangements. When families perceived these deficiencies to threaten the achievement of personal educational aspirations, they commonly sought private tutoring to maintain or improve pupils' chances of accomplishing educational aspirations. Furthermore, findings suggested that the professional competences of teachers and therefore teaching practices were strongly related to parental and pupil decisions concerning private tutoring use.

The examination of individual pupil characteristics influencing the decision concerning private tutoring indicated that pupils' motivation for learning in school was an important element influencing the decision on private tutoring use. However, the relationship was not straightforward, as both lower and higher levels of motivation lead to an increased tendency to use private tutoring services. Parental perspectives on education and parenting styles also played vital roles in decision making. Parental dissatisfaction with the perceived deficiencies of the formal system of education was particularly pertinent. Parental obligations and multiple professional and social roles made parents feel less willing or able to support their children' educational needs. In most contexts, use of tutoring had become a social norm.

The following account offers methodological insights from this complex study by research teams in five countries. It begins with the broad framework of qualitative and comparative orientations. It then describes the research design, including participant selection and procedures for interview development, data collection, and analysis. Conclusions offer more general perspectives on methodological issues related to this type of research.

Qualitative and Comparative Orientations

Numerous scholars have called for research on shadow education from a range of methodological approaches (e.g. Bray 2009, 2010; Manzon & Areepattamannil 2014). To date, quantitative research has dominated and was part of the background for the present study (Silova et al. 2006). In the domain of private tutoring, as in educational studies more generally, qualitative research has been less common. While substantial debates about private tutoring and exploration of its foundations and implications are not possible without robust quantitative data, it is also impossible to understand the complexity of private tutoring without rich qualitative data. This observation is consistent with the writings of Gorard and Taylor (2004), who suggested that when examining complex topics, quantitative research should provide answers to questions of 'what' and 'how many', while qualitative research should answer questions of 'how' and 'why'.

Another strong feature of the project was its comparative orientation. Bray's (2010) overview of methodology in private tutoring research stressed the value of comparative endeavours but also made several critiques. His concerns about at large global assessment programmes focused on deficiencies in the formulation of items about private tutoring (see also Bray & Kobakhidze 2014). These items, he argued, commonly neglected the existing body of knowledge on private tutoring. If used non-selectively and without careful contextualisation, such items can lead to erroneous conclusions. Bray (2010) called for more precise definitions and cautious consideration of the units of analysis in comparative cross-national and cross-cultural research.

The need for thorough understanding of what is being meant by concepts in different settings was evident in the initial quantitative study (Silova et al. 2006). In the qualitative follow-up, clear definition of focus became even more important; and to secure common understanding of concepts and contexts, research teams held numerous face-to-face and online meetings. This brought financial strain to the project, but was essential for its success.

The study had two general aims. The first was to develop conceptual understanding of private tutoring within and across contexts, and within and across groups of stakeholders. Second, the research aimed to ameliorate public policy and practice in each context by identifying tailored policy options based on the data analyses. Intrinsically related to these aims was the issue of purpose in the use of comparisons. The research was mainly interpretative, but it also had a causal-analytic purpose (Manzon 2014, p.98).

The interpretative purpose focused on understanding the phenomenon in the five countries. For this goal, the methodological decisions could be related to Bereday's four-step model for comparative studies: description, interpretation, juxtaposition, and simultaneous comparison (Bereday 1964, p.28). The juxtaposition phase, in which the criteria upon which valid comparisons could be made, was especially important. While the parameters for initial comparability of the chosen units of analysis were partly taken from the earlier project, the parameters were developed throughout the research. A systemic attempt was made by all involved to avoid mechanical identification of similarities and differences between contexts and stakeholders, and to establish domains for comparison in a more contextual manner with emphasis on the complexities surrounding private tutoring. This goal demanded labour-intensive discussions by teams on each element of the research design, and emphasised the extent and reasons for commonalities and differences.

Concerning the causal-analytic purpose, although it was clear that the design and methodological choices did not permit establishment of true causality, the project aimed to formulate models of causal relationships within the conceptual framework and the coding scheme. For this purpose, the three-step approach developed by Ragin (1987, pp.47-48) was informative:

- find underlying similarities among units of comparison that have common outcomes;
- determine whether these similarities are causally relevant to the phenomenon of interest; and
- on the basis of identified similarities, formulate a general explanation.

Consideration of links between the units of analysis was also crucial. The project adopted the three-dimensional approach developed by Bray and Thomas (1995) for categorising foci, conceptualised as a cube. In the geographic/locational dimension, levels in this model were identified ranging from individuals to world regions/continents. The second dimension covered non-locational demographic groupings and included ethnic, age, religious, gender and other groups as well as whole populations. The third dimension addressed educational and social elements such as curriculum, assessment, financing, and teaching methods. The manner in which the present research can be fitted to this multilevel model was as follows.

- *Geographic/locational dimension*. At the most direct level, the study compared decisions on use of private tutoring in five sovereign states. Bray et al. (2014) rightly observed that the sovereignty of states does not guarantee the validity of comparisons and that intranational differences are also important. Azerbaijan, Croatia, Estonia and Georgia, although showing substantial differences, had centrally-governed education systems that allowed cross-national comparison. Bosnia & Herzegovina had a different structure of governance and demanded special attention because its inclusion brought both insights and complications. The constitution of Bosnia & Herzegovina defines the country as a state consisting of two entities, the Federation of Bosnia & Herzegovina and the Republic of Srpska, in addition to the separate administrative unit of Brčko District. Further, the Federation of Bosnia & Herzegovina consists of 10 cantons. Education in Bosnia & Herzegovina is under the autonomous rule of its separate entities (comprising the two aforementioned entities and 10 cantonal ministries of education). Each of the 12 administrations has its own ministry of education, laws, policies, and budgets. In order to gain a more complete grasp of the political and educational complexity of the country, the research design envisaged a larger number of participants from Bosnia & Herzegovina as well as targeted inclusion of spheres from both entities and several cantons.

At a higher level of generalisation, the five participating countries were initially grouped and discussed in several ways. In the first instance, a distinction was made between the Western Balkan countries (Bosnia & Herzegovina and Croatia) and the three remaining countries. This distinction was geographic, but also cultural and political based on shared history and strong linguistic connections. Although these groupings were made on a sound conceptual basis, they did not manifest clearly in the data. From this perspective, one lesson would be that if the research attempts to make comparisons at these higher levels of generalisation, substantially more geographic research contexts are needed.

- *Non-locational demographic groupings*. The research solicited the views of various groups of stakeholders, including teachers, parents and politicians. This arrangement allowed for a discussion of the views of such groups both generally and across the contexts.
- *Aspects of education and of society*. As emphasised in the description of the conceptual framework, the decision concerning the use of private tutoring services has been placed within an ecological system comprised of several subsystems. Multiple aspects of education and society, ranging from the most proximal level of pupil to the most distant level of wider society, influence the decision to use private tutoring, and were discussed separately.

The three-dimensional approach proved conceptually sound. Examination of relationships in each ecological subsystem with the decision concerning the use of private tutoring services allowed comparison according to different geographic and demographic groupings as well as with regard to specific elements characteristic to each subsystem. This permitted various ways of comparison, from two dimensional such as the role of assessment practices in five contexts to three dimensional such as specific types of stakeholders' views on parental roles. The applicability of the three-dimensional approach depended on the selection of the participants and subsequent data collection procedures described below.

Research Design

This section first explains the identification of stakeholders and the sampling strategy. It then describes the development and content of the interview and focus group schedules, data collection procedures, and efforts to secure consistency and allow comparisons across countries.

Identification of stakeholders
The first step for identification of stakeholders was decision-making on the spheres from which perspectives should be sought. This was part of the *non-locational demographic* grouping in the three-dimensional approach. The inclusion of individuals and organisations from varied contexts permitted more comprehensive exploration of the causes and effects of private tutoring. The following paragraphs elaborate on the rationales for each sphere.

Persons responsible for educational governance
As governance holds a central regulatory role, the conceptualisations and awareness of private tutoring among persons in this sphere were a critical component. Each of the five countries had different governance structures, characterised by varying roles and responsibilities at central and regional levels. As such, representatives in charge of educational governance from both levels were included. The sample in each country included senior Ministry of Education officials and counterparts in the regional and/or local governments. Differences in governance structures and internal structures of the governing bodies demanded thorough discussion on the equivalence of the positions. In Bosnia & Herzegovina, the local authorities exercised more power than those at higher levels.

Other political representatives
Representatives from parliamentary groups were included in order to secure a more complete array of political views. While the formal system

of educational governance to some extent reflected the views of the political parties in power, the perspectives of other politicians were also important. The Georgian researchers were unable to secure interviewees in this group despite considerable effort, which had implications for both the national dataset and the ability to compare across geographical locations and types of stakeholders.

Educational professionals
Officials from professional institutions and organisations in education were another core group. With variations in each context, they included representatives from bodies such as Institutes of Education, curriculum authorities, assessment centres, pedagogical institutes, and inspectorates. Perspectives from this sector were sought on the assumption that knowledge of the educational context and its characteristics would deepen insights into the underlying causes and effects of private tutoring.

Academics engaged in educational research and teacher training
The perspectives of academics were similarly important. They provided important information on conceptualisations and the causes and effects of private tutoring. Their inclusion was also valuable because they could be critical of governance and practices within schools.

NGOs and IGOs dealing with education
Non-Governmental Organisations (NGOs) and Inter-Governmental Organisations (IGOs) dealing with education were included as potentially valuable sources of information. Because personnel in such bodies do not participate in formal governance, they can in some instances offer critical perspectives on education. Further, such organisations are commonly key players in the initiation of change to public policy and in public discourse. The Croatian research team could not find respondents in this group despite repeated invitations. Several NGOs and IGOs declined to participate because they felt that they did not have enough knowledge or expertise on the topic. Paradoxically, the high profile of the research team in the topic of private tutoring contributed to that, as rejection was often accompanied with statements that the researchers were the most knowledgeable about it.

Teachers' unions
As central organisations promoting the professional position of teachers,

unions possess expert contextual knowledge that was deemed highly relevant. Further, because teachers are among the primary providers of private tutoring, it was important to include the perspectives of unions regarding the causes and effects of private tutoring in general, with particular attention to the provision of tutoring by teachers employed in schools.

School principals
The executive roles of principals in school leadership, together with their knowledge of the needs of educational organisations, teachers, pupils and parents, made their perspectives important. In addition, principals bridged educational policies determined at the central or regional levels and educational practice in schools. They provided valuable information on the potential for change in schools and on the regulation of private tutoring.

Private tutoring providers
The perspectives of private tutoring providers were an essential element. Providers can be expected to be in a good position to describe the features and organisation of tutoring in their settings. Further, they can assess the elements in schooling that potentially contribute to the decision concerning private tutoring use. The roles of providers offer insight into the motivations of pupils and parents to use private tutoring services. Because factors were heterogeneous in the participating countries, the researchers aimed to include the perspectives of both directors of established institutions and individual private tutors, most of whom were not teachers at the time of the data collection.

Teachers
Teachers are among the most knowledgeable sources of information on private tutoring. They can offer perspectives on the reasons for pupils' and parents' decisions to use the services of private tutors and on the features of the systems that contribute to the emergence and growth of private tutoring. Further, teachers are among the main providers of private tutoring and commonly the main channel of communication to pupils and parents regarding such services.

Parents
Most often, the parents are the deciders whether their children need pri-

vate tutoring, and also pay for the service. As such, their perspective on the causes and effects of private tutoring and their personal roles in the decisions concerning the use of private tutoring services were central to the study.

Pupils
Inclusion of pupils' perspectives was made an optional element, chiefly because the previous project (Silova et al. 2006) was based primarily on pupils' perspectives. While the predominantly quantitative nature of the previous project allowed for initial insight into pupils' perspectives, the option for each team in the present research to include pupils offered an opportunity to probe their perspectives and understanding of the complexities of private tutoring.

Sampling strategy
The participant spheres were determined and agreed by all country teams. To permit necessary flexibility, the teams were allowed to add layers to the overall sampling strategy if considered desirable for specific settings. For example, if in some contexts the pupil organisations were established and their perspective was considered important, research teams were allowed to include them. Country teams were also allowed to omit data collection from segments that were deemed inapplicable in specific settings.

Participants were selected from each sphere through both criterion and purposive sampling. Each team identified the institutions and individuals whose perspectives should be included on the basis of roles and positions held by the individuals within specific organisations (e.g. State Secretary for General Education, Director of the National Curriculum Body) or the individuals' experience and/or expertise in relation to private tutoring (e.g. director of a centre providing private tutoring services, researcher on private tutoring). Purposive sampling was applied in the recruitment of participants for teacher and parent focus groups, where research teams were advised to contact schools, teachers and parents who they knew had experience with private tutoring. As with any research employing purposive sampling, this strategy had implications for the generalisability of the findings and conclusions.

Once agreement on the sampling strategy had been reached, each team independently identified participants in its country. Considerable attention was devoted to the challenging task of securing adequate comparability of participants across countries, while at the same time ensuring strong national contextualisation. Through ongoing and thorough discussion and comparisons of the organisational structures and missions of the organisations that employed interviewees, these seemingly contradictory goals gradually became less disparate. Table 4.1 indicates the number of interviews and focus groups in each country.

Table 4.1: Interviews and Focus Groups, by Country

Educational stakeholders	Azerbaijan	Bosnia & Herzegovina	Croatia	Estonia	Georgia
Educational governance – ministerial level	1	3	1	2	1
Educational governance – regional/local level	1	6	1	1	1
Other political representatives	1	2	2	1	-
Education professionals	3	6	5	2	5
Academics engaged in educational research and teacher training	1	1	4	1	2
NGOs and IGOs dealing with education	5	3	-	2	4
Teachers' unions	-	3	2	2	2
School principals	2	-	2	1	4
Private tutoring providers	2	4	5	2	2
Teachers	2 FG	2 FG	1 FG	2 FG	2 FG
Parents	2 FG	2 FG	1 FG	3	2 FGs
Pupils (optional)	2 FG		Nat. C'ttee of Pupils	Pupils' union	
TOTAL	16 + 6 FG	27 + 4 FG	23 + 2 FG	18 + 2 FG	21 + 4 FG

Note: FG = Focus Group

In total, 105 individual interviews and 18 focus group discussions (with individuals different from those interviewed) were conducted, providing approximately 230 hours of recorded material. Table 4.1 shows the high level of consistency between research contexts, but also omissions from some groups of stakeholders. In order to protect the anonymity of the individuals who participated in the study, the roles of the respondents in each stakeholder group were described only generally when reporting. Furthermore, due to ethical considerations, every attempt was made to protect the anonymity of the stakeholders participating in the study.

The data collection did not stray significantly from the plan. As such, it allowed for both cross-national and intra-national comparison as well as for comparison between groups of stakeholders. While the sampling procedure did not permit grand generalisations, it did allow an exploration of the elements influencing decisions about the use of private tutoring.

Data collection techniques and methods
Data from all sampling spheres except teachers and parents were collected through semi-structured interviews. The decision to conduct semi-structured rather than structured and open-ended interviews was informed by Patton's (2002) observation of the lack of mutual exclusivity between different types of interviews, as well as Bogdan and Biklen's (2007) comparison of the advantages and disadvantages of different interview forms. Use of semi-structured interviews was justified by the complexity of the topic and variety of professional backgrounds of the participants. Some structure was required to ensure a constant focus on the topic and comparability across contexts (Fontana & Frey 1998). However, as with the sampling procedures, some freedom for the researchers was needed to make the data collection flexible, to adjust interview discussions to the characteristics of private tutoring in specific contexts, and to probe interesting responses that had potential to add depth.

For teachers and parents, it was agreed that most data would be collected through focus groups. This decision reflected the researchers' wish to include multiple perspectives from these heterogeneous groups. The economical nature of this data-collection technique permitted gathering varied perspectives in a short time. Focus groups were also expected to encourage teachers and parents to engage more fully and to interact with varied perspectives, perhaps becoming more willing to discuss sensitive issues. Although the presence of peers might have constrained participants from discussing and sharing experiences, this did not appear to be the case. This lack of constraint was indicative of the growing acceptability of the phenomenon.

In the interests of comparability of findings across countries, all data collection was carried out between May 2009 and September 2010. Consistency in data collection was ensured through specific protocols and procedures for contacting potential participants and for conducting interviews and focus group discussions. These processes are described more fully below.

Semi-structured interviews

Interview schedules were developed by country teams working together. They incorporated aspects of existing knowledge on private tutoring within the conceptual framework. The source interview schedule was developed in English and then translated into the languages of the participating countries. The development of the interview schedules had two stages. First, themes were identified, and then specific questions or probes under each theme were agreed while allowing country teams to develop further probes specific to their contexts. In the initial phase of interview schedule development, 12 interview themes were formulated.

Once interview themes had been agreed by all research teams, the aims for each theme and suggested approaches during interviews were developed. These elements were an important guide for interviewers, helping to make processes consistent across countries (Table 4.2).

Table 4.2: Themes, Aims and Suggested Approaches for Interviews

Themes	Aims	Approaches
1. Personal association with private tutoring	Interview opener; relating private tutoring to the personal experiences of the interviewee	Unstructured and open; allow interviewee space to describe his/her associations/history with private tutoring
2. Perception of the scope of private tutoring	Explore interviewee's impression of prevalence of private tutoring. An opening question, setting the scene for other probing.	Direct; accept short answers.
3. Relationship between private tutoring and different educational levels	Probing perspectives on functions of private tutoring at different educational levels.	Open; encourage a personal perspective; probe for perspectives concerning different educational levels if not mentioned.
4. Forms of private tutoring	Probe perspectives on forms of private tutoring and their functions.	Lead from the previous question; probe for various types of private tutoring and the interaction between type and organisation.

As with other components, the schedule for the semi-structured interviews was developed commonly by the research teams. The suggested procedure began with an official invitation to the stakeholder to participate. Upon agreement, an interview time was set up; and in most cases interviews took place in the workplaces of interviewees. The interviewers provided previously-agreed information, and then used the schedule and approach guidelines to conduct the interviews. At the outset participants were asked to consent to recording of the interviews, and all agreed.

Focus groups
Focus group protocols were also commonly developed through the mutual collaboration of research teams. Because focus group discussions were administered with both teachers and parents, two schedules were developed. Once again, general themes were first agreed and then followed by the formulation of more specific questions and probes. Focus group protocols were initially developed in English and then translated.

Country teams were permitted to modify the protocols if they chose to focus on specific groups, e.g. of elementary or secondary teachers. In order to ensure adequate triangulation with data collected through semi-structured interviews, focus group protocols included similar themes and approaches to those in the interview schedule. Teams also had flexibility to develop specific probes or questions.

The process of development of data collection instruments and procedure protocols was among the strengths of the study. From the outset it was clear that the common understanding was essential and that formalisation would partially be through the instruments and procedures. The research teams devoted much time to this matter, laboriously going through different versions of the schedules and protocols.

Data Analysis
The data from all five countries were deposited into a database and analysed using NVivo software (NVivo 2010). All iterations of the coding scheme were developed commonly and applied to the data from all five contexts. Some codes were pre-determined based on the project's conceptual framework and data collection instruments, while others were developed in response to the data. As an example, Figure 4.1 presents the coding scheme for the Level 2 code 'Users and providers'.

Figure 4.1: Coding Scheme for the Level 2 Code 'Users and Providers'

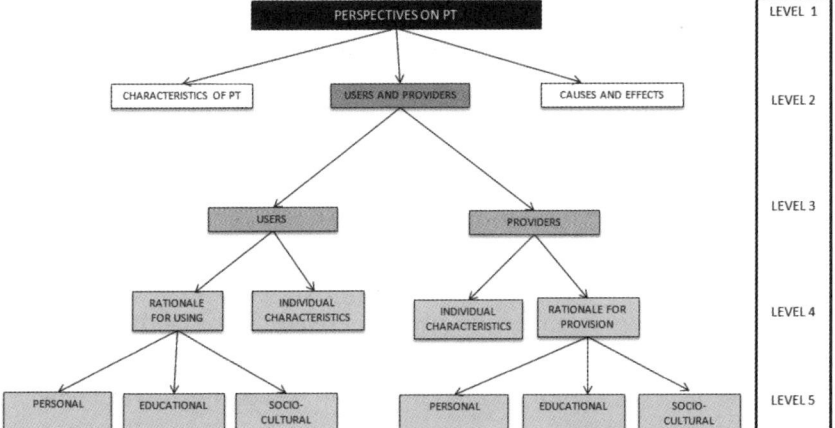

The coding was conducted in three waves. The first wave was based on thematic coding at relatively general levels, while a more interpretative approach to coding was adopted in the subsequent waves. From the outset, teams agreed that the same data could be classified under more than one code. The basis for this decision was that codes did not represent orthogonal structures, and there was significant overlap between different elements of the coding scheme. Multiple coding allowed for more complex and intricate representation of the data and the manner in which varying elements represented in the coding scheme were interrelated. Each research team coded its own data, and results were entered into commonly agreed matrices which were shared between groups.

Verification procedures
Because the research aimed to gain insight into the individual perspectives of educational stakeholders, the verifiability of the research findings was considered by ensuring and examining trustworthiness, confirmability, transferability, credibility and dependability. These were the qualitative equivalents for the psychometric indicators of reliability and validity in quantitative data (Lincoln & Guba 1985).

In this procedure, first the strength of the argument housed in the reported findings should demonstrate both transferability and credibility (Strauss & Corbin 1998). Here, transferability of data occurs at two levels: the extent to which the findings are transferable to other elements of the specific contexts, and the extent to which the findings are transferable to other contexts. The dependability of findings relates to the issue of ensuring that data collected are stable and consistent over time, a condition that was met in the present research by the application of two data collection periods. The dependability and confirmability of the present research were enhanced by audio-taping and verbatim transcriptions (Maxwell 1996). Arguably, confirmability is also evident in the manner in which sufficient details of the research design are presented to allow for external assessment and reproduction of the data. The trustworthiness of the data was strengthened by the use of multiple methods and by the inclusion of a relatively large number of interview participants able to provide supporting evidence. Finally, the credibility of the findings was strengthened by the consideration, analysis and exposure of cases opposite to the general patterns emerging from the findings (Patton 2002; Miles & Huberman 1994).

Conclusions

In addition to collecting new data, the research addressed some methodological deficiencies in the field. Through its close relationship with the initial private tutoring project which had included four of the five countries in this new project, a basis for a methodologically more complete consideration was established. This augmentation of quantitative data with qualitative data addressed some concerns of others who had been researching private tutoring. Further, in order to gain a holistic understanding of the decision to use private tutoring the design included stakeholders with potentially contrasting views.

As a complex collaborative effort of teams in five countries, the research offered methodological lessons about coherence and control. In order to establish the foundation for coherence, common understanding of the research concepts and design elements was essential. While it may seem obvious, this demanded communication and understanding between teams and leadership. The need to communicate, elaborate and understand the similarities and differences within and between contexts was present from the first day of the project, and required numerous face-to-face and online meetings. The process increased the consistency of team members' understandings as well as the joint sense of ownership of the project and its outcomes. However, the demands slowed the pace of work and caused budget strains.

The research design emphasised consistency and comparability across contexts while allowing flexibility. Consistency and comparability were established through agreement on the sampling, interview schedules, and even data collection procedures. All research teams were held responsible to adhere to agreements as closely as possible. Nevertheless, teams had freedom to adapt data-collection instruments and samples. The design therefore sought a delicate balance between consistency and flexibility. Achievement of this balance was assisted by the researchers' pre-existing understanding of the topic, gained from previous research and by the decision that all data should be collected by members of the research teams themselves. This decision placed a strain on the researchers, but the common view was that if data collection had been outsourced or carried out by less experienced persons, the necessary balances and rigour might not have been achieved.

Although the basis for the comparison between geographical locations had been carefully established, in this domain too some issues might provide lessons for other researchers. First, the complex governance structure of Bosnia & Herzegovina demanded special consideration, with sampling of larger numbers of stakeholders and limitations in generalisation of findings. Second, future comparative efforts should include more contexts if the intention is to provide meaningful higher-level geographical comparisons.

The project also encountered challenges in the data analysis phase. Transcription demands much time and money, and multiple languages made matters even more complex. The intention had been to translate all of the transcribed materials to English as common language, but costs were too high. Researchers in comparable projects should be mindful of the budgetary demands if they have similar goals.

Lessons from design and implementation presented in this chapter are indicative of the complexity and labour-intensive nature of a qualitative comparative exploration of private tutoring in five countries. They emphasise the need to balance firmness and flexibility of structure in all phases. More importantly, these lessons indicate the importance of common understanding, commitment and open communication between and within research teams. Some compromises are inevitable, but the findings and the methodological lessons from this project provide fertile ground for future studies both in the five countries and more widely.

References

Bereday, George Z.F. (1964): *Comparative Method in Education*. New York: Holt, Rinehart & Winston.

Bogdan, Robert C. & Biklen, Sari Knopp (2007): *Qualitative Research for Education: An Introduction to Theories and Methods*. 5th edition, Boston: Allyn & Bacon.

Bray, Mark (2009): *Confronting the Shadow Education System: What Government Policies for What Private Tutoring?*. Paris: UNESCO International Institute for Educational Planning (IIEP).

Bray, Mark (2010): 'Researching Shadow Education: Methodological Challenges and Directions'. *Asia Pacific Education Review*, Vol.11, No.1, pp.3-13.

Bray, Mark; Adamson, Bob & Mason, Mark (2014): 'Different Models, Different Emphases, Different Insights', in Bray, Mark; Adamson, Bob & Mason, Mark (eds.), *Comparative Education Research: Approaches and Methods*. CERC Studies in Comparative Education 19, 2nd edition, Hong Kong: Comparative Education Research Centre, The University of Hong Kong, and Dordrecht: Springer, pp.417-436.

Bray, Mark & Kobakhidze, Magda Nutsa (2014): 'Measurement Issues in Research on Shadow Education: Challenges and Pitfalls Encountered in TIMSS and PISA'. *Comparative Education Review*, Vol.58, No.4, pp.590-620.

Bray, Mark & Thomas, R. Murray (1995): 'Levels of Comparison in Educational Studies: Different Insights from Different Literatures and the Value of Multilevel Analyses'. *Harvard Educational Review*, Vol.65, No.3, pp.472-490.

Bronfenbrenner, Urie (1979): *The Ecology of Human Development: Experiments by Nature and Design*. Cambridge: Harvard University Press.

Fontana, Andrea & Frey, James H. (1998): 'Interviewing: The Art of Science', in Denzin, Norman K. & Lincoln, Yvonna S. (eds.), *Collecting and Interpreting Qualitative Materials*. London: Sage, pp.47-78.

Gorard, Stephen & Taylor, Chris (2004): *Combining Methods in Educational and Social Research*. Maidenhead: Open University Press.

Husremović, Dženana & Trbić, Dženana (2006): 'Private Tutoring in Bosnia & Herzegovina', in Silova, Iveta; Būdienė, Virginija & Bray, Mark (eds.), *Education in a Hidden Marketplace: Monitoring of Private Tutoring*. New York: Open Society Institute, pp.143-168.

Jokić, Boris (ed.) (2013): *Emerging from the Shadow: A Comparative Qualitative Exploration of Private Tutoring in Eurasia*. Zagreb: Network of Education Policy Centers.

Lincoln, Yvonna S. & Guba, Egon G. (1985): *Naturalistic Inquiry*. London: Sage.

Manzon, Maria (2014): 'Comparing Places', in Bray, Mark; Adamson, Bob & Mason, Mark (eds.), *Comparative Education Research: Approaches and Methods*. CERC Studies in Comparative Education 19. 2nd edition, Hong Kong: Comparative Education Research Centre, The University of Hong Kong, and Dordrecht: Springer, pp.97-138.

Manzon, Maria & Areepattamannil, Shaljan (2014): 'Shadow Educations: Mapping the Global Discourse'. *Asia Pacific Journal of Education*, Vol.34, No.4, pp.389-412.

Matiashvili, Anna & Kutateladze, Nino (2006): 'Private Tutoring in Georgia', in Silova, Iveta; Būdienė, Virginija & Bray, Mark (eds.), *Education in a Hidden Marketplace: Monitoring of Private Tutoring*. New York: Open Society Institute, pp.191-210.

Maxwell, Joseph Alex (1996): *Qualitative Research Design: An Interactive Approach*. Thousand Oaks: Sage.

Mazawi, André E.; Sultana, Ronald G. & Bray, Mark (2013): 'Beyond Shadows: Equity, Diversity, and Private Tutoring', in Bray, Mark; Mazawi, André E. & Sultana, Ronald G. (eds.), *Private Tutoring Across the Mediterranean: Power Dynamics and Implications for Learning and Equity*. Rotterdam: Sense, pp.205-216.

Miles, Matthew B. & Huberman, A. Michael (1994): *Qualitative Data Analysis*. 2nd edition, Thousand Oaks: Sage.

NVivo Qualitative Data Analysis Software; QSR International Pty Ltd. Version 9, 2010.

Patton, Michael Quinn (2002): *Qualitative Research and Evaluation Methods*. 3rd edition, Thousand Oaks: Sage.

Ragin, Charles (1987): *The Comparative Method: Moving beyond Qualitative and Quantitative Strategies*. Berkeley: University of California Press.

Ristić Dedić, Zrinka; Jokić, Boris & Jurko, Lana (2006): 'Private Tutoring in Croatia', in Silova, Iveta; Būdienė, Virginija & Bray, Mark (eds.), *Education in a Hidden Marketplace: Monitoring of Private Tutoring*. New York: Open Society Institute, pp.169-190.

Silova, Iveta; Būdienė, Virginija & Bray, Mark (eds.) (2006): *Education in a Hidden Marketplace: Monitoring of Private Tutoring*. New York: Open Society Institute.

Silova, Iveta & Kazimzade, Elmina (2006): 'Private Tutoring in Azerbaijan', in Silova, Iveta; Būdienė, Virginija & Bray, Mark (eds.), *Education in a Hidden Marketplace: Monitoring of Private Tutoring*. New York: Open Society Institute, pp.113-142.

Strauss, Anselm & Corbin, Juliet (1998): *Basics of Qualitative Research*. 2nd edition, Thousand Oaks: Sage.

5

Ethical Dilemmas in Shadow Education Research: Lessons from a Qualitative Study of Learners' Experiences in Lecture-type Tutoring in Hong Kong

Kevin W.H. YUNG

Introduction

Ethical considerations arise at every stage in the research process – planning the study, recruiting and engaging participants in data collection, analysing the data, and publishing. The principal ethical considerations are causing no harm to participants and a commitment to moral integrity and participants' rights, consent and confidentiality (Watts 2006; Vainio 2013). However, researchers face dilemmas if strict adherence to specific ethical rules affects what is being studied – perhaps even to the extent of making it impossible to conduct research of the type envisaged (Homan 1991; Wiles et al. 2006; Hammersley 2015). Social research, particularly qualitative research, has experienced controversy because ethical guidelines are sometimes intentionally vague to allow researchers flexibility to adopt a "situational relativist" approach in which researchers make ethical decisions based on their own ethical or moral standards. Yet while ethical issues have been considered important and influential in research, they "usually remain detached or marginalized from discussions of research projects" (Hesse-Biber & Leavy 2011, p.59).

Bray, Mark; Kwo, Ora & Jokić, Boris (eds.) (2015): *Researching Private Supplementary Tutoring: Methodological Lessons from Diverse Cultures*. Hong Kong: Comparative Education Research Centre (CERC), The University of Hong Kong, and Dordrecht: Springer. © CERC

This chapter discusses ethical issues in a one-year qualitative study of Secondary 6 students' English learning experiences in lecture-type tutoring in Hong Kong. As ethical dilemmas are usually context-specific in social research (Goodwin et al. 2003; Wiles et al. 2006), the chapter first describes the context of the study. It then outlines the research design, and describes the data collection process in the pilot and main study. The section on ethical issues includes focus on informed consent, incentives, building relationships, researcher positioning, and confidentiality and anonymity.

The Context

Hong Kong is a competitive city for both higher education admissions and job market opportunities (Watkins 2009; Yung 2015). The Diploma of Secondary Education (DSE) examination taken at the end of Secondary 6 exerts much pressure on students. Many Hong Kong students attend tutorial classes in the hope of performing better in the examination and then securing university places.

Among the various types of shadow education, lecture-type tutoring in large tutorial companies is the most popular among students in the last grade of secondary schooling. Zhan et al. (2013) found that among 657 Secondary 6 respondents in 13 schools who had received private tutoring within 12 months prior to their study, 54.2 per cent had enrolled in live lecture-style classes and 61.7 per cent in video-recorded lecture-style classes. Students sit in classrooms with a maximum of 45 students as regulated by the Educational Ordinance (Bray & Kwo 2014, p.37), but the classrooms walls may be made of glass so that over 100 students can have lessons together and see the tutor (see Yung 2011 for details). Popular tutors in large tutorial companies are usually called "star tutors" or "kings and queens" (Kwo & Bray 2011). They are like "stage actors" (Ng 2009), dressing in a stylish manner and using trendy vocabulary to appeal to youngsters. They advertise on the exterior of buses and buildings. Some appear to be millionaires, claim that they have over 10,000 students, and boast about their students' achievements in public examinations.

The study reported in this chapter limited the context to lecture-type tutoring because it is a dominant form in this age group. The tutorial company for the study was selected because it was large and well known for this type of tutoring. Secondary 6 learners were chosen because they were in their final year of secondary school and preparing for the university entrance examination. Nevertheless, as noted by Bray (2010, p.6), in the shadow education industry both tutors and tutees may be unwilling to provide data. Tutors may not want to reveal their "secret" teaching methods or materials; and tutees, especially those in senior forms who need to sit public examinations at the end of the academic year, may not have the time or incentive to participate in a study.

Research Design

The research study investigated the extent to which the ideologies of teaching and learning English as a second language in shadow education conflicted with or complemented those in senior secondary mainstream education. It explored and explained the situation of English teaching and learning in lecture-type tutoring from a sociocultural and psychological perspective. The study mainly adopted a qualitative research paradigm, albeit using a questionnaire, through a one-year study to gain understanding of Secondary 6 students' English learning experiences. These experiences were shaped by their formal schooling, social environments, private supplementary tutoring, and their strategies, beliefs and motives for learning English.

A case study approach of the tutorial company was used to obtain "a thick description of a complex social issue embedded within a cultural context" (Dörnyei 2007, p.155). In addition, as noted by Atkins and Wallace (2012, p.108), case studies permit researchers "to capture or interrogate the 'real world' – be that a situation, an organisation or a set of relationships – in all its complexity". While only one tutorial company was selected as the starting point for data collection, the students had a wide range of school backgrounds, levels of English proficiency, and home environments.

With experience of teaching in large tutorial companies for four years, my insider knowledge of the tutorial industry helped me to understand the context. I spent a period of one year to examine and gather detailed information about the case in its natural surroundings. As Dörnyei and Ushioda (2011, p.240) suggested, looking at a case from different angles can "achieve an elaborate and comprehensive understanding of a complex matter". I utilised a combination of research instruments so that the study could more effectively generate a full picture of the target phenomenon. It also triangulated the findings to validate the conclusion by presenting converging results obtained. The various instruments planned for the study included a student questionnaire, a series of tutor and student individual interviews, classroom observations at tutorial centres, and student reflective writing. Details are described below.

The questionnaire
The questionnaire was used to elicit preliminary information about the students' backgrounds, learning practices, and beliefs about English teaching and learning. It was written in Chinese, the participants' first language, to minimise the danger of respondents misunderstanding the questions because of lower English proficiency. The first part of the questionnaire was a consent form, outlining the title, purpose and procedures of the study. It stated that the study had no potential risks and that the participants could benefit from their reflection on their learning experiences. I also assured them of the confidentiality of their information. The students could choose to respond only to the questionnaire or to participate in the whole study including follow-up interviews. The questionnaire served as an invitation for the respondents to participate in the second part.

Before answering the behavioural and attitudinal questions, respondents were asked to provide background information, including their genders, medium of instruction at school, self-evaluation of their English proficiency, modes of tutoring, target grades for the DSE English examination, and durations of participating in private supplementary tutoring in English. Then, they would proceed to their opinions about the importance of learning English, their reasons for receiving private supplementary tutoring in English, their reasons for choosing lecture-type tutoring, and their beliefs about teaching and learning English in both private supplementary tutoring and formal schooling. Seventy Likert-scale statements were listed, and participants were asked to indicate the extent to which they agreed or disagreed with a number of statements. They were given six options (strongly agree, agree, slightly agree, slightly disagree, disagree, and strongly disagree) so that they would be 'forced' to be discriminating in response because the neutral option was not available.

Interviews
After responding to the questionnaire, the respondents who consented to

participate in the second stage were contacted for one-to-one interviews. Interviews were one of the main research instruments in the study with both tutors and learners. All the interviews were planned to be conducted in a one-to-one, face-to-face format because the study focused on individual experiences of learners instead of commonalities in larger groups. With face-to-face interviews, participants' reactions could be noticed, showing when they were enthusiastic or otherwise about a particular point in the discussion (Savin-Baden et al. 2010, p.165). The interviews were semi-structured, with broad questions developed in advance. The questions were designed to encourage the interviewees to talk freely. The interviews were audio-recorded to avoid distraction by the taking of notes. They were conducted in Cantonese, the interviewer's and interviewees' first language, so that we could talk comfortably and generate accurate and rich data without language barriers.

Classroom observations
Classroom observations can generate extensive descriptive data of the tutors' instructional behaviours, classroom discourse and student engagement patterns. Direct observation can provide a more objective account of events and behaviours than second-hand self-reported data, and it has been considered an important research instrument for case study research (Dörnyei 2007; Yin 2009). In the study, I was a "non-participant-observer" doing "unstructured observation" because the observations were qualitative in nature (Dörnyei 2007, p.179). I took narrative field notes, and the lessons were audio-recorded to allow me to revisit the data when necessary. The data were also used as stimuli in the interviews to ask participants to explain their classroom behaviours.

Reflective writing
Learners' reflective writing was used as a research instrument in two ways. First, before the interviews the participants were asked to write reflective essays in which they narrated their English learning experiences in formal schooling and private supplementary tutoring and their beliefs about the two English learning contexts. This not only provided written data but also allowed the participants to organise and formulate their experiences prior to the interview. Second, the reflective writing allowed me to prepare relevant interview questions and stimulate the participants to recall and explain what they had written through deeper articulation of their learning experiences and beliefs. The reflective writ-

ing was also used for recruitment purposes in the main study, because the participants could be attracted by "writing training" in which I offered language feedback on their writing (see below).

Data Collection

Before the main study, a pilot study was conducted to test the research instruments, namely the questionnaire and interview probes. Throughout the process, a research diary was kept to maintain "an ongoing dialogue between collecting data, writing and analysis" (Holliday 2010, p.102) and allow me to reflect on the data collection experience as well as the issues raised at different stages. This section describes the data collection process and reflections in the pilot and main study.

Pilot study

My work as an English tutor in a large tutorial company for four years had provided a network in the industry. I sought help from a former colleague who was an English tutor. I requested to observe one of his classes, to deliver the questionnaire to his students, and to recruit participants for the interview. Sixteen students had enrolled in the course, but only eight attended the lesson. The eight students filled out the questionnaire, but no one was willing to be interviewed. One reason might have been that the tutor was not particularly helpful: he did not sound encouraging when he asked his students to "think very carefully whether [they] really wanted to participate". Another reason might have been that some students were in a hurry to leave and did not fill out the questionnaire seriously.

I then sought help from a friend who was a mathematics tutor running a small centre, asking him to deliver the questionnaire to his students who were receiving English lecture-type tutoring. Twelve of his students were willing to fill out the questionnaire but not to be interviewed. In the end, I offered HK$50 (US$6.40) cash to those willing to participate, and two consented. I also asked two cousins, one studying Secondary 4 and one Secondary 6, to join. The four participants were asked to think aloud while filling out the questionnaire. The participants were trained to do this in advance to ensure that they could articulate what they were thinking during the process as much as possible. In a feedback session, I asked the participants to comment on the quality of the questionnaire and whether they could understand what had been written. The whole process was audio-recorded so that I could revisit the participants' thinking processes and comments for revising the questionnaire. The participants were then interviewed and asked to write a reflective essay about their English learning experiences. In the end, two of the four interviewees submitted essays.

The pilot study raised several concerns for the main study. First, I was worried about how I could attract participants. I wondered whether offering money was a good strategy, because I might have attracted participants who were extrinsically motivated and might not engage fully in the research process. I also revised the layout and wording of the questionnaire. One concern was the length of the questionnaire and the 'attractiveness' of the invitation for interview. I considered the four-page questionnaire, with a full-page consent form listing the objectives and procedure of the study and 70 questionnaire items, to be too exhausting. I also thought about how I could engage the tutor so that he could be interested in the study and encourage his students to join. Through these considerations, a number of strategies were adopted to revise the research instruments for the main study.

Main study
Before the beginning of the academic year, I arranged through my personal network to meet the head of a large tutorial company. He was one of the most popular English tutors in the industry. We discussed the objectives and procedure of the study and the logistics for data collection. He then invited two colleagues to join the study. One was a very popular English tutor, and the other was less popular. I conducted the first meeting with these two tutors to explain the study and logistics. Finding the study educationally meaningful, and attracted by the fact that I could bring them the students' voices about their teaching effectiveness, the two tutors and the head were willing to distribute the questionnaire to their students in their live classes. In addition, one popular tutor with video classes asked his teaching assistants to administer the questionnaires and encourage students to complete them; and the other made a short video to explain the study, highlighting participants' benefits such as extra writing training and a certificate of appreciation awarded by the University of Hong Kong. This video was played before the lesson video.

Among the 2,500 questionnaires prepared, 2,216 completed questionnaires were returned, in which 547 respondents consented to participate in the study. One hundred potential participants were purposefully selected based on their questionnaire responses. The 100 'applicants' were contacted via telephone, and participated in a telephone interview. They were asked in more detail why they learned English and had enrolled in tutorial classes, in order to validate and elaborate on their questionnaire responses. I also used the interview to hear how passionate they were about participating in the research. In the end, with an original target of 10, I selected 22 students to participate and thus allow room for drop-outs. We became 'friends' on Facebook for better and more instant communication online. I also used Facebook as a platform to recommend some English learning resources and sustain our relationships. When participants dropped out from the study, they were removed from my Facebook so that they would not see any posts related to my study or worry about keeping contact with me as Facebook 'friends'.

The participants were asked to write reflectively about their English learning experiences, and to come to my office for the first face-to-face individual interview. The interview elicited their English learning history inside and outside school, including private tutoring. The first classroom observations and tutor interviews were conducted before the first student face-to-face interviews for me to understand more deeply the teaching and learning situations in the research context. Two months after the first round of face-to-face interviews, the two participants who did not submit any reflective writing withdrew, and one more said that his parents no longer allowed him to take part in the study. The remaining 19 were interviewed on the telephone about their English learning experiences in private tutoring during the previous three months. This round of telephone interviews was conducted after the second classroom observations. Seven of the student participants in four different classes sat next to me so that the observed learner classroom behaviours could be explained during the interview. One participant indicated during the interview that she would withdraw from the study because she had enrolled in another tutor's class and felt that she had "betrayed" her original tutor. However, a participant who had changed to another tutor's class in the same tutorial school helped me to invite her tutor to participate in the research study, so a new tutor participant joined. The second tutor interviews were conducted in the same period.

At the end of the tutorial courses, the remaining 18 participants were asked to write two pieces: one about their English learning experiences in private tutoring during the academic year, and one about their views on learning English through private tutoring. The essays were sent to me before we had the second face-to-face individual interviews, which elicited participants' reflections on their English learning experiences in private tutoring. The third round of classroom observations was conducted three months later and followed by the third tutor interviews. The final round of student and tutor interviews was conducted after the release of the public examination results. At that time the participants reflected on the teaching and learning experiences in private tutoring during the whole academic year.

Ethical Issues
Seeking informed consent from the participants' perspectives
According to Flynn and Goldsmith (2013, p.10), informed consent generally means that participants understand the risks and benefits of participating in the research before they agree to participate. Prior to data collection, informed consent forms had been prepared for different types of participants, including the head of the tutorial company, tutors and students; and a passive consent form had been prepared for the parents of the student participants who were aged below 18 and thus considered mature minors. Having already agreed to participate after my verbal description, the head and the tutors read the consent form patiently. However, I worried that the students might find it too time-consuming and tiresome to read the whole form, considering that they had paid to attend the tutorial lessons and did not expect to spend time doing things not related to their learning. From my experience in the pilot study, students tended not to read the whole form carefully; and the formality made the form boring and unable to attract them to join the interviews.

Procedurally, participants should read the consent form in detail before they decided to sign to participate. However, as others have noted (e.g. Wiles et al. 2006, p.286), such "bureaucratization of research" can be off-putting. Therefore, in the main study I decided to give the students the full consent form after explanation of the study and their selection for participation in the study. I simplified the wording by including only basic procedures and highlighting participants' benefits, but ensured that the information was sufficient as a basis for them to make a judgement in giving or refusing consent. More detailed information about the study was given in the first telephone conversations with the 100 selected potential participants, and verbal consent was obtained before recordings for the first telephone interviews. The full written informed consent was signed when I met the 22 finally-selected participants for the first face-to-face individual interviews.

The revised process made the research more interesting and thus made the recruitment more effective. I ensured that the process fitted within ethical procedures through clear verbal communication with the participants. For example, I stressed that the training in writing had a dual purpose of reflection for my data and advice on their writing. This could be considered a necessary flexibility in the recruitment. Corrigan (2003, p.770) has highlighted the danger of "empty ethics" in which participants cannot easily make sense of procedures despite signing agreement in informed consent. Also, as noted by Wiles et al. (2006, p.295), procedures that do not take into account the social context may leave the researcher and the participants with "potentially different understandings of what is to take place".

Using appropriate incentives to recruit participants
Another issue related to the offer of incentives to participants. Several commentators (e.g. Grant & Sugarman 2004, p.718; Singer & Couper 2008, p.50) have queried whether using incentives in research is ethically appropriate because they may be considered a form of coercion or undue influence. Incentives are an extrinsic benefit intentionally designed to motivate people to choose to do what they may otherwise do. They may be effective when the response rate is low because the study is not interesting and does not offer other persuasion.

As noted, following the extremely low response rate in the pilot, I offered monetary reward to each participant who was willing to be interviewed. Grant and Sugarman (2004, p.721) argue that there are ethical and unethical forms of incentives, and that the main factor determining which form a researcher is using is the exercise of power. Issues include the purposes of offering incentives, the voluntariness of accepting the offers, and the effects on the researcher and the researched. While money was used to motivate participants, I made sure that it did not cause undue influence or coercion. I offered HK$50 to each participant because this amount was not irresistible to the extent of impairing potential participants' ability to make decisions or blind them to potential risks. I also invited my friend to help recruit the participants, and asked him to stress that participation was entirely voluntary.

Although monetary reward was used ethically in the pilot study and attracted some participants, the response rate was not boosted dramatically. This experience made me reflect on the meaning of offering incentives, and how I should proceed to the main study. Monetary reward may serve as a motivator to attract participants and a compensation for their time and contribution, but it may make the recruitment and research process a form of trade and alter the nature of research endeavour (Braun & Clarke 2013, p.61). It may lead to commodification of research, and the sample may be skewed by attracting mainly lower income or extrinsically motivated individuals. Then I considered that incentives did not need to be monetary, and that it would be more important to make the study more salient and interesting to the participants. Therefore, in the main study, instead of paying money I offered participants training in writing, a certificate of appreciation, and the chance to increase their English proficiency through reflecting on their own learning experience. Grant and Sugarman (2004, p.722) suggested that "incentives may induce people to do the right thing, but for the wrong reason, and thus undermine responsibility, altruism, or other important values". To avoid this situation, I explained to the participants the purposes of the incentives and the value of the research study. The emphasis was on their contribution to research rather than on what they could get in return.

Balancing closeness and distance in researcher-participant relationships
In addition to informed consent and using incentives to recruit participants, establishing a trusting relationship at the beginning is an important step in data collection. Among all the participants, the gatekeeper can be considered the most important at this stage.

To build rapport with the head of the tutorial centre, I discussed common topics such as postgraduate studies and experiences in English teaching. Then I explained the objectives and procedure of my research. During the discussion, I raised several concerns about data collection and sought to address them together. One was my background and work experience in the tutorial industry, since I faced a dilemma of how much I should expose myself to him. Interviewing tutors and observing their classes would mean I could know their 'secret' professional strategies. Should I hide my identity so that the tutors would not be cautious when telling me their secrets? If so, would they find out during the process? What would be their reaction if they found out? Since the meeting aimed to establish trust which needed to last for the whole period of study, I chose to confront the matter. I was frank to him and I told him I realised that it would be a sensitive issue, but reassured him that all the data would be kept confidential and used for research purposes only. I also emphasised that I was no longer involved in the tutorial industry. Such self-disclosure built trust, and the head appreciated my honesty. The trusting relationship assisted with the validity of the data collected.

In addition to building trust with the head and the tutors, I needed to build trust with my student participants. This process was slightly different, because I also needed to establish my credibility as a researcher and an English teacher/tutor who could help with their English. Pitts and Miller-Day (2007, p.181) argue that researchers can gain rapport with their participants by giving them "more respect, power and control". This involves "reception formations" – i.e. the ways in which the researcher and participants accept each other – which are shaped by constructs such as gender, ethnicity, class, and age. While I might have power over the student participants in terms of knowledge of English, I desired to minimise the impact of those power relations on their responses. I appeared youthful to them and spoke in their language style, showed understanding as someone who knew the studying situation and the tutoring industry in Hong Kong by disclosing some of my learning experiences, and applauded their willingness to share their learning experiences and reflections. Such a process of rapport building and power balancing requires personal skills and "maintenance of something personal to develop a relationship, which, through personal commitment, extends beyond the research" (Pitts & Miller-Day 2007, p.181).

When a trusting relationship has been developed, an ethical challenge concerns the balance between the closeness and distance in that relationship. Taylor (2011, p.11) suggests that close relationships with participants increase the opportunities for the researcher to generate rich data because of better perception related to participants' non-verbal communication cues and affect in interviews, sensitive topics, rationality and participants' self-image. At the beginning of the study, after obtaining their consent, I asked my student participants to add me on Facebook, and we started communicating with each other online. Facebook gave me a platform to announce information such as when I would contact them for interviews. I also posted useful English learning materials, and encouraged them to share their personal lives through Facebook statuses and photographs. Sometimes I 'liked' their photos and left comments in order to build more personal connections. Knowing about their lives would also stimulate me to ask relevant questions in interviews and be aware of sensitive issues. At one point, however, I was worried about knowing too much about their personal lives. For example, one student participant posted pictures taken with her father who had just passed away, writing goodbye to him. I did not comment, because I considered it too personal. However, this made me conscious that when I contacted her for a parent interview, I would not say I wanted to talk to one of her parents. Instead, I would say "I want to talk to your mom". Another incident arose when a few participants tried to use my English expertise to help them with further language support. I rejected their request softly by making them understand our relationship as researcher-participants or research collaborators instead of tutor-students. This avoided participants' abusing the researcher as a resource for excessive help with instrumental tasks and hence distorting the nature of research through greater intimacy.

Building and sustaining relationships with research participants is crucial in studies where the researcher needs to meet the participants multiple times, but the issues of trust and closeness can be complex. Hesse-Biber and Leavy (2011, p.75) warn that: "Personal engagement with research subjects on an interpersonal level can lead to unanticipated and unintended deception that can actually raise even more the possibility of undue power, influence, and authority in the research process." The researcher must strike a balance and confront the ethical issues which may emerge.

Being both an insider and outsider researcher
Issues of researcher positioning as an insider or outsider in qualitative research have been discussed extensively (e.g. Hellawell 2006; Watts 2006; Breen 2007; Mercer 2007; Taylor 2011). An insider can be understood as a person who belongs to the research domain and has deep understanding of the research context and culture. By contrast, an outsider can be regarded as one who does not belong to the group under study and has no prior knowledge of the research community.

There are pros and cons of being either an insider or an outsider in qualitative research. Paechter (2013, p.75) suggested that starting as an insider makes the initial processes easier by using the researcher's prior knowledge to identify appropriate research questions and to access, select and establish rapport with the participants. The researcher can also collect richer data by prompting participants to say more through insider knowledge, and hence generate thicker descriptions in the research report. However, an insider researcher may take things for granted, and may be blinded by prior knowledge about the research problem (Mercer 2007; Taylor 2011; Creswell 2014). This may lead to bias in data analysis, and ethical problems about objectivity when reporting the 'truth'.

In practice the insider-outside dichotomy is not clear-cut, and the best way to collect and analyse data is to balance the insider-outsider continuum. In this study, I considered myself to be both an insider and an outsider. Having experienced learning English in tutorial centres as a secondary school student years ago and having later worked in the industry, I had insider knowledge. The experiences inspired me to generate research questions and explore relevant information. However, in the tutor interviews I needed to be cautious about what insider knowledge I could share with the tutor participants. Projecting myself too much as an insider might discourage the tutors from sharing their 'secrets' with me because of the fierce competition in the industry. In addition, sharing too much of my past tutoring experience might put my ex-colleagues at risk, exposing their own professional 'secrets'. I needed to keep reminding myself of my role as a researcher who was familiar with the industry but was no longer involved in it. This could also make me "go observationalist" (Paechter 2013, p.75) by distancing myself from the phenomenon, allowing me to analyse the data through a reasonably objective and neutral lens. This involved "unlearning" and "objectification" (Taylor 2011, p.16). Moving along the continuum back and forth during the entire research process to find the right balance at different stages increased the extent of obtaining rigorous, valid and reliable data and analysing and interpreting them objectively. More importantly, researchers need to confront their subjectivity as an ethical strategy and explicitly reflect on how it may affect research.

Ensuring data confidentiality and anonymity of participants
Confidentiality and anonymity are routinely granted to research participants prior to data collection. This seems straightforward and sensible, but can be complex, especially in qualitative research. Wiles et al. (2008, p.418) define confidentiality in research as: "(1) not discussing information provided by an individual with others, and (2) presenting findings in ways that ensure individuals cannot be identified (chiefly through anonymisation)". Vainio (2013, p.685) added that anonymity "is one of the core principles of research ethics and is usually regarded as the mechanism through which privacy and confidentiality are maintained". It is one of the main ways to operationalise confidentiality.

One of the complicated domains for ensuring confidentiality concerns online data from Facebook. Wiles et al. (2006) suggested that promises of confidentiality in research are related to who has access to what data and how they are used. While Facebook was set up as a communication platform between the participants and me, I occasionally saw some other posts which could contribute valuable research data. Baker (2013, p.137) described Facebook as an excellent tool to obtain surprising data. However, a dilemma was whether it was ethically legitimate for me to use these data, even though consent had been obtained before the participants added me on Facebook. Participants might not be always conscious that I as a researcher could see their posts and might use them as research data. Moreover, tutors often posted their teaching philosophies and sometimes personal experiences on Facebook, which can be considered public; but they might write them for promotion purposes and thus might not necessarily be reliable. Therefore, I decided not to cite anything directly from their Facebook but to ask them relevant questions in our formal interviews. Ethical guidelines regarding the use of online data in research have not been fully developed (Beneito-Montagut 2011). It is the researcher's responsibility to ensure that privacy is not invaded and that participants know exactly how their information will be used and give informed consent in advance.

An ethical dilemma in anonymity is the balance between protecting the participants' identity and keeping their original "voice" for "social justice goals" (Braun & Clarke 2013, p.63). The 'celebrity tutors' participating in the main study were well known in the industry, and some of their features were potentially identifiable. As Mellick and Fleming (2010, p.307) suggested, identity may be disclosed through the uniqueness of the case and the aggregation of separate details. Even if pseudonyms were used, tutors' identities may be deduced from descriptions of their qualifications, gimmicky teaching strategies, appearance, and relations to others. These were important data, especially when explaining their popularity and detailing their uniqueness in the industry. Hiding or distorting these features would mean modifying the data or leaving out some of the best data. While Vainio (2013, p.691) argued that anonymity can force researchers to generalise the findings and "shift the focus from the particularities of the case to a more abstract level", it can be problematic in narrative research which focuses on participants' detailed and individualistic lived experience, as generalising them may lose the original flavour of participants' stories. Wiles et al. (2006, p.292) suggested discussing with the participants how the data will be presented before they are submitted for publication, but they also acknowledged that "the logistics of doing this are prohibitive". Josselson (2007, p.539) proposed "an ethical attitude" when dealing with this dilemma in narrative research, securing balance between honouring and protecting participants "while still maintaining standards for responsible scholarship". Such an attitude had been maintained throughout the writing process. I disguised individuals by adjusting some distinct characteristics, provided that such an adjustment did not affect the integrity of the data. However, if there was still a risk that the participant would be identified, especially when revealing that part of data might cause harm to the participant, I would choose to discard it. It is the researcher's responsibility to protect participants from potential harm.

Nevertheless, sometimes participants do not want to be anonymous. In such circumstances, as noted by Hesse-Biber and Leavy (2011, p.70), different ethical dilemmas arise – especially when participants want their identified voices to be heard in order to gain empowerment. Before data collection, the head of the tutorial centre once suggested showing his and other tutors' real names in the acknowledgements. While he claimed that it was not for his advertising purposes, this request made me consider a number of questions: Should I impose anonymity despite the participants' request to show their identity? What would be the consequences if I revealed their real names? Knowing that their identity might be revealed, participants might deliberately say something positive and hide the negative, and hence lower the trustworthiness of the responses. In the end, I explained to the head that keeping their identity confidential would mean protecting participants' privacy and allowing them to express their views freely without caring about who they really were.

In most qualitative research, confidentiality and anonymity can be problematic and hardly be assured, especially in the presentation of findings. It is the researcher's responsibility to address this issue and reflect on the process of data collection, analysis and writing up.

Conclusion

Ethics in shadow education research, as much as in other domains, can be complex. This is especially likely in qualitative studies in which the researcher is a key instrument and needs to establish relationships with the participants. In this reflection about my study of students' English learning experiences in a large tutorial centre in Hong Kong, I have discussed ethical issues that emerged at different stages.

While there are always ethical dilemmas in research, it is the researchers' responsibility to integrate ethics into the entire process. However, as Flick (2014, p.43) suggested, taking ethical dilemmas into account should not prevent researchers from doing research. Rather it should encourage them to be more reflective in research processes by considering participants' perspectives at different levels and the impact every ethical decision may have on different parties. The processes should not be limited by institutional bureaucratisation on ethical approval but guided by ethical principles beyond informed consent. This chapter does not aim to object the procedural chores, but to bring out their practical meanings and to note the dangers when the intended meanings are not actualised despite procedural correctness. Those ethical principles should be reflexive through engaging in researchers' internal dialogues with their own ethical standards and embedded in all researchers and scholarly practices.

References

Atkins, Liz & Wallace, Susan (2012): *Qualitative Research in Education*. London: Sage.
Baker, Sally (2013): 'Conceptualising the Use of Facebook in Ethnographic Research: As Tool, as Data and as Context'. *Ethnography and Education*, Vol.8, No.2, pp.131-145.
Beneito-Montagut, Roser (2011): 'Ethnography Goes Online: Towards a User-Centred Methodology to Research Interpersonal Communication on the Internet'. *Qualitative Research*, Vol.11, No.6, pp.716-735.
Braun, Virginia & Clarke, Victoria (2013): *Successful Qualitative Research: A Practical Guide for Beginners*. London: Sage.
Bray, Mark (2010): 'Researching Shadow Education: Methodological Challenges and Directions'. *Asia Pacific Education Review*, Vol.11, No.1, pp.3-13.
Bray, Mark & Kwo, Ora (2014): *Regulating Private Tutoring for Public Good: Policy Options for Supplementary Education in Asia*. Hong Kong: Comparative Education Research Centre, The University of Hong Kong, and Bangkok: UNESCO.
Breen, Lauren J. (2007): 'The Researcher 'in the Middle': Negotiating the Insider/Outsider Dichotomy'. *The Australian Community Psychologist*, Vol.19, No.1, pp.163-174.
Corrigan, Oonagh (2003): 'Empty Ethics: The Problem with Informed Consent'. *Sociology of Health and Illness*, Vol.25, No.7, pp.768-792.

Creswell, John W. (2014): *Research Design: Qualitative, Quantitative, and Mixed Methods Approaches*. 4th edition, Thousand Oaks: Sage.

Dörnyei, Zoltán (2007): *Research Methods in Applied Linguistics: Quantitative, Qualitative, and Mixed Methodologies*. Oxford: Oxford University Press.

Dörnyei, Zoltán & Ushioda, Ema (2011): *Teaching and Researching Motivation*. Harlow: Longman.

Flick, Uwe (2014): *An Introduction to Qualitative Research*. Los Angeles: Sage.

Flynn, Leisa Reinecke, & Goldsmith, Ronald E. (2013): *Case Studies for Ethics in Academic Research in the Social Sciences*. Thousand Oaks: Sage.

Goodwin, Dawn; Pope, Catherine; Mort, Maggie & Smith, Andrew (2003): 'Ethics and Ethnography: An Experiential Account'. *Qualitative Health Research*, Vol.13, No.4, pp.567-577.

Grant, Ruth W. & Sugarman, Jeremy (2004): 'Ethics in Human Subjects Research: Do Incentives Matter?' *Journal of Medicine and Philosophy*, Vol.29, No.6, pp.717-738.

Hammersley, Martyn (2015): 'On Ethical Principles for Social Research'. *International Journal of Social Research Methodology*. Vol.18, No.4, pp.433-449.

Hellawell, David (2006): 'Inside-Out: Analysis of the Insider-Outsider Concept as a Heuristic Device to Develop Reflexivity in Students Doing Qualitative Research'. *Teaching in Higher Education*, Vol.11, No.4, pp.483-494.

Hesse-Biber, Sharlene Nagy & Leavy, Patricia (2011): *The Practice of Qualitative Research*. Thousand Oaks: Sage.

Holliday, Adrian (2010): 'Analysing Qualitative Data', in Paltridge, Brian & Phakiti, Aek (eds.), *Continuum Companion to Research Methods in Applied Linguistics*. London: Continuum, pp.98-110.

Homan, Roger (1991): *The Ethics of Social Research*. London: Longman.

Josselson, Ruthellen (2007): 'The Ethical Attitude in Narrative Research: Principles and Practicalities', in Clandinin, Jean (ed.), *Handbook of Narrative Inquiry: Mapping a Methodology*. Thousand Oaks: Sage.

Kwo, Ora & Bray, Mark (2011): 'Facing the Shadow Education System in Hong Kong'. *The Newsletter*, International Institute for Asian Studies (IIAS), Vol.56, p.20.

Mellick, Mikel & Fleming, Scott (2010): 'Personal Narrative and the Ethics of Disclosure: A Case Study from Elite Sport'. *Qualitative Research*, Vol.10, No.3, pp.299-314.

Mercer, Justine (2007): 'The Challenges of Insider Research in Educational Institutions: Wielding a Double-Edged Sword and Resolving Delicate Dilemmas'. *Oxford Review of Education*, Vol.33, No.1, pp.1-17.

Ng, Yuk-Hang (2009): 'Tutors Are Like Actors'. *Deccan Herald*. 1 June. http://www.nytimes.com/2009/06/01/business/global/01iht-cramside.html?_r=0, accessed 10 January 2015.

Paechter, Carrie (2013): 'Researching Sensitive Issues Online: Implications of a Hybrid Insider/Outsider Position in a Retrospective Ethnographic Study'. *Qualitative Research*, Vol.13, No.1, pp.71-86.

Pitts, Margaret Jane & Miller-Day, Michelle (2007): 'Upward Turning Points and Positive Rapport-Development across Time in Researcher-Participant Relationships'. *Qualitative Research*, Vol.7, No.2, pp.177-201.

Savin-Baden, Maggi; Gourlay, Lesley & Tombs, Cathy (2010): 'Researching in Immersive Spaces', in Savin-Baden, Maggi & Major, Claire Howell (eds.), *New Approaches to Qualitative Research: Wisdom and Uncertainty*. London: Routledge, pp.162-171.

Singer, Eleanor & Couper, Mick P. (2008): 'Do Incentives Exert Undue Influence on Survey Participation? Experimental Evidence'. *Journal of Empirical Research in Human Research Ethics*, Vol.3, No.3, pp.49-56.

Taylor, Jodie (2011): 'The Intimate Insider: Negotiating the Ethics of Friendship When Doing Insider Research'. *Qualitative Research*, Vol.11, No.1, pp.3-22.

Vainio, Annukka (2013): 'Beyond Research Ethics: Anonymity as 'Ontology', 'Analysis' and 'Independence''. *Qualitative Research*, Vol.13, No.6, pp.685-698.

Watkins, David A. (2009): 'Motivation and Competition in Hong Kong Secondary Schools: The Students' Perspective', in Chan, Carol K.K. & Rao, Nirmala (eds.), *Revisiting the Chinese Learner: Changing Contexts, Changing Education*. CERC Studies in Comparative Education 25, Hong Kong: Comparative Education Research Centre and Dordrecht: Springer, pp.71-88.

Watts, Jacqueline (2006): ''The Outsider Within': Dilemmas of Qualitative Feminist Research within a Culture of Resistance'. *Qualitative Research*, Vol.6, No.3, pp.385-402.

Wiles, Rose; Charles, Vikki; Crow, Graham & Heath, Sue (2006): 'Researching Researchers: Lessons for Research Ethics'. *Qualitative Research*, Vol.6, No.3, pp.283-299.

Wiles, Rose; Crow, Graham; Heath, Sue & Charles, Vikki (2008): 'The Management of Confidentiality and Anonymity in Social Research'. *International Journal of Social Research Methodology*, Vol.11, No.5, pp.417-428.

Yin, Robert K. (2009): *Case Study Research: Design and Methods*. Thousand Oaks: Sage.

Yung, Kevin Wai-Ho (2011): *Shadow Education in Hong Kong: The Experience of Learners of English*. Master of Arts in Applied Linguistics dissertation, The University of Hong Kong.

Yung, Kevin Wai-Ho (2015): 'Learning English in the Shadows: Under- standing Chinese Learners' Experiences of Private Tutoring'. *TESOL Quarterly*. Vol.49. DOI: 10.1002/tesq.193.

Zhan, Shengli; Bray, Mark; Wang, Dan; Lykins, Chad & Kwo, Ora (2013): 'The Effectiveness of Private Tutoring: Students' Perceptions in Comparison with Mainstream Schooling in Hong Kong'. *Asia Pacific Education Review*, Vol.14, No.4, pp.1-15.

6

Classroom Practices and Private Tuition in the Maldives: Methodological Reflections on an Ethnographic Study

Maryam MARIYA

Introduction

This chapter presents methodological dimensions of a study of what in the Maldives is called private tuition and elsewhere is called private tutoring. The study compared the settings of private tuition and mainstream classrooms (Mariya 2012). I wished to know why students opted for private tuition even though they received instruction in mainstream classrooms. The study particularly focused on teaching and learning of English Language.

An ethnographic approach was used to illuminate everyday activities (Hammersley 1997). The research techniques included observations, field notes, journal entries, document analysis, and photographs. In addition, I used interviews to find out in more detail the participants' *hows* and *whys* of doing things in socially complex contexts (Talmy 2010).

The Maldives is a small country, with a population of 395,000 scattered over 1,200 islands formed through 26 atolls in the Indian Ocean. Approximately one third of the population lives in the capital, Male'. The research on which this chapter reports was conducted in Male' and in a more distant atoll.

Bray, Mark; Kwo, Ora & Jokić, Boris (eds.) (2015): *Researching Private Supplementary Tutoring: Methodological Lessons from Diverse Cultures*. Hong Kong: Comparative Education Research Centre (CERC), The University of Hong Kong, and Dordrecht: Springer. © CERC

The study is grounded in my own history and identity. I had received private tuition in mathematics when in Grade 10, joining friends in a group in the house of a tutor called Ms Sam three times a week. Later I became a teacher and gave supplementary private classes in English for students sitting the Ordinary Level examinations. I worked at a tuition centre, and since I was working at school in the mornings I provided private tuition in the afternoons and sometimes in the evenings. Later I became a senior teacher in the system. That facilitated the research reported in this chapter, but also required care. The teachers whose views I was researching saw me as a figure of authority because I had previously been their supervisor. That dimension may have made them think that I could impart the knowledge to higher sources, including the Ministry of Education. Nevertheless, I was able to generate trust which considerably facilitated the study.

Methodology

For this research I conducted an ethnographic study of:

- two Grade 8 classrooms, two Grade 10 classrooms and four teachers in a secondary school in Male' which will henceforth be called the City School; and
- one Grade 8 classroom, two Grade 10 classrooms and two teachers in what will henceforth be called the Atoll School.

Different number of classrooms and teachers were selected from the two schools according to the accessibility of the teachers and their private tuition settings. Further variation arose because I respected the assistance of the heads of department in the schools in choosing the teachers and classrooms.

I observed activities in these classrooms over a period of nine months for about three to four hours each week. Observations and field notes were taken for each lesson of 35 minutes. I met with the principals of both the schools, heads of departments, supervisors, teachers in the English departments, other teachers whom I met occasionally in the staff rooms, a number of students, and some parents.

In addition to these two school sites, I explored the private tuition setting. It was difficult to gain access to private tuition sessions, because few teachers were willing to let me watch them tutor. Only one teacher,

Naomi, from the City School willingly agreed. In addition, I visited a student's home three times a week over a period of two months.

Although most teachers were reluctant to let me watch them teach in their private tuition settings, I was able to have informal talks and interviews about their tutoring. In addition to observing and interviewing teachers, I interviewed four parents and many students who received private tuition both from the City School and the Atoll School.

Several random interview sessions were conducted with each interview participant from both the schools and private tuition settings, with each session lasting around five minutes. By contrast, in-depth informal meetings lasted more than 15 minutes. The interviews with principals and other senior staff were held in their offices. In both schools, the interviews with students and teachers were held before and after school hours in different locations. The interviews with parents were also held before and after school hours, in the office spaces allocated to me by the schools and in their own homes.

I collected and analysed the data by daily analysis: fleshing out, reading, and re-reading field notes and journal entries; listening to and transcribing audio tapes; looking for patterns of actions and meanings in the data; and reflecting on the data with the help of excel sheet recordings. By colour coding the words, I was able to find emerging patterns. When the patterns emerged, I obtained feedback from the informants about them. This was done by asking the informants to give their opinions about the transcribed conversations. Having done so, I identified themes by reading the notes again and again. Once the themes had been collected and the notes had been studied, I was ready to formulate theme statements to develop a story line.

In summary, the analysis enabled me to generate a description of the classroom practices of both classroom streams of the City School and Atoll School and the private tuition settings I observed.

Ethical considerations
The research on which this chapter reports was undertaken for doctoral studies at Massey University in New Zealand. The University system required me to seek ethical approval for the research approach and instruments. Later, permission was also obtained from the Maldivian Ministry of Education and the school principals, teachers, parents and students.

accurate information about all aspects of the study and to assure them of "maintaining participants' anonymity".

Moosa (2013), who also conducted research on education in the Maldives, reminds readers of the complexity of the notion of anonymity, and questions whether promises of anonymity are always necessary or valid. She points out that some participants seek recognition – i.e. do not wish to be anonymous. She also notes that where the pool of potential participants is small, anonymity cannot really be guaranteed. This, indeed, is a feature of small states in which everybody seems to know everybody else and social actions require forms of 'managed intimacy' (Bray & Packer 1993, p.39). Nevertheless, I told the participants of the measures I would take to attempt to maintain their anonymity, and none expressed concern about this issue. I stressed that pseudonyms would be used instead of their real names, and added that all documents, including interview transcripts, field notes and journal notes, would be kept in a safe place and destroyed later. Figure 6.1 shows the whole approval process.

Figure 6.1: Approval Route for the Study of Private Tuition in the Maldives

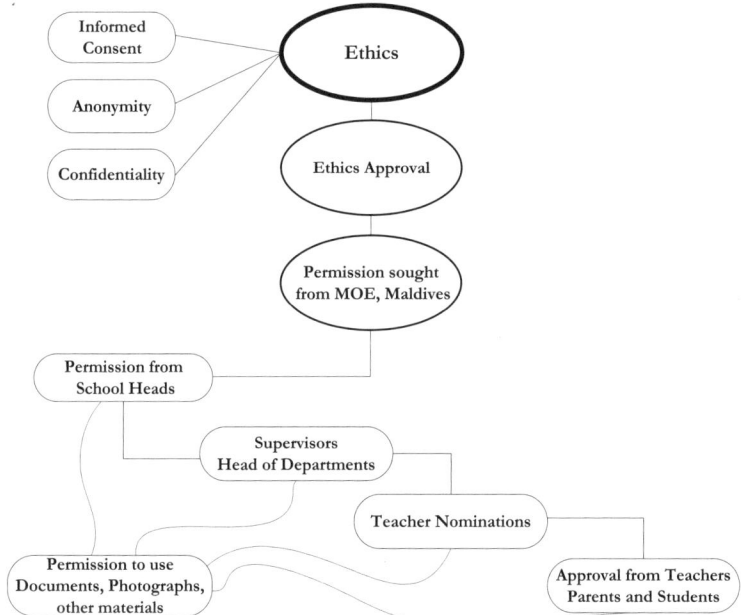

In conducting this study, I had the advantage of being an experienced teacher who was familiar with the school setting and the people. It was therefore easy to approach the informants and negotiate a project timeframe. Gaining access to the schools was easy because I was very familiar with the way the institutions worked. I had all the necessary contacts, and knew the procedures to get permissions and access to data.

Approval to study the Atoll School was gained by telephoning a friend from the school and later calling the principal and assistant principal to fix a date. The participant teachers in both schools were nominated by their heads of department, and were randomly chosen from a pool of teachers who were willing to participate in the research.

By contrast, gaining admission to the private tuition settings was not easy and I only visited one home where private tuition was carried out. The teacher who volunteered to let me observe her private tuition sessions was a former colleague who later was part of my supervision team. This relationship was one reason she let me come and watch her. The teacher sought permission from the parents and the students. On the first day, I briefed the parents and students about the research and they informed me that they were glad to help.

During the data collection process, I explained the nature and contents of the study, and the anticipated benefits to the Maldives and to the participants. The participants were willing to talk to me because they perceived me to understand their school situations. They appeared to trust me, and considered themselves part of the research project. They were in no way compelled to give any information. However, considering my role as an insider researcher (in the City School), all necessary measures were taken to ensure that the standard ethical principles were followed. This included care in use of data obtained from interviews, documents and photographs.

In addition to addressing the standard procedures, I took special measures to address ethical issues, particularly those related to informed consent, anonymity and confidentiality (Cohen at al. 2007). Hammersley and Atkinson (2007), two of the best-known authors in the field of ethnography, stress four major areas in research ethics: ensuring that informed consent is obtained; ensuring that privacy is protected; protecting participants from harm and exploitation; and considering consequences for future research. Bearing these themes in mind, I used face-to-face meetings to ensure that participants of all three settings had clear and

Why ethnography in this study?

An ethnographic approach was chosen because of its flexibility and range. Data collection included all kinds of experiences in different places and different instances in the City School, the Atoll School and private tuition settings. I found data everywhere, including personal experiences, observations, and conversations that were part of everyday life. Data collection occurred in everyday discussions in the supervisor's room, the classroom, the staff room, the canteen, the school compound, the school office, the corridors, the printing room, and the school hall.

I tried to get thick descriptions with many details. When culture is examined from an ethnographic perspective, researchers face a set of interpretations of life and of common sense understandings that are complex and difficult to separate from each other. As a key instrument in the study, I, as an ethnographer, had to equip myself with an insider's view, with extensive communication with the observed, and with continuous discourses with others and myself. In other words, I needed to engage in dynamic participation and self-examination. I viewed ethnography as the glue that bonded students from all walks of life. It strengthened the ideology that the classroom can be viewed as a "microcosm of social order" that reflects a broader concept of a social world (Pennycook 2001, p.103).

The place of interview within the study

In choosing to use interviews in this study, I maintained awareness of their function as social practice, i.e. in dialogue with interviewees rather than just treating them as a source of information on predetermined questions (Talmy 2010). To find out about the nature of classroom and private tuition settings, I interviewed teachers, students, and parents. The four teachers in the City School and the two in the Atoll School were selected by the school administrators or heads of department, and one teacher volunteered to let me collect data from her private tuition setting. The small number of teachers interviewed was intentional as it allowed me to gather rich data and perform more sensitive analyses than would have been possible with a greater number of informants.

In addition, I gained data from students during library periods, breaks, and other free times. Sometimes students themselves started conversations, while on other occasions I invited students to talk in more formal interview settings. In addition, I met three students at home in a private tuition setting, weekly over one and half months for approximately an hour each time. Connected with this, I interviewed the parents to find out details of the children's lives inside and outside school and to understand parents' interpretations of their children's learning at school during the private tuition. Interviews were also conducted with some academics and the school administrators. These meetings were generally pleasant and meaningful, though the meetings with students were a little more difficult, despite my explanations of purpose – i.e. that I was undertaking research study on classroom practices, trying to understand how teachers teach, students learn, etc.. The students perhaps saw me as an outsider who was asking questions that did not concern them. However, with time they accepted me in their circle of life, and became more open in sharing their thoughts and feelings. In this respect my experiences matched those of Garton and Copland (2010).

My role as a researcher
At the beginning of the research, I strongly identified myself as a teacher. I had accumulated 10 years of English-language teaching experience, mostly in secondary schools. The teachers I interviewed and observed were effectively, from my viewpoint, colleagues in the sense that they were teaching the same subject and age groups that I had previously taught. In this sense, I saw myself as an *insider*, able to immediately take an emic perspective with the teachers in the school.

While I inhabited the role of the researcher for the duration of my field work, on occasion I simultaneously inhabited other roles due to the familiarity with the settings and the participants. In the context of interviewing at the City School in which I had worked preceding my research, the relationship between interviewer and interviewee was always very familiar. My prior relationships with some teachers and administrators greatly contributed to rapport for the interviews. Along the lines advocated by Roulston et al. (2001, p.748), I was able to lead the teachers to produce certain types of talk which were useful for my study. For instance, Naomi shared with me her daily lesson plans and the note book that she carried for private tuition, and freely discussed what and how she planned to teach in private tuition settings on particular days.

Data analysis
Analysis was on-going throughout the observation sessions. Data were reviewed in terms of both the most common emerging themes and the themes that were more narrowly represented. The expanded notes were coded manually with attention to the emergent themes and categories.

The aim of the analysis was to gain deeper understanding of the situations under observation and to provide reasonable explanation along the lines recommended by Miles and Huberman (1984).

A number of factors were involved in analysing the interview data, determining the nature of the interview as social practice. Attention was paid to both the practical *hows* and the substantive *whats* of interviewing in reporting the results for the co-construction of the meaning which has significant implication for data analysis (Talmy 2010). In this respect, Holstein and Gubrium's (2003) active interviews align with interview as social practice where interviewers are interested in the content as well as the "interactional [and] narrative procedures of knowledge production" (p.68).

Also, the voices and opinions of the interviewees were considered as social action, the manner in which the interviewees spoke, their moods, and their gestures and other actions. The relationship between the interviewer and interviewee was also studied and used as context for examination of the aforementioned attributes. These factors were written out qualitatively, identifying extracts that were significant in some way (Borg 2001). I recorded instances, for example, when I learned something new about the interviewees, where plans were made for future interviews and/or social situations, and when events that occurred in the interviewees' presence were discussed.

Findings

Classroom settings - schools

In the Maldives, teachers are placed in schools not only to impart knowledge to students but also to serve as moral embodiments for students to follow. Parents expect teachers not merely to ensure that the students learn but also to guide children to develop as persons in the society. This is part of the traditional respect for teachers, as valued elders transmitting knowledge and wisdom to subordinate juniors. Nevertheless, while this is the ideological and idealised position, in the pressure of the weekly workload it is often lost from sight.

Although the City School and Atoll School had achieved many successes throughout the years, the teachers and students faced many demands. The teachers had to meet the expectations of their heads, and they refrained from group work with students first because they were concerned about losing teaching time and second because they were worried that students would be noisy and disruptive. In consequence, much learning was passive in an examination-oriented, teacher-dominated mode. Most teachers in both schools provided private tuition. The interest they showed in the tuition class was due to factors like a change of environment, fewer students, and lack of pressure on the teachers to adhere to time and syllabuses.

These factors may be illustrated by some teachers' statements: "Well…classroom atmosphere is not good…. Children are not attentive" (Mariya 2012, p.16). Four teachers claimed that they did not offer tuition to gain money but as a service to the students and to impart their knowledge. In some cases, teachers indicated that they provided tuition in response to parents' requests and peer pressure: "We also need to give tuition as everyone else is giving" (Mariya 2012, p.179).

Private tuition settings
One of the most striking characteristics of private tuition was the relaxed and friendly atmosphere. This was very clear in Naomi's tuition classes. It was also reported from other tuition centres, and matched my own experience as a tutor. The students could openly discuss their doubts with the teachers without feeling inhibition. The teachers were open to talk about what the students wanted, and were not afraid to stray from the lesson plans. I was impressed by the teachers' openness to questions and suggestions. The classes were interesting, and the teachers could easily explain topics with which the students had trouble. The teachers did everything to make the students feel comfortable, and ensured that the students learned at their own pace. Further, the classes were small and enjoyed by the students. In the tuition classes that I observed, tutors were able to teach to high standards, providing one-to-one sessions and using needs-based lessons and activities whilst simultaneously making them interesting, student-centred and relaxing.

The rooms in which the classes were held included a kitchen, a bedroom and a living room. During the time of tuition, the rooms were transformed into a tuition space by the use of small tables, chairs and stools. The silence contrasted with the noise in schools which mostly had open classroom structures in which students and teachers had to cope with the noise from classes next door. During these tutoring classes, the students were able to concentrate more easily.

The teachers also gained a lot from the private classes. Secondary school teachers did not earn high salaries, and private tuition provided a way to supplement their earnings. Most teachers earned the equivalent of approximately US$1,000 per month, which was barely enough to cover their daily expenses. From private tuition, they could earn between US$500 and US$1,000 per month on top of their official salaries. This possibility helped to retain some quality teachers in the profession.

Although it was heavy on the pockets of parents, private tuition was reported to reap rewards at the end of the day. One parent, for example, stated that:

> Last year, my daughter got a B in English in the final term.... With tuition, she has improved and gained an A. (Parent from Atoll School; Mariya 2012, p.184)

Although the Atoll School parents were satisfied with the teaching in the school, the parents wanted to supplement their children's learning by providing them with private tutors. The parents of both schools worked hard and made sure that their children were not deprived of tuition. They felt that if their children received tuition, as parents they did not need to worry.

I observed that private tuition settings, at home and at tuition classes, were much more conducive to learning than the mainstream classrooms. The teachers' enthusiasm to teach and relatively relaxed attitude left me wondering about the matter. There was no one to dictate to them, and so they were free to use the most appropriate material that the students needed. They dealt with the students with much ease; they were very friendly, and laughed and enjoyed the time with the students. They did not have to look at their watches constantly or time the students' work progress repetitively. Thus students found tuition a place where they could learn things that they did not learn at school in a more relaxed and friendly atmosphere. This caused me to consider further the imperative of private tuition and matters of private and personal space.

The imperative of private tuition

In the Maldives, almost all teachers offer some form of private tuition. Teachers spend most of their free time going from house to house earning significant amounts of money. According to the teachers, without the extra money, it would be hard to live on their government salaries. Further, the teachers I interviewed enjoyed the tuition and were pleased with what they had done to boost the students' performance. As exemplified by one of Naomi's statements (Mariya 2012, p.195): "I try to cater to the skills of the students...and do interesting vocabulary...of a higher level." The teachers also had freedom to choose the learning tasks for particular students and to spend time on specific topics until the students understood the materials. Providing tuition also affirmed the teachers' status, though some teachers provided tuition because of peer pressure. As reported by teachers in one group interview (City School; Mariya 2012, p.179), some teachers desired to show their peers that they could do it too: "[We] give tuition as everyone else is giving... [We use it to show] that we are up to the mark... We need to upkeep our status."

The parents' motivation in seeking tuition for their children was diverse. Some parents feared that if they did not provide their children with tuition, the children would be failures. The parents basically felt forced to provide extra help for their children. They were unsettled by a lack of confidence in local schools arising from perceptions of falling standards, traditional teaching methods, large classes and under-qualified teachers.

As can be ascertained from these remarks, parents of various financial means make sacrifices to pay for tutors. Peer pressure among children also plays a part: students are influenced by their classmates into wanting tutors. There is more competitiveness and pressure for tuition than before. When more children get top grades in the Ordinary Level and Advanced Level examinations, parents naturally want to do the best for their children. Especially just before the examinations begins, children who are about to sit their Ordinary Level examinations are more likely than any others to have extra tutoring after school.

At the same time, tuition provides several further benefits to parents. Parents can gain more information on their children's progress, as they can freely discuss matters with the tutors. In addition, tuition is a social marker for 'doing the right thing'. Not securing tuition for their children would seem an anomaly, suggesting that the parents are not concerned; that they cannot afford tuition; that the school is sufficient; or that the parents have less long-term investment in education.

The trend also has negative backwash on schooling. Shauna, a student in the City School, made a sharp point when she stated that students pay less attention in class because they feel that they can catch up in tuition. Also parents feel that because teachers see tuition as a source of income, they teach less in class and more in tuition sessions. This action effectively makes tuition compulsory for students.

Private and personal space

In classrooms, children are bound by the levels and attitudes of the people that surround them. Private tuition is more personalised to the levels of the students. Classrooms may be paced too quickly or too slowly, but in private tuition scenarios the pace is set by the students and the teachers. Naomi shared how she helps in both group and individual tuition:

> I try to cater to the skills of the students. If it is a very weak student, I try to give work that is not very challenging. I give simple exercises, like fill in the blanks, comprehension and vocabulary that is one or two levels below their standard. I get them to write simple paragraphs and explain how to write simple sentences first and then make them write complex ones. For a good student, I make them do challenging ones. If it is a grade eight student, I try to find practice exercises a bit higher than their level. For example, I make them do grade ten type of comprehension and also do interesting vocabulary exercises of a higher level. I also use the Singapore text books which have work for different levels.

At the same time, I found that the atmosphere in the tuition classes commonly very creative and very private. In private tuition, only a few students are together with the tutor for that particular time, so the tutor can concentrate on the set of students at all times. An example of the relaxed atmosphere is in the following transcript concerning Shauna (S) and Azza (A). They were sitting around the table with the teacher, learning with ease, giggling, enjoying and gaining the maximum from the lesson:

> S: *Miss, can you tell me another word for hurt?*
> A: *pain? Harm? I wrote pain..*

The students were writing an essay on a disaster.

> Teacher: *Remember, the brainstorming strategy I told you? Write sentence with hurt and think of other words that mean the same that would fit the sentence. Look at your thesaurus if you are stuck.* [Takes out the thesaurus and flips through the pages]
>
> S: *Yes Miss, yes, let's do that!* [thrilled]
>
> A: *Oh yes!* [smiling] *I found one already, here* [pointing at her thesaurus]. *I got hurt. I got injured. Wounded? Miss, ok tha?*

Unlike school, there was no noise from outside and the children could concentrate. Also the students were permitted to pause, ask questions or take a break as frequently and as lengthily as they deemed appropriate. There was no negative peer pressure, and the teacher identified the learning problems and swiftly dealt with them. She geared tasks exactly to the students' abilities and experience, as recorded in my notes:

> At the end of the second term, Shauna got 63 in English, which is a grade C. She is very happy with her achievement and hopes 'to work for a B or an A next term,' she said with enthusiasm. She adds: Naomi Miss is a very good teacher. Me and Azza like her a lot. She listens to us and helps us improve our comprehension and writing. She corrects our essays and tells us how to use new vocabulary in our essays. Shauna and her friends do not speak in English in the class, at the tuition sessions or at home. She enjoys English lessons at school but 'we don't get much speaking practice.'

Students like Azza and Shauna also believe that at tuition they can be more relaxed and ask anything they want. Shauna stated (Mariya 2012, pp.186-187) that:

> I can ask anything I want. I am shy at school to ask questions. I cannot take my hands up. But at tuition, we can talk and ask everything we don't know.

The private tuition also provided opportunities for personalised feedback.

Conclusions

The marriage of ethnography with interview as social practice enriched my research in helping to illuminate the complexities in teaching and learning in both classroom practices and private tuition settings. Interview as social practice enhanced the participants' willingness to share, and brought many dimensions to light. My prior relationships with the participants allowed me "to access resources that might not have been available in traditional interviews" (Garton & Copland 2010, p.548). Most importantly, I was able to bring the voices of the participants of the City School, the Atoll School and the private tuition settings to the foreground in an informative way.

Through the use of the ethnographic method of data collection and interview as social practice, I was able to uncover issues related to the classroom practices in the two classroom settings and the private tuition settings. The teachers and students in the City School felt pressured to deliver the curriculum in a timely manner, and the rigidly-governed subject committee unintentionally discouraged enthusiasm for innovation. The sustained mini-examination sessions of teaching and learning were a further stress for both teachers and students. The teachers also felt that the physical structures of the classrooms obstructed placing students in groups and pairs; and they feared that their large classes would become noisy and unmanageable with group and paired work.

The teachers also felt time pressures. In response to these pressures, they preferred to dominate the classrooms, making them teacher-centred and leaving the students bored with monotonous lessons. The teachers in the City School felt subjected to a hierarchical structure of decision-making on teaching and learning, in contrast to their counterparts in the Atoll School. Due to these reasons and in combination with pressures from low salaries, many teachers spent much of their free time – mornings before school, evenings after school, and weekends – on private tutoring by going to students' homes or tuition centres, in which they provided learners with what they had missed in the mainstream classrooms.

One of the most telling findings of this study was the number of students who described school lessons as dull and lacking the sort of individual attention that they could secure in private tuition. Students and their parents sought private tuition in order to learn with greater flexibility and comfort, and to understand the lessons in a more meaningful manner.

On the basis of the findings, this study confirmed that teachers in the Maldivian classroom do things the way they do because it is what is expected of them. The solution to the problems with classroom practice is therefore contingent upon addressing the factors mentioned in this chapter. Attention to these complexities for teachers in ensuring better classroom practice should be taken into consideration and finding a solution would be valuable for teaching and learning in the Maldives and beyond.

References

Borg, Simon (2001): 'The Research Journal: A Tool for Promoting and Understanding Researcher Development'. *Language Teaching Research*, Vol.5, No.2, pp.156-177.

Bray, Mark & Packer, Steve (1993): *Education in Small States: Concepts, Challenges and Strategies*. Oxford: Pergamon Press.

Cohen, Louis; Manion, Lawrence & Morrison, Keith (2007): *Research Methods in Education*. 6th edition. London: Routledge.

Garton, Sue & Copland, Fiona (2010): 'I like this Interview; I get Cakes and Cats!': The Effect of Prior Relationships on Interview Talk'. *Qualitative Research*, Vol.10, No.5, pp.533-551.

Hammersley, Martyn (1997): *Reading Ethnographic Research: A Critical Guide*. New York: Longman.

Hammersley, Martyn & Atkinson, Paul (2007): *Ethnography: Principles in Practice*. 3rd edition. London: Routledge.

Holstein, James A. & Gubrium, Jaber F. (2003): 'Active Interviewing', in Gubrium, James A. & Holstein, James A. (eds.), *Postmodern Inter- viewing*. Thousand Oaks: Sage, pp.67-80.

Mariya, Maryam (2012): *I Don't Learn at School, so I take Tuition: An Ethnographic Study of Classroom Practices and Private Tuition Settings in the Maldives*. PhD thesis, Massey University.

Miles, Matthew B. & Huberman, A. Michael (1984): *Qualitative Data Analysis: A Sourcebook of New Methods*. Newbury Park: Sage.

Moosa, Dheeba (2013): 'Challenges to Anonymity and Representation in Educational Qualitative Research in a Small Community: A Reflection on my Research Journey'. *Compare: A Journal of Compara- tive and International Education*, Vol.43, No.4, pp.483-495.

Pennycook, Alastair (2001): *Critical Applied Linguistics: A Critical Intro- duction*. London: Lawrence Erlbaum.

Roulston, Kathryn J.; Baker, Carolyn D. & Liljestrom, Anna (2001): 'Analyzing the Researcher's Work in Generating Data: The Case of Complaints'. *Qualitative Inquiry*, Vol.7, No.6, pp.745-772.

Talmy, Steven (2010): 'Qualitative Interviews in Applied Linguistics: From Research Instrument to Social Practice'. *Annual Review of Applied Linguistics*, Vol.30, No.1, pp.128-148.

7
Researching Shadow Education in Iran: Methodological Experiences in an Islamic Republic

Abbas MADANDAR ARANI

Introduction

At the time of the 1979 Islamic Revolution in Iran, I was a Grade 9 student participating in demonstrations against Shah – though I admit that I viewed these activities mostly as a hobby and a way to shut down our classes. Due to the political turmoil, all universities were closed for what turned out to be three years. Even longer was the war between Iran and Iraq that lasted for eight years.

The end of my upper secondary schooling coincided with the reopening of the universities, I was fortunate to be among the first group of students to pass a difficult national university entrance examination and political filtering called *Ghoziynesh*. Eight years later, having gained a bachelor's and a master's degree, I was hired at a state university and commenced an academic career.

From these remarks it will be evident that I am a part of the 'revolutionary generation'. During the decades since entering school I have experienced an Islamic revolution, closure of universities, a terrible

---

Bray, Mark; Kwo, Ora & Jokić, Boris (eds.) (2015): *Researching Private Supplementary Tutoring: Methodological Lessons from Diverse Cultures.* Hong Kong: Comparative Education Research Centre (CERC), The University of Hong Kong, and Dordrecht: Springer. © CERC

war, political training, external economic blockades, teaching of new generations, and opportunities to contribute to research.

These experiences have brought different lessons, but two in particular set a context for this chapter on approaches to research in contemporary Iran. First, Iran's education system in all dimensions and at all levels remains strongly under political influence. The government is very mindful of the role of schooling in shaping attitudes, and pays close attention to educational structures and processes. As a result, the organisational climate in all education offices and schools is conservative. Administrators and teachers behave with considerable caution towards subjects or persons coming from outside the mainstream education system – including researchers.

Second, for years the relationship between the Ministry of Education with universities and research centres was disconnected. Especially in the initial decade following the revolution, few people responsible for education valued research. Subsequent decades brought some shift, but relationships are still far from optimal. As a result, researchers need to be strongly aware of political discourses, the overt and unspoken views of government officials, and the overall climate of schools. This requires researchers to pay close attention to channels for cooperation. It also leads researchers to avoid topics that might be considered risky.

Structure of the School System

Iran has a 6+3+3 model for primary, middle and upper secondary schooling. When a pupil reaches Grade 9, the sensitivity and attention of parents usually increases because students are sorted into different types of upper secondary schools according to their examination performance in the core subjects of mathematics, science and literature. In upper secondary education, there are three branches, i.e. theoretical, vocational/technical and manual. Usually the high achievers go to theoretical schools. Again, there is a highly competitive environment among students, especially in Grade 12 to prepare for the tough national university entrance examination known as the *Konkur*.

At all levels, schools for boys and girls are separate. In general, the teachers also follow the gender divide, i.e. with male teachers for boys' schools and female teachers for girls' schools.

Embarking on Research about the Private Sector

In 2012/13 I conducted a study of privatisation of education for the Ministry of Education which in an indirect way increased my familiarity with shadow education (Madandar Arani 2014). Subsequently I visited the Comparative Education Research Centre (CERC) at the University of Hong Kong (HKU), and gained a clearer understanding of international patterns on this topic. I realised that many features of Iran's education system that I had taken for granted were distinctive and deserved further investigation.

The private sector in Iran's education system has a long history but with a break in the last part of the 20th century. The rise in oil prices and therefore government revenue during the early 1970s permitted the Shah to consider modernising society along the lines of some other Middle Eastern countries (Najmabadi 1987). However, at the time less than half of Iran's population was literate. The Shah envisaged strengthening both public and private schooling, but his dream was never realised because he suddenly lost his kingdom and Iran became a country with an Islamic revolutionary regime.

In 1979, the new regime immediately closed all private schools and tutorial centres on the grounds that they maintained and exacerbated social inequalities and had too much independence from the government. The Islamic Parliament adopted a new constitution and approved a law that education should be compulsory and free up to the end of higher secondary education (Islamic Parliament of Iran 1979). Many politicians supported this law (see e.g. Akrami 2013).

After a decade, the restrictions were gradually eased. Two factors, which were relevant not only to the re-emergence of private schools but also to the development of shadow education, were the government's population policy and the Iran-Iraq war. The government encouraged families to have more children, and the population growth rate increased from 2.7% in 1979 to 4.3% in 1987 (Kazemipour 2010). Schools then faced shortages of teachers and space. The Iran-Iraq war consumed massive amounts of the budget, and left little for other sectors including education (MohsaniNeya 1999). The combination of expanded population and budget cuts reduced the quality of education. As a result, the government had to relax its prohibition not only of private schools but also of tutorial centres.

In the contemporary era, private tutoring is widespread. Few data are available on its nature, scale and intensity, but recent studies give a snapshot. In Tehran, Aryan (2011) found that 35% of sampled Grade 5 students and 38% of sampled Grade 12 students received some sort of supplementary help. In Sannadaj city, West Iran, Shirbagi (2011) found that 61% of sampled upper secondary students had received some type of private tutoring; and in Ahwaz, Southwest Iran, NajadMosavi (2012) found an enrolment rate of 48%.

When I returned from my 2013 visit to Hong Kong, I translated into Farsi Bray's 2009 book on shadow education, and launched a research project to investigate shadow education in Khorramabad, West Iran. This city was chosen because it was the location of my work at Lorestan University. Although, the city has some minor cultural differences from counterparts elsewhere in Iran, the *Konkur* follows the same procedure everywhere and thus can be assumed to have a similar impact. Bray (2009, p.25) pointed out that "a student is more likely to receive private tutoring at transition points in education systems". With this in mind, students in Grades 9 and 12 were targeted for this research. The remainder of this chapter presents the team and a summary of the findings, and indicates some of the challenges in the conduct of the research.

The Team and Summary Findings

The survey was carried out in the 2012/13 school year in 15 schools in the two districts of Khorramabad. According to official data, the total number of students in Grades 9 and 12 was 8,946. The research data were derived from 249 Grade 9 students and 231 Grade 12 students, representing 5.4 per cent of the total student population, through multi-stage stratified sampling.

I was assisted by four of my MA students (two men and two women) at Lorestan University. Before distribution of questionnaires between selected participants, we had three two-hour sessions. In the first session, the research assistants received information about the purpose of the study, relating it to their own experiences of shadow education. In the second session, the content of the questionnaire was explained and they learned how to answer queries that might come from the schools and students. In the third session, I explained how the research assistants should contact and relate to the principals, teachers and students.

The survey indicated that 74.1 per cent of male respondents and 67.8 per cent of female respondents had received some sort of private tutoring during the previous 12 months. Most had received lecture-style tutoring, but some had received one-to-one tutoring. The most popular subjects were English, Arabic and mathematics. Over 60 per cent of respondents stated that the cost of private tutoring was a financial burden for their families.

Challenges in Design of Research Tools

Among the first challenges for a researcher is securing or preparing appropriate instruments for collection of data. I took the Hong Kong questionnaire for students designed by Bray and colleagues (see Chapter 8, Appendix 8.1), and adapted it. I translated the questionnaire into Farsi, and it was then back-translated into English by a colleague in the Department of English at Lorestan University to check if the meanings had remained constant. In addition, the questions were checked and answered by five of my first-year students in the field of educational sciences who had received some form of private tutoring before admission to university.

The questionnaire was then piloted in a Khorramabad upper secondary school in which one of my former students was principal. With his help, 15 Grade 12 students completed the questionnaire. As distribution of research tools among students is prohibited without an official letter from the local Educational Organisation, this pilot study was based on the principal's trust.

I made the following changes to the questionnaire after translation and piloting.

1. I added the name of God at the beginning of the questionnaire according to the common practice in Iran, in which Islam is the official religion.
2. I asked two mainstream school teachers who both had over 15 years of service to check the questions from the perspective of Islamic Republic law and regulations, since there are many circulars on such matters and the teachers might have known about some important dimensions which I had overlooked. The teachers did not recommend any changes.
3. I added a request to students to answer questions patiently and carefully, and to ask any questions that they might have.
4. I divided Question 2 "Why did or didn't you take private supplementary tutoring in the past 12 months?" into two separate ques-

tions. I did this because during the pilot study, some students inappropriately answered both sections, i.e. both why they did and why they did not take tutoring. I also instructed the research assistants to explain these two questions when administering the questionnaire, for increasing of the accuracy of responses.
5. Questions 3 and 4 of the Hong Kong questionnaire referred to specific subjects in the Hong Kong curriculum. To fit the Iranian curriculum I deleted Chinese language/literature, and added Arabic language which is compulsory for students in Grades 7 to 12. I also removed Business and Liberal Studies, and added Chemistry, Physics and Biology in place of Science. I retained the open option of "Others", to allow for subjects not specifically named.
6. Question 13 of the Hong Kong questionnaire referred to classes taught by a "Tutorial King or Queen". I removed this question because the vocabulary did not fit the Iranian context.
7. I also deleted Questions 23 and 24, which asked about birthplace and nationality, since I anticipated that few students in Khorramabad would have been born outside Iran or have non-Iranian nationality.

Even with these adjustments, the administration of the final version of the questionnaire encountered some challenges. First, Grade 9 students in particular found the questionnaire rather long. Some questions (for example Questions 3 and 4) had multiple sub-questions which were demanding. Second, even after the separation of Question 2 into two parts for students who did and did not receive tutoring, some respondents still answered both parts. Third, respondents – especially in Grade 9 – commonly did not have exact information or accurate knowledge for Question 8 about the amount of money spent and for Question 16 about household monthly incomes. And fourth, respondents in the Iranian cultural context may have been shy to respond on whether they did not take any tutoring because they did not have the money (Question 2) or whether they had part-time jobs (Question 29). I recognise that questionnaires are the most common research instrument among Iranian scholars, in part because of the ease and speed of data collection; but my decades of experience suggest to me that some questions might be addressed more effectively through interviews.

Interpersonal Relationships

The research demanded collaboration with several categories of people. The following sections focus on the educational administrators, principals and teachers at the school level, and the students who responded to the questionnaires.

Educational administrators

Iran's education system was completely centralised in the initial years following the 1979 revolution. In 1986, some decentralisation was brought by a Law on Formation of Educational Councils in provinces, cities and districts (UNESCO 2000). Each province, city and district has an Education Organisation responsible for local administration. The Ministry of Education retains supervision through these organisations, but local personnel have some authority for planning, financing and administration of schools.

Aristotle once said that "All who have meditated on the art of governing mankind have been convinced that the fate of empires depends on the education of youth" (Weinberger 1975, p.21). The approaches of Iranian education policy makers and executive officers are commonly consistent with this aphorism. These personnel aim not only to control the education system but also to protect it from the influences of people outside the Ministry of Education. Researchers are among such people. In the suspicious organisational climate, negotiation of access and distribution of a research instrument is demanding. As Fazali, one of the best known Iranian researchers in the field of sociology, has pointed out (Fazali & Mozayen 2013, p.148):

> Different authorities must decide on your entry to school. Much of the researcher's energy goes in this way. Even when access to school has been gained, many principals are unwilling to cooperate. Photography is prohibited, and access to documents is difficult.

The procedure for approval has three stages. At the outset, the researchers should be ready to indicate who they are and why they want to do the research. Usually, this part is handled by a formal letter of introduction from each researcher's university or research organisation.

The second stage is approval of the content of research instruments by the Security Office of the city and/or district Education Organisation. The major concern of this office is with the 'political and moral' dimensions. If the Security Office finds any problem in the research subject or instrument, the researcher has to make changes. It helps for researchers to have good connections with people in this office. Fortunately for the research on which this chapter reports, private supplementary tutoring was not considered politically or morally sensitive.

In the third stage, all questionnaires must be marked with an official stamp on every page. For this project, the questionnaire had six pages and a planned sample of 500 students. To save time, the Security Office stamped only the original version of the questionnaire and required the researchers to make copies of this version for the schools. Nevertheless, it was the responsibility of the school principal to check that all questionnaires had the official stamp. This procedure is another good reason for having a short questionnaire, and also discourages researchers from considering large samples. The process assures the principals, teachers and students that they are not being asked to respond to an uncontrolled questionnaire.

This procedure also tends to steer researchers away from questionnaires and towards interviews. Because interview questions are usually fewer in number and more general, getting permission from the Security Office may be easier. Also, for research that has political or cultural dimensions, interviews may be a better way to secure deep data – though of course researchers are careful how they present their findings.

After completion of these three stages, usually the Education Organisation prepares a letter to introduce the researchers to the school principals. The researcher is then ready to move to the next step.

School staff
The permission letter from the Director of the local Education Organisation is the main key to access schools. Of course, principals can still determine their own degree of cooperation, and can even decide to reject the permission letter. Thus researchers and their assistants commonly need to use their social capital (Gray 2004), and should convey a positive impression to principals. It is helpful for someone who is familiar with the principals to make an introduction. One reason is that even in Iran schools are increasingly burdened by "researcher traffic". The volume of research is much lower than in many other countries, but government efforts to promote the country's scientific position through expansion of postgraduate courses and publication has led to a significant increase of activities compared with the past (Azar et al. 2013). School principals are mindful of pressures not only from the curriculum but also from partici-

pation in social and political ceremonies. In such circumstances, principals may not welcome additional demands from researchers.

Once researchers have secured cooperation from the principals, their next challenge concerns the teachers. Teachers are commonly pressed for time, especially in mathematics and science subjects. Perhaps even more important, teachers may not consider research to be of value – and may even see it as threatening, e.g. if the teacher is working in parallel as a private tutor. Teachers may also be status-conscious, and insist on the presence of the main researcher rather than an assistant.

Despite these challenges, two points should be noted. First, in recent years the Ministry of Education has stressed the value of training teachers as a 'Teacher Researchers', and organises an annual competition at district, provincial and national levels. To encourage participation, the Ministry issues certificates and provides financial rewards. As a result, some teachers are keen to learn about research and like to keep copies of questionnaires for themselves. Second, some teachers, especially towards the end of the school day, like to leave the classroom as soon as possible and therefore accept researchers willingly. In this case, a negative feature of teachers' desire to depart might have a positive benefit for researchers.

Students

The final step demands the attention and collaboration of the students. In the author's experience, younger respondents (in the present research, Grade 9 students compared with Grade 12 students) are more cooperative in completing questionnaires, but may have weaker understanding of the themes. In contrast, older respondents have more understanding but less enthusiasm. One factor for the Grade 12 students is the pressure of the impending national university examination (YarMohammadian et al. 2003).

A second factor, alongside age, is the gender of both respondents and researchers. As mentioned above, all schools in Iran are single-sex, even at primary level, which creates challenges for research access. Young people in particular, which in this case included my research assistants, cannot go to schools of the other sex. This restriction derives from Islamic beliefs and values which do not permit any type of relationship between the two sexes prior to marriage (Motahari 2001).

There can be ways to overcome this challenge. One is for the research assistant to be accompanied by a parent or sibling matching the gender of the school and a permission letter from the Education Organisation. This strategy secures 'peace of mind' for all sides (research assistant, respondent and school authority) since everything has been managed through a family environment. The second method is to find a teacher in the school who knows the researcher personally, is willing to talk to the principal, and is also willing to come to the class during data collection. A third way is to persuade the principal that the researcher is influential and/or that the research is valuable, in which case the principal may be willing to accompany a researcher of the 'wrong' sex to the classroom.

These constraints are particularly strict for young researchers and for investigations in government secondary schools. Older researchers of the other sex may be tolerated more easily, and primary and non-government schools are less sensitive. For the present research, it was decided that male research assistants would be used for boys' schools and female research assistants for girls' schools. However, some collaboration was still needed within the team. Since the questionnaires were heavy, the male research assistants carried the questionnaires to the gates of the girls' schools and then waited nearby until the completed questionnaires were brought out to be carried back to the university.

The gender dimension also influenced the research in another way. Particularly in the Grade 12 classes, the girls were usually more co-operative and asked more questions about the research than the boys. This may have been because the research assistants were MA students and the Grade 12 students saw them as role models. By contrast, the Grade 12 boys were less willing to complete the questionnaires, especially when research assistant was young and not accompanied by the main researcher.

The greater interest of the girls in the research may also reflect wider forces. The proportions of female students taking the *Konkur* and attending university have risen in recent years. In 2014, 59 per cent of *Konkur* candidates were female (Tavakoli 2014) and 64 per cent of university students were female (Vista News Hub 2015). In turn, this may be linked to the structure of the labour market. Since in general the labour market favours males, females see education as the main way to strengthen their competitive edge (Shavarini 2005).

Conclusion

This chapter has focused on some challenges of research on shadow education in Iran to provide insights about the processes of data collection in an Islamic Republic. My basic assumption for preparation of this chapter was that the first step towards high quality research is an understanding of the possibilities, available facilities, and strengths and weaknesses of the society for conducting research. In Iran many researchers have examined such matters at both macro and micro levels. At the macro level, Iran's strengths include the large number of universities and research institutions and abundance of young researchers. According to SCImago (2013), which is a portal that includes the journals and country scientific indicators developed from information in the Scopus® database, Iran ranked 23 which was higher than Austria (24), Denmark (25), Finland (26) and Greece (27).

Despite this quantitative performance, few studies have had practical benefits. As pointed out by Moradi et al. (2013) and Mousavi and ZaerSabet (2011), this is because Iran does not have a strongly institutionalised culture of research and its application at various levels of politics, economics, culture and education. There are several reasons for this. Enayati et al. (2012) believe that the most important reason is lack of perceived need for research because of fatalist approaches to life and resistance to innovation among the authorities. Because of lack of real belief in research, in 2014 Iran allocated only 0.4 per cent of its Gross Domestic Product (GDP) to research, while the global average was 1.5 per cent and the figure for the Republic of Korea was 4.0 per cent (Ravanshadniya 2014). Despite numerous problems requiring research, research priorities are not well articulated and even the research has been and is being done mostly relies on form rather than content.

At the micro level and in the realm of education, one of the major problems is that most school principals and teachers focus only on their educational tasks and have limited incentives for collaboration with researchers. Enayati et al. (2012) investigated the main research barriers from the teachers' perspectives in the north of Iran, noting economic challenges, the lack of research culture, organisational constraints, and lack of belief in research among teachers.

With these matters in mind, I offer some suggestions that might assist researchers in Iran and perhaps similar countries:

- Avoid research topics that have been repeated by many scholars. Saki (2006) found that many research topics in education were repeated with only minor changes. To reduce this challenge, recently Iran's Ministry of Science, Research and Technology has established an online system to check repetition of research themes.

Despite the growth of the shadow education in Iran, little research has been investigating this phenomenon. This could provide an opportunity for researchers to work on a new topic and seek more contribution from administrators, teachers, parents and students.

- Avoid the use of repetitive forms of Likert scale questionnaires as a research tool. One of the most common problems in educational research in Iran is the excessive use of questionnaires presenting many options in monotonous rows. Respondents who have received many of these questionnaires find them boring, and in my experience commonly tick the boxes without having read the questions carefully. Fortunately shadow education as a research topic has potential to be investigated through a combination of research instruments.
- I also alluded to the expansion of postgraduate education and therefore of research. While it may still be modest compared to some other countries, the expansion is very evident in comparison with earlier periods in Iran. In this situation, I recommend university students and novice researchers to select their native places or small cities as sites for research.

At the end of this chapter, I call readers' attention to the work of Canen (1995, cited in Manzon 2014, p.109). Canen compared education in Brazil and the United Kingdom, and found that despite the huge contextual differences, both countries faced similar challenges imposed by the multicultural natures of their societies. A similar remark may be made in the present chapter. Iran is very different from other countries, but the challenges faced by researchers have much in common. Therefore, expression of challenges does not mean that all settings have massive resistance to research. Further, I cannot ignore the enjoyable fact that during the past two decades many students, teachers and principals have welcomed me with open arms.

References

Akrami, Syed Kazam (2013): *I was against Non-Governmental Schools: An Interview with Former Minister of Education.* http://fararu.com/fa/.../می‌اکرمی-مخالف-مدارس غیرانتفاعی-بود..., [in Farsi]

Aryan, Khateje (2011): *Effective Factors on Tendency of Students, Parents, and Teachers toward Private Supplementary Tutoring and its Consequences*, Unpublished Research, Tehran: AllameTabatabaie University. [in Farsi]

Azar, Adel; KholamRezaie, Davood; DanaeeFard, Hasan & Khodadad Hosayni, Hamid (2013): 'An Analysis of Higher Education Quality in the Fifth Development Plan'. *Journal of Strategy for Culture*, Vol.21, pp.139-173. [in Farsi]

Bray, Mark (2009): *Confronting the Shadow Education System: What Government Policies for What Private Tutoring?* Paris: UNESCO International Institute for Educational Planning (IIEP). Farsi translation by Abbas Madandar Arani published 2013 by Tuloo Edarnesh, Tehran.

Canen, Ana (1995): 'Teacher Education in an Intercultural Perspective: A Parallel between Brazil and the UK'. *Compare: A Journal of Comparative Education*, Vol.25, No.3, pp.227-238.

Enayati, Teraneh; Zamani, Farshideh & Ghorbani, Talate (2012): 'A Survey on Research Barriers from Middle Secondary School Teachers' Perspectives in Behshare'. *New Approach in Educational Management*, Vol.3, No.4, pp.189-205. [in Farsi]

Fazali, Namatollah & Mozayen, Farahsteh (2013): 'Interpretations of Female Students about School Uniform in Higher Secondary Schools of Tehran'. *Journal of Sociology*, Vol.14, No.2, pp.123-152. www.isa.org.ir/magazine-article/6050 [in Farsi]

Gray, Anne (2004): 'The Social Capital of Social Researchers', in Edwards, Rosalind (ed.), *Social Capital in the Field: Researchers' Tales*. London: London South Bank University, pp.8-10. http://www1.lsbu.ac.uk/ahs/downloads/families/familieswp10.pdf

Islamic Parliament of Iran (1979): *Constitution of the Islamic Republic of Iran*. http://parliran.ir [in Farsi]

Kazemipour, Shahla (2010): 'Development and Composition of Population in Iran: A Prospective Approach', *Quarterly Journal of Second Interpretation*. Vol.7, No.11-12, pp.75-108. http://www.ensani.ir/storage/Files/20120504165135-9013-3.pdf [in Farsi]

Madandar Arani, Abbas (2014): 'The Role of Institutions, Organizations and Individuals in Suspension of Non-Governmental Schools: A Semantic Reconstruction'. *Quarterly Journal of Educational Innovations*, Vol.13, No.51, pp.73-96. [in Farsi]

Manzon, Maria (2014): 'Comparing Places', in Bray, Mark; Adamson, Bob & Mason, Mark (eds.), *Comparative Education Research: Approaches and Methods*. CERC Studies in Comparative Education 19, 2nd edition, Hong Kong: Comparative Education Research Centre, The University of Hong Kong, and Dordrecht: Springer, pp.97-138.

MohsaniNeya, Mohammad Javad (1999): 'Budget and Budgeting in Education'. *Quarterly Journal of Management in Education*, Vol.6, No.22, pp.71-93. http://www.ensani.ir/storage/Files/20120506095817-7077-18.pdf [in Farsi]

Moradi, Mahmoud; Dustar, Mohammad; Ghaderifar, Esmaeil & Zanjani, Behnaz (2013): 'Identifying and Prioritizing the Barriers to Research: Case Study of

Research Centers of Ministry of Science, Research and Technology'. *Journal of Science and Technology Policy*, Vol.6, No.1, pp.35-47. [in Farsi]

Motahari, Mortaza (2001): *Women's Rights in Islam*, Tehran: Sadra. http://www.aviny.KeyWords/library/motahari/for/nezamezan [in Farsi]

Mousavi, Yaghob; ZaerSabet, Forough (2011): 'A Sociological Study of Structural and Human Barriers on Development of Applied Social Research in Iran'. *Journal of Iranian Social Development Studies*, Vol.3, No.2, pp.7-34. [in Farsi]

NajadMosavi, Sayed Ali (2012): *Parents and High School Students' Perspectives on Private Supplementary Tutoring and its Relationship with Family Costs: A Case Study in Ahwaz City*, MA Thesis, Kurdistan University. [in Farsi]

Najmabadi, Afsaneh (1987): 'Iran's Turn to Islam: From Modernism to a Moral Order'. *Middle East Journal*, Vol.41, No.2, pp.202-217.

Ravanshadniya, Mehdi (2014): 'Research Challenges in Iran'. Tehran: Aftab News Agency. http://aftabnews.ir/fa/news/275808/ [in Farsi]

Saki, Reza (2006): Educational Research and its Challenges, *Quarterly Journal of Education*, Vol. 22. No. 1, pp. 65-106, [in Farsi]

SCImago (2013): *SJR — SCImago Journal & Country Rank*. http://www.scimagojr.com/countryrank.php

Shavarini, K. Mitra (2005): 'The Feminisation of Iranian Higher Education'. *Review of Education*, Vol.51, No.4, pp.329-347.

Shirbagi, Naser (2011): 'Increasing Tendency on Private Supplementary Tutoring: Students, Parents and Teachers' Views'. *Journal of Educational Studies*, Vol.7, No.13, pp.73-102. [in Farsi]

Tavakoli, Hossain (2014): 'Details of the Konkur', JameJam News Agency , June 3. http://www.jamejamonline.ir/newspreview/1517262385521423940

UNESCO (2000): *The EFA 2000 Assessment: Country Report - Iran*. http://www.unesco.org/education/wef/countryreports/iran/rapport_2_4.html

Vista News Hub (2015): *Quota for Boys' University Entrance*, 3 January. http://vista.ir/.../دانشگاه سهمیه بندی برای ورود پسران به[in Farsi]

Weinberger, W. Caspar (1975): 'Social Goals and Individual Freedom'. *Presidential Studies Quarterly*, Vol.5, No.4, pp.19-23.

YarMohammadian, Ahmad; Sohrabi, Nadere & Arizi, HamidReza (2003): 'A Comparison of the Konkur's Influence on Universities' Accepted and Rejected Students and Their Families'. *Psychological Studies*, Vol.1, No.2, pp.119-136. [in Farsi]

Expanding Perspectives with
Mixed Approaches

8

Designing and Implementing Mixed Approaches to Shadow Education Research: Experiences and Lessons in Hong Kong

Mark BRAY and Ora KWO

Introduction

This chapter reports on dimensions of a research journey. The journey was a project entitled 'Private Supplementary Tutoring: Scale, Nature and Implications for Secondary Schooling in Hong Kong'. It was chiefly concerned with the experiences of students in Grades 9 and 12 (i.e. what in the Hong Kong education system is called Secondary Form 3 and Secondary Form 6). Readers may compare the commentary on the journey with that in other chapters of this book and with the wider literature not only on research methods in general (e.g. Johnson & Christensen 2012; Creswell 2014) but also specifically in the domain of shadow education (e.g. Bray 2010; Jokić 2013; Zhang & Bray 2013).

The chapter begins with the project design, including its objectives and the personnel. This section provides information on the research questions, the intended sample, and the procedure for securing ethical clearance. The chapter then turns to the ways in which the project was implemented. It describes the preparation and piloting of instruments,

---

Bray, Mark; Kwo, Ora & Jokić, Boris (eds.) (2015): *Researching Private Supplementary Tutoring: Methodological Lessons from Diverse Cultures.* Hong Kong: Comparative Education Research Centre (CERC), The University of Hong Kong, and Dordrecht: Springer. © CERC

and identifies the actual sample and the reasons for difference from the intended sample. This section also notes issues arising in the administration of questionnaires and conduct of interviews.

Once data have been collected, they have to be processed. Challenges commonly arise at this stage too, and the project described here was no exception. The chapter summarises on dimensions of processing first of quantitative data and then of qualitative data. Data processing is of course linked to the themes of analysis, which are also addressed. The findings are not presented in this chapter, but are available elsewhere (Bray 2013; Zhan et al. 2013; Bray et al. 2014; Kwo & Bray 2014; Bray & Kobakhidze 2015).

Personnel, Objectives and Design

The team

The project team had five core members at the University of Hong Kong (HKU). This team brought together longstanding international knowledge of the literature on shadow education (Mark Bray); strong social capital in Hong Kong schools (Ora Kwo, and to some extent Mark Bray); mother-tongue fluency in Cantonese, the dominant spoken dialect of Chinese in Hong Kong (Ora Kwo); mother-tongue fluency in Putonghua, the dominant and official spoken form of Chinese in Mainland China (Wang Dan, Zhan Shengli); mother-tongue fluency in English (Mark Bray, Chad Lykins); excellent quantitative skills (Zhan Shengli); strong expertise in the sociology of education and qualitative research (Wang Dan); and parallel grounding in dimensions of philosophy relating to research (Chad Lykins).

The team was supported by a Project Manager (Emily Mang). She had excellent administrative skills and mother-tongue fluency in Cantonese. In addition two Year 4 BEd students provided research assistance; and along the way a number of PhD students both contributed and gained experience for their own work.

Research questions

The project aimed to investigate "the scale and nature of supplementary private tutoring and its implications for mainstream schooling as perceived by students and teachers". The overarching question was:

> From an ecological perspective, what are the nature and implications

of the relationship between private supplementary tutoring and the experience of secondary schooling in Hong Kong?

The "experience of secondary schooling" was considered wider than just teaching and learning. It included social relationships outside the classroom, which may be relevant to pupils who attend (or do not attend) tutoring classes together. The researchers hypothesised that in addition to shaping the received curriculum tutoring in mainstream schooling, tutoring shapes peer relationships (e.g. in the canteen, the sports field and the journey home from school) as well as relationships between pupils and teachers.

From the main question flowed sub-questions at the school level:

1. What tutoring is received by the pupils, and why?
   [For some pupils, the answer to the first part was expected to be zero; and then the question for the second part was expected to be "Why not?" rather than "Why?"]
2. How, in the perception of pupils, has the tutoring [or absence of tutoring] shaped the pupils' secondary schooling experiences?
3. How do the teachers view and respond [or not respond] to the existence of the different forms of tutoring?

In turn, the answers to these questions were expected to help identify the implications for policy and practice at system, institutional and classroom levels.

Sampling and sequencing
In order to contain costs while still achieving statistical rigour, when designing the project the team decided to use cluster sampling rather than simple random sampling. The design commenced with random selection of schools, within each of which the research would focus on Grades 9 and 12. From each grade, two classes would be randomly sampled, and all students in these classes would be surveyed. Grades 9 and 12 were chosen because they were transition points in Hong Kong's 6+3+3+4 education structure (six years of primary, three years of lower secondary, three years of upper secondary, and four years for a basic university degree).

In the first step of sampling, the team decided to calculate the base sample size of students as if a simple random sample would be drawn. Official statistics indicated that in 2011, approximate Grade 9 and 12 enrolments would be 80,000 and 83,000 students. Accordingly, for a random sample the minimum size for each grade would be 382 at the .05 margin of error and 95% confidence level. To account for the design effect of multi-stage sampling, in line with accepted practice this base sample size would be doubled. To allow for contingencies (non-responses), the researchers would inflate the sample size by 5%. This created a target sample of 802 students in each grade (382 x 2 x 105%).

In the next step, the researchers calculated the number of schools to be selected. On the assumption that average class size would be 35 in both Grade 9 and Grade 12, a sample of 802 students in each grade would require a sample of 23 classes. Since the researchers planned to sample two classes in each grade in each school, the sample size at the school level would be 12. Within each school, the classes would be randomly sampled from each grade unless there were only two classes in the targeted grades.

In 2009/10, Hong Kong had 523 secondary schools of which 498 were in the local system and 25 were English Schools Foundation (ESF) and other international schools. The research design envisaged random selection of 12 schools from the local system and one international school. This approach aimed to provide useful contrasts across school systems and cultures.

In summary, the team aimed to sample 13 schools, two grades in each school, and two classes in each grade. This gave a total of 1,820 (35 x 2 x 2 x 13) students in Grade 9 (910) and Grade 12 (910). Despite its random nature, the sampling was expected to deliver schools in a range of locations around the territory. While the whole of Hong Kong may be considered urban, and has excellent public transport, different schools serve different socio-economic groups. The sample was thus expected to show some variations in clienteles. The sample would also show variations in achievement bands (Band 1 being the highest achievers, and Band 3 the lowest achievers).

The above paragraphs explain the samples of *schools* and *students*. The sample of *teachers* was to be drawn from the same schools. Four teachers of Grade 9 and four of Grade 12 were to be randomly selected from each of the 13 schools, making a total of 104 teachers. The sample was likely to generate a range of ages and subject specialisations. It would also bring data from both males and females, thereby permitting the researchers to ask whether variations existed according to such characteristics.

Year 1 was devoted to collecting data from students through both quantitative (questionnaire) and qualitative (interview) methods. Year 2 was for collecting data from teachers, again through quantitative and qualitative methods; and a further six months in the project were allocated to data analysis and writing.

Ethical approval
HKU requires such projects to be approved by the Human Research Ethics Committee for Non-Clinical Faculties (HRECNCF). The application procedure demanded submission not only of the research framework but also of proposed consent forms and instruments to collect data from students. The procedure required:

- passive consent (non-objection) from the parents of the targeted students from whom the team aimed to collect anonymous data through questionnaires and interviews;
- active consent from the students themselves.

The consent forms indicated that the schools had already given permission, and thus that the project was already anchored at the institutional level. When in due course the project reached the stage of collecting quantitative and qualitative data from the teachers, forms for active consent were required – i.e. the teachers themselves were required to sign forms indicating willingness for the data to be used anonymously for research purposes.

Experiences in Implementation
Preparation of instruments
Team members spent much time devising instruments, with lengthy meetings over many rounds. The final versions of the questionnaires are presented in Appendices 8.1 and 8.3. The student questionnaire was especially demanding since it was multifaceted and bilingual in English and Chinese. The teacher questionnaire was prepared only in English since all teachers were assumed to have adequate competence in that language. The interview guides (Appendices 8.2 and 8.4) were only prepared in English since interviewers who chose to work in Chinese felt that they did not need separate scripts.

Efforts were made to keep the questionnaire to six pages, so that it would not seem intimidating in length. Care was taken with layout and sequencing, e.g. to ask about the different types of tutoring in Question 1 so that the students would at the outset gain some idea about the parameters of the questionnaire.

Piloting

The instruments were piloted in two schools before finalisation. These schools were identified through the professional networks of team members.

The piloting led to changes in the questionnaire and, even more significantly, in the process for interviewing of students. The proposal had envisaged interviews in groups of four on the grounds that the students would stimulate each other and collectively produce a more detailed picture of the nature and impact of tutoring. During the piloting, the researchers realised that students were unwilling to talk on the topic in front of their peers because they might be perceived as purchasing an unfair advantage and/or as being slow learners unable to cope without supplementary support. The interview sample was therefore changed four students in each grade of each school interviewed individually:

- one boy receiving tutoring during the last 12 months,
- one boy not receiving tutoring during the last 12 months,
- one girl receiving tutoring during the last 12 months, and
- one girl not receiving tutoring during the last 12 months.

Securing sample schools, students and teachers

The final sample was of 16 rather than 13 schools. This number resulted from a combination of disappointment with achieving a truly random cluster sample and success in securing replacement schools for those originally desired.

Elaborating, while researchers in the comfort of their offices may desire random samples and prepare mathematical designs for selecting institutions, the real world may be replete with rejections. Because the researchers were based in a university rather than the government or another body with direct lines of authority, for access to institutions they had to use invitation and persuasion rather than instruction. One negative side effect of the fact that research in Hong Kong schools has become much more extensive has been that the institutions experience 'research fatigue'. Institutions may be especially adverse to invitations that seem to invite disruptions without corresponding benefit. As a result, although the researchers commenced with their desired sample of 13 schools, one school said that they could collect data in Grade 9 but not Grade 12 (because it did not want the Grade 12 students to be disturbed at this point in their academic careers) and four institutions rejected the invitation altogether. The team received a rejection even from a school which was headed by a former university colleague.

Fortunately for the project, the team had a back-up mechanism which benefitted from the social capital of members who had worked for several decades in the Hong Kong education system. This work had generated many connections through alumni and other forms of partnership. The team was able to replace the institutions that had rejected the invitations with others that were deemed sufficiently similar to retain the overall integrity of the project. Indeed in addition to the target number of 13 schools a further three were brought into the project in response to the enthusiasm of senior personnel in the schools and because the team wanted a further Direct Subsidy Scheme (DSS) school to strengthen the representativeness of that group.

The final sample was not consistent across all components of the project. As shown in Table 8.1, three schools granted permission only for Grade 9 and not Grade 12; two schools granted permission only to survey the students rather than the teachers; and when it came to the actual implementation in one school only the questionnaires for teachers were administered, without follow-up interviews. Nevertheless, the final sample was deemed adequate to meet the need.

Further variations occurred in the sampling within schools. For sampling of students, the two main reasons for variation arose from the attitudes of the school administrations and the roles of classroom teachers. Some teachers were very helpful, stressing to their students the value of the research. In these cases the samples within the target classrooms were relatively high. In other cases the researchers found a less positive climate. Students tended to see the completion of the questionnaire as chore of little direct benefit to themselves, and when they saw that they could opt out, some of them did so. Group dynamics led to proportions of opting out being greater in some classes than others.

While having to allow variation in the numbers of student questionnaires completed, the smaller numbers envisaged by the sampling frame for the student interviews team permitted that component to be secured in a more straightforward manner. Thus Table 8.1 shows that in almost all cases four students were interviewed in each grade. In the schools where only three students were interviewed, it was usually because proportions of students receiving tutoring were very high and it was difficult to find a student of the desired gender who was not receiving tutoring.

Different factors underlay the variations in the sample of teachers. One major factor concerned processes to feed the findings back to the schools. The team felt a responsibility to let the schools know the profiles of their students and the comparisons of these profiles to the total sample. In some cases the data were simply sent back to the schools, but in other cases team members joined staff meetings or even ran briefing workshops. In the latter cases, the samples of teachers who completed the questionnaires and who volunteered for interview were larger. The team was careful to administer the questionnaires and conduct the interviews before providing the data from the students, because the team realised that the student data would have shaped the perceptions of the teachers in the questionnaire responses and interviews.

Table 8.1: Final Sample of Schools, Students and Teachers in the Hong Kong Study

School ID	Band/ type	Grade 9 students sampled (questionnaire)	Grade 12 students sampled (questionnaire)	Grade 9 students interviewed	Grade 12 students interviewed	Teachers sampled (questionnaire)	Teachers interviewed
1	2	55	56	4	4	16	5
2	1	55	59	4	4	8	6
3	3	34	18	4	4	27	9
4	3	60	52	4	4	9	0
5	ESF	47	19	4	4	9	4
6	3	74	62	4	3	10	3
7	1	35	65	4	4	9	3
8	3	57	35	4	4	9	3
9	DSS	69	45	4	4	10	3
10	1	67	66	4	3	9	3
11	3	59	33	4	3	10	3
12	DSS	60	21	4	4	10	4
13	1	55	n.p.	4	0	n.p.	n.p.
14	3	116	128	0	0	15	0
15	2	99	n.p.	4	0	n.p.	n.p.
16	DSS	27	n.p.	4	0	8	2
Total		969	659	60	45	160	48

Notes: ESF = English Schools Foundation; DSS = Direct Subsidy Scheme; n.p. = not participate.

Administering the student questionnaires
In each school, part of a lesson was allocated to the research. This required the support of the principal and the teacher, and the team was mindful that it was to some extent disruptive. The team had to accept the time slots granted by the schools and teachers. These slots did not always fit with convenient timetabling for the four target classes, but the necessary compromises were of course acceptable even if they required the team to make more than one visit to the school.

Because of the need for multiple tasks, including handing out and collecting questionnaires, answering queries and negotiating interviews, the student questionnaires were always administered by at least two team members. The team was keen on the one hand to make use of the authority of teachers when distributing the questionnaires, but on the other hand to assure the students that their answers would not be read by the teachers. In ideal circumstances, the teacher introduced the researchers and then left the room. When the teacher did not leave the room, an additional benefit from having more than one team member was that one person could administer the questionnaires while another could take responsibility of ensuring that the teacher's behaviour was not intrusive to the students as they wrote their answers.

The team was aware that the demeanour of the researchers when administering the questionnaires would shape the extent to which the students took the activity seriously. An initial introduction by one of the team members explained the content and purpose and allowed students to ask questions. Team members who had experience of teaching and classroom management were particularly effective in this role and generally took the lead.

Conducting the student interviews
To select students for interview, the team members first briefed the whole class and then conducted a "lucky draw" at the time of the distribution of the questionnaires. Students ticked boxes on a pre-printed piece of paper to indicate if they were (a) male or female, (b) had or had not received private tutoring during the previous 12 months, and (c) were or were not willing to be interviewed. If they were willing, they then provided their names. The forms were collected from the students, and then the questionnaires were distributed. While the students were completing the questionnaires, one team member sorted the papers into piles and then randomly selected one male and one female who had received tu-

toring, and one male and one female who had not received tutoring. The students selected in the process were informed when the questionnaires had been collected.

In most cases, at least some interviewing was undertaken immediately. However, this required removal of the students from the classrooms, which caused those students to miss the lessons that their classmates were receiving. Thus in many cases alternative arrangements were made, such as interview during a vacant lesson, during a break, or even after the end of school time. This again required flexibility for the researchers since schedules could not always fit tightly.

The interviews commonly took place in an empty classroom, a corner of the library, or the preparation room for a science laboratory. Depending on the linguistic competence and preference of the people concerned, some interviews took place in English while others were in Cantonese or Putonghua. The team was aware that different types of interviewer (male or female, older or younger, Cantonese-speaking or non-Cantonese-speaking, etc.) would have different types of impact on the interview process. To promote consistency, the team operated with standardised guidelines. Before beginning the research team members undertook role plays with mutual critique; and during the research processes the team members compared impressions and experiences.

Administering the teacher questionnaires
The teacher questionnaires were administered in somewhat more diverse circumstances. Some were completed during meetings, while others were completed independently and then brought back to a central collection point. Each pattern had merits: if done during a meeting, the purpose and content of the questionnaire could be explained by the research team or other responsible person, and queries could be answered. Also, the focused time set aside for the questionnaire responses may have been beneficial. If, by contrast, the questionnaires were completed separately, the respondents could work at their own speed and perhaps choose a location free of distractions.

Most teachers were selected by the schools according to the criteria requested by the research team, i.e. that the teachers should have been teaching at least one class of either Grade 9 or Grade 12, even though those teachers may also have been teaching other grades. Beyond this criterion, no stipulations were made on age, gender, subject specialisation, nationality, etc.. However, in the case of School 3, in which 27 teachers completed the questionnaire, some respondents did not teach either Grade 9 or Grade 12. The large number of respondents in School 3 reflected the school's decision to ask the teachers to complete the questionnaire during a staff meeting. The team felt that the data provided by the teachers were very useful, and decided to retain the data even from the teachers who were not specifically teaching either Grade 9 or Grade 12.

The team did review the questionnaire responses to see if the administrative arrangements appeared to have made a significant difference to the nature of the responses, including whether some groups abandoned the questionnaire part way through, etc.. No obvious differences were evident. Similarly, the fact that larger numbers of teachers in some schools completed the questionnaire does not seem to have greatly changed the balances in the types of responses.

Conducting the teacher interviews
With the Grade 9 and Grade 12 students, it was felt permissible and perhaps even advantageous for at least some interviews to be conducted by the HKU BEd students who were providing research assistance. These BEd students were senior to the secondary school students but were relatively close in age and the interviews and related conversations could proceed naturally. However, it would not have been appropriate for the teachers to have been interviewed by BEd students. The interviews of teachers were therefore all conducted by the professoriate members of the research team, by the project manager, and in some cases by the PhD students.

As with the students, teachers were interviewed individually in quiet locations on the school premises. In some cases this meant an empty classroom, while in other cases it meant a corner of the staff room, an office or another location.

Data Processing and Analysis
The quantitative data
The quantitative data had to be coded, inputted to the computer system, and cleaned. This work was mostly undertaken by the BEd student assistants under the supervision of the project manager. The postdoctoral fellow reviewed the data to identify domains demanding double-checking. The quantitative data were analysed using the Statistical Package for the Social Sciences (SPSS).

The qualitative data

The qualitative data were in some respects more challenging to process. First, the team decided that a common language was necessary for analysis and therefore that interviews conducted in Chinese (either Cantonese or Putonghua) should be translated into English. Such translation inevitably brings some slippage, depending on the skills and the care of the translators. Most of the translation was undertaken at the time of transcription by the BEd student assistants, and then checked by the project manager.

Second, even English-language transcription is not always easy. Interviews contain many half sentences, apparently superfluous phrases of politeness, repetition, etc.. The team wished to adhere to the actual spoken word as much as possible, but recognised that this was sometimes demanding and that in any case compromises had already been made with the transcriptions from translated Chinese.

Once the transcriptions had been completed, they were analysed with NVivo software. This required agreement on codes, which in turn required agreement on the sorts of messages which the researchers sought from the interviews. Further, at the analysis stage the challenges of having different interviewers with different personalities and awareness of nuances became evident. Even though all interviewers had a standard guide and undertook to ask all questions even if not necessarily in the sequence set out in the guide, the clarity with which the questions were asked and answered was not always consistent. Nevertheless, the transcripts did provide many insights.

Methodological Lessons for the Wider Research Community

This Hong Kong research was in many respects innovative. It drew on an existing literature to identify the focus, but was at a cutting edge in the field. Other chapters in this book have noted that researchers elsewhere have adapted some aspects of the instruments for use in their own settings (see in particular Chapter 12). The Hong Kong questionnaire was designed specifically for use in Hong Kong, and as such had some questions (e.g. about Tutoring Kings and Queens) that would not be relevant elsewhere. Nevertheless, insofar as shadow education has become a global phenomenon, clearly some generic components can also be identified. In the present book, this has been noted in the chapters about Malaysia, Iran, India and Jamaica.

The Hong Kong work was undertaken by a team, which brought not only human resources but also diversity in skills and perspectives. As such, it had an advantage over work conducted by individual masters and doctoral students, for example. Yet the team was limited in size and scope, and was not comparable to those undertaking large international projects such as the Trends in International Mathematics and Science Study (TIMSS) or the Programme for International Student Assessment (PISA) (see e.g. Mullis et al. 2013; OECD 2014).

The mixed-methods design was clearly beneficial for this work. The quantitative component covered large numbers of students and teachers while the qualitative component helped to show the personalised sorts of characteristics that shape individual decisions and experiences. At the same time, the team was mindful of limitations in the sampling. The work was not achieved with a truly random sample, and the types of experiences recorded to some extent reflected not only the respondents but also the investigators.

The design also has limitations in the extent to which individual data points can fit together. In a few cases student interviewees identified their questionnaire response sheets so that interviewers could have the basic information when conducting the interviewees, but in most cases the questionnaire and interview processes were kept separate. Further, the teacher questionnaires and interviews were conducted during the academic year following the student questionnaires and interviews, and therefore could not be linked to the experiences of specific groups of students.

In addition, of course, the data sets include only students and teachers. They do not include directly-collected data from parents or other family members, from tutors, or from policy-makers, administrators and managers at school and system-levels.

Many of the achievements and challenges of the research implementation were common to all research in social science domains in the scale undertaken here and in the nexus between a university-based team and social institutions in the community (see e.g. della Porta 2008; Johnson & Christensen 2012; Creswell 2014). The distinctive features arising from the focus on shadow education included that the subject matter was in some ways difficult to define with precision, and many students and teachers had not previously thought very clearly about the phenomenon. Also, some dimensions were sensitive to the respondents. Students who were receiving private tutoring might not wish to appear to gain an unfair advantage over their peers, and teachers might not wish to appear either influenced by or indirectly encouraging of the private sector activities. Nevertheless, it is clear from the findings (Bray 2013; Bray et al. 2014; Kwo & Bray 2014; Zhan et al. 2013) that many new insights were obtained.

Acknowledgement: The research reported in this chapter was funded by the General Research Fund (GRF) of the Hong Kong Research Grants Council (RGC), project 741111.

References

Bray, Mark (2010): 'Researching Shadow Education: Methodological Challenges and Directions'. *Asia Pacific Education Review*, Vol.11, No.1, pp.3-13.
Bray, Mark (2013): 'Benefits and Tensions of Shadow Education: Comparative Perspectives on the Roles and Impact of Private Supplementary Tutoring in the Lives of Hong Kong Students'. *Journal of International and Comparative Education*, Vol.2, No.1, pp.18-30.
Bray, Mark & Kobakhidze, Magda Nutsa (2015): 'Evolving Ecosystems in Education: The Nature and Implications of Private Supplementary Tutoring in Hong Kong'. *Prospects: Quarterly Review of Comparative Education*, in press.
Bray, Mark; Zhan, Shengli; Lykins, Chad; Wang, Dan & Kwo, Ora (2014): 'Differentiated Demand for Private Supplementary Tutoring: Patterns and Implications in Hong Kong Secondary Education'. *Economics of Education Review*, Vol.38, No.1, pp.24-37.
Creswell, John W. (2014): *Research Design: Qualitative, Quantitative, and Mixed Methods Approaches*. 4th edition, Thousand Oaks: Sage.
della Porta, Donatella & Keating, Michael (eds.) (2008): *Approaches and Methodologies in the Social Sciences: A Pluralist Perspective*. Cambridge: Cambridge University Press.
Johnson, Burke & Christensen, Larry (2012): *Educational Research: Quantitative, Qualitative, and Mixed Approaches*. Los Angeles: Sage.
Jokić, Boris (ed.) (2013): *Emerging from the Shadow: A Comparative Qualitative Exploration of Private Tutoring in Eurasia*. Zagreb: Network of Education Policy Centers.
Kwo, Ora & Bray, Mark (2014): Understanding the Nexus between Mainstream Schooling and Private Supplementary Tutoring: Patterns and Voices of Hong Kong Secondary Students. *Asia Pacific Journal of Education*, Vol.34, No.4, pp.403-416.
Mullis, I.V.S.; Martin, M.O.; Smith, T.A.; Garden, R.A.; Gregory, K.D.; Gonzales, E.J.; Chrowstowski, S.D. & O'Connor, K.M. (2003): *TIMSS Assessment Frame-*

works and Specifications 2003. Chestnut Hill: International Study Center, Lynch School of Education, Boston College.

OECD (Organisation for Economic Co-operation and Development) (2014): *PISA 2012 Technical Report*. Paris: OECD.

Zhan, Shengli; Bray, Mark; Wang, Dan; Lykins, Chad & Kwo, Ora (2013): 'The Effectiveness of Private Tutoring: Students' Perceptions in Comparison with Mainstream Schooling in Hong Kong'. *Asia Pacific Education Review*, Vol.14, No.4, pp.495-509.

Zhang, Wei & Bray, Mark (2013): 'Researching Supplementary Education: Plans, Realities, and Lessons from Fieldwork in China', in Aurini, Janice; Davies, Scott & Dierkes, Julian (eds.), *Out of the Shadows: The Global Intensification of Supplementary Education*. Bingley: Emerald, pp.67-94.

Appendix 8.1: Questionnaire for Students

Questions on Private Supplementary Tutoring
補習問卷調查

> **Private supplementary tutoring** is the additional support in academic subjects (Chinese, English, Mathematics, Sciences, Humanities, Business, and Liberal Studies) which is received in exchange for payment. It does not include extra-curricular activities such as piano or basketball. Thank you for your help.
> 私人補習是通過付費獲得對學校學業科目（如：中文、英文、數學、科學、其他文科、商科、通識科）的額外支持。它不包括鋼琴、籃球等校外活動。謝謝您的幫助。

Please tick the boxes below or write the most suitable answers.
請於下列各題適合的方格內填 "✓" 或填寫內容。

General information 基本資料

Gender 性別： ☐ $_1$Male 男　　☐ $_0$Female 女

Age 年齡 ：＿＿＿＿＿＿

Class form 年級： ☐ $_1$S.1　☐ $_2$S.2　☐ $_3$S.3　☐ $_4$S.4　☐ $_5$S.5　☐ $_6$S.6　☐ $_7$S.7

1. Have you received the following types of private supplementary tutoring in the past **12 months**? (can tick more than one) 在過去的 **12個月內** 你曾否參加過以下形式的補習？（可選多於一項）

   ☐ $_a$ Private one-to-one 一對一私人補習　　☐ $_b$ Internet tutoring (including Skype) 互聯網補習
   ☐ $_c$ Small group 小規模補習班　　☐ $_d$ Lecture style by tutors (live) 大教室由補習老師現場授課
   ➤ the number of students in your group is:＿＿
   　小規模補習班的學生人數是：＿＿＿＿
   ☐ $_e$ Lecture style (video recording) 在課室通過錄影學習
   ☐ $_f$ Others 其他 (Please state 請注明: ＿＿＿＿＿)　☐ $_g$ None of the above 沒有參加任何補習

2. Why **did** or **didn't** you take private supplementary tutoring in the past 12 month? (can tick more than one)
   你 **參加或不參加** 上述各種類型補習的原因是什麼？（可選多於一項）

   I took some, because: 有補習，其原因為：

   ☐ $_1$ I want to learn subjects better.
   　　我希望透過補習更好地學習各個學科。
   ☐ $_2$ I want to improve my exam scores.
   　　我希望透過補習提高考試成績。
   ☐ $_3$ I was attracted by the tutoring advertisement.
   　　我受補習廣告宣傳所吸引。
   ☐ $_4$ My parents chose it for me.
   　　我家長為我安排的。
   ☐ $_5$ Many of my friends are doing it.
   　　我好多朋友都參加補習。
   ☐ $_6$ My teachers recommended it.
   　　我學校老師建議我參加補習。
   ☐ $_7$ Others (Please state 請注明:＿＿＿＿
   　　＿＿＿＿＿＿＿＿＿＿＿＿＿＿＿）
   If "**took some**", please go to **Question 3**.
   如回答 "有補習"，請繼續回答第 **3** 題。

   I did not take any, because: 沒有補習，其原因為：

   ☐ $_1$ I am already doing well enough in school.
   　　我在學校的表現已經夠好了。
   ☐ $_2$ None of the available private tutoring seems to suit my needs. 現有的補習沒有適合我需要的。
   ☐ $_3$ Not many of my friends are doing it.
   　　我的朋友中參加補習的不多。
   ☐ $_4$ I don't have time. 我沒有時間參加補習。
   ☐ $_5$ I don't have the money. 我沒有錢參加補習。
   ☐ $_6$ My school teachers are knowledgeable enough.
   　　我學校的老師已經足夠有知識了。
   ☐ $_7$ My parents don't want me to do it.
   　　我家長不想我參加補習。
   ☐ $_8$ It doesn't seem worth the money. 補習不值得花錢。
   ☐ $_9$ My teachers said it is not useful.
   　　我學校老師認為補習沒有用。
   ☐ $_{10}$ Others 其他 (Please state 請注明:＿＿＿＿
   　　＿＿＿＿＿＿＿＿＿＿＿＿＿＿＿）
   If "**did not take any**", please go to **Question 10**
   如回答 "沒有補習"，請直接跳至回答第 **10** 題。

For students who are receiving private supplementary tutoring Q3-Q9 僅參加了補習的同學回答：

3. How many hours **per week** do you receive private supplementary tutoring in the following subjects? (If you do not receive any tutoring in some subjects, please write "0" [zero].)
下列科目，你**平均每週**參加多少**小時**的補習？（如果你沒有參加有些科目的補習，請填寫 "0" [零].）

Subject(s) 科目	During the ordinary term-time per week (hours) 平常學期期間每週（小時）	During test/exam periods per week (hours) 考試/測驗期間每週（小時）	During holidays/vacation periods per week (hours) 放假期間每週（小時）
Chinese language/ literature 中國語文/文學			
English language/ literature 英語/英語文學			
Mathematics 數學			
Business 商科			
Humanities 其他文科			
Sciences 理科			
Liberal Studies 通識科			
Others 其他(please state 請注明:___)			

4. Do the following activities happen in your tutoring course(s)? 你的補習課是否有下列活動？

Subject(s) 科目	My tutoring session(s) follow the school curriculum. 我的補習課內容與學校課程一致。		I have homework from my tutor(s). 我的補習老師給我家課。		I take test or mock exam(s) in my tutoring course(s). 我的補習課會有測驗或/和模擬考試。	
	Yes 是	No 否	Yes 是	No 否	Yes 是	No 否
Chinese language/ literature 中國語文/文學	□1	□0	□1	□0	□1	□0
English language/ literature 英語/英語文學	□1	□0	□1	□0	□1	□0
Mathematics 數學	□1	□0	□1	□0	□1	□0
Business 商科	□1	□0	□1	□0	□1	□0
Humanities 其他文科	□1	□0	□1	□0	□1	□0
Sciences 理科	□1	□0	□1	□0	□1	□0
Liberal Studies 通識科	□1	□0	□1	□0	□1	□0
Others 其他(please state 請注明:___)	□1	□0	□1	□0	□1	□0

5. To what extent do you agree that private supplementary tutoring has **improved** your: (Tick ONE each)
你在多大程度上同意補習**提高/改善**了你的：（每一項只選一個）

	Strongly disagree 非常不同意	Disagree 不同意	Agree 同意	Strongly Agree 非常同意	No opinion 沒有意見
a. Examination grades 考試成績	□1	□2	□3	□4	□0
b. Relationship with school teachers 與學校老師的關係	□1	□2	□3	□4	□0
c. Confidence in examinations 對考試的信心	□1	□2	□3	□4	□0
d. Revision skills 複習技巧	□1	□2	□3	□4	□0
e. Confidence in school performance 對自己在學校表現的自信	□1	□2	□3	□4	□0
f. Learning strategies 學習策略	□1	□2	□3	□4	□0

6. Where did you get the information about tutoring and/or tutoring courses? (can tick more than one)
   你從甚麼渠道得知補習的資訊？（可選多於一項）

   ☐₁ my family and relatives 家人親戚   ☐₂ friends and classmates 同學朋友
   ☐₃ teachers in my school 本校老師   ☐₄ advert. on TV or newspaper 電視報紙上的廣告
   ☐₅ Internet 互聯網   ☐₆ advert. on buildings, supermarkets or buses 大廈、超市和巴士上的廣告
   ☐₇ promotion activities of tutoring centers 補習社宣傳活動
   ☐₈ Others 其他 (Please state 請注明: _____)

7. To what extent do you agree with the following comparison about your school teachers and your tutors? (Tick ONE each) 你在多大程度上同意下列關於學校老師和補習老師的比較？(請每一項選擇一個)

	Strongly Disagree 非常不同意	Disagree 不同意	Agree 同意	Strongly Agree 非常同意	No opinion 沒有意見
a. My tutors are more knowledgeable. 我的補習老師更有知識。	☐1	☐2	☐3	☐4	☐0
b. My tutors are less inspiring in teaching. 我的補習老師教學較少具有啟發性。	☐1	☐2	☐3	☐4	☐0
c. I have more interaction with my tutor(s). 我與補習老師有更多的互動。	☐1	☐2	☐3	☐4	☐0
d. My tutors are less supportive. 我的補習老師給學生的支持更少。	☐1	☐2	☐3	☐4	☐0
e. My school teachers are more patient with me. 我的學校老師對我更有耐心。	☐1	☐2	☐3	☐4	☐0
f. My school teachers provide more guidance and counseling about my life. 我的學校老師為我提供更多生活上的指引和輔導。	☐1	☐2	☐3	☐4	☐0
g. My school teachers help me to learn knowledge and skills other than exam. 我的學校老師教我更多考試以外的知識和能力。	☐1	☐2	☐3	☐4	☐0
h. My school teachers advise me more on my behavior. 我的學校老師對我的日常行為提供更多的建議。	☐1	☐2	☐3	☐4	☐0
i. My school teachers are more likely to make me confident in my studying. 我的學校老師更容易使我對學習有信心。	☐1	☐2	☐3	☐4	☐0

8. The amount of money you/your parents spend on private supplementary tutoring on the average **per month** is :你/你的家長**平均每月**的補習支出大概是：HK$_____
   (Please provide your best estimate.) (請估算.)

9. To what extent do you agree that "Private supplementary tutoring is a financial burden to you and your family"? 你在多大程度上同意 "補習對你和你家庭來說是一種經濟負擔"？

   Strongly Disagree 非常不同意 ☐₁   Disagree 不同意 ☐₂   Agree 同意 ☐₃   Strongly Agree 非常同意 ☐₄   No opinion 沒有意見 ☐₀

FOR ALL RESPONDENTS Q10-Q29 請所有學生都回答

10. How would you rate the effectiveness of the following types of private supplementary tutoring? (Tick ONE each)
    你如何評價下列各種類型補習的效果？（請每一項選擇一個）

	No Effect 沒有效果	Small Effect 效果很小	Medium effect 效果中等	Large Effect 效果很大	No Opinion 沒有意見
a. Private one-to-one 一對一私人補習	□1	□2	□3	□4	□0
b. Small group 小規模補習班	□1	□2	□3	□4	□0
c. Internet tutoring 互聯網補習	□1	□2	□3	□4	□0
d. Lecture style by tutors (live) 在大教室由補習老師現場授課	□1	□2	□3	□4	□0
e. Lecture style (video recording) 在課室通過錄影學習補習課程	□1	□2	□3	□4	□0

11. To what extent do you agree with the following statements about "Tutorial Kings and Queens"? (Tick ONE each) 你在多在程度上同意下列對"補習天王和天后"的評價？(請每一項選擇一個)

	Strongly Disagree 非常不同意	Disagree 不同意	Agree 同意	Strongly Agree 非常同意	No opinion 沒有意見
a. They help their students to raise exam scores. 他們幫助學生提高考試分數。	□1	□2	□3	□4	□0
b. They have few effects on the improvement of students' real ability. 他們對學生真正能力的提高作用很小。	□1	□2	□3	□4	□0
c. They mislead students by focusing only on exam. 他們誤導學生過於看重考試。	□1	□2	□3	□4	□0
d. They introduce better exam tips than school teachers. 相比於學校老師，他們介紹更好的考試貼士。	□1	□2	□3	□4	□0
e. They help students to build their confidence. 他們幫助學生建立自信。	□1	□2	□3	□4	□0

12. Did you receive private supplementary tutoring earlier in your schooling? If yes, which grades? (If no, please write "0" [zero].) 你以前參加過補習嗎？如果是，在哪幾個年級？（如果沒有參加過，請填寫"0"[零].)

    e.g. Secondary 中學: S. __1-3, 5, 7__

    Kindergarten 幼稚園 : K. _____

    Primary 小學 : P. _____

    Secondary 中學 : S. _____

13. Have you ever enrolled in a class taught by a "Tutorial King or Queen"?
    你是否曾參加過"補習天王或天后"的補習課程？
    □1 Yes 是   □0 No 否

14. According to your estimate, what is your academic achievement level compared with all students of your grade in your school? (please tick one) 你認為你的成績在全校同年級中屬於（請選擇其中一項）：

Excellent 優秀	Good 良好	Fair 一般	Poor 差	Very Poor 很差
□1	□2	□3	□4	□5

15. What are your father and mother's highest levels of education? 你父親和母親的最高教育水準是：

	Father 父親	Mother 母親
Completed primary education or lower 小學或以下	☐₁	☐₁
Completed secondary education 中學	☐₂	☐₂
Matriculation or postsecondary education 預科或專上教育	☐₃	☐₃
Completed university 大學學士	☐₄	☐₄
Postgraduate degree 碩士或以上	☐₅	☐₅

16. Your household's recent **average gross monthly income is** 你家裏最近**每月的平均總收入**是：

    ☐₁ <HK$4,000   ☐₂ HK$4,000-5,999   ☐₃ HK$6,000-9,999
    ☐₄ HK$10,000-14,999   ☐₅ HK$15,000-19,999   ☐₆ HK$20,000-24,999
    ☐₇ HK$25,000-34,999   ☐₈ HK$35,000-59,999   ☐₉ HK$60,000-79,999
    ☐₁₀ HK$80,000-99,999 ☐₁₁ >=HK$100,000（Please state 請注明：_____）

    Among them your **father's monthly income** is about 其中，你父親的**每月收入**大概是：HK$ _____.
    your **mother's monthly income** is about 你母親的**每月收入**大概是：HK$ _____.
    (Please provide your best estimate. If no income, please write zero.) (請儘量估算。如果沒有收入,請寫 0.)

    For questions below, if the answer is "no" or zero, please write "0".
    以下問題,如果回答是"沒有"或"零",請填寫"0"。

17. Please state the numbers of the following rooms in your home. 請填寫你家裡的房間數。

    a) living/dining room(s) 客/飯廳：____間；   b) bedroom(s) 睡房：____間
    c) toilet(s) 廁所：____間   d) other room(s) 其他（Please state 請注明：____）：____間

18. Do you live in public housing? 你住在公屋嗎？
    ☐₁ Yes 是   ☐₀ No 否   ☐₉ I don't' know 我不知道

19. Does your family receive Comprehensive Social Security Assistance from Hong Kong government?
    你家有沒有領取綜援？
    ☐₁ Yes 有   ☐₀ No 沒有   ☐₉ I don't' know 我不知道

20. Please state the number of domestic helper(s) your household has 你家裡有家庭傭工：____個

21. Please state the number of private car(s) your family owns 你家裡有私家車：____輛

22. How many brothers and sisters do you have? 你的兄弟姐妹有：_____個

23. In which country/region were you born? 你的出生地是：_____

24. Please state your nationality (for most people it will only be ONE) and the country/region you lived most of your life. 請選出或填寫你的國籍（一般只選其中一個）和你居住時間最長的國家/地區。

	your nationality 你的國籍	country/region you lived most of your life 你居住時間最長的國家/地區
a) China (Hong Kong SAR) 中國（香港特別行政區）	☐₁	☐₁
b) China (Mainland) 中國（大陸）	☐₂	☐₂
c) Another Country/region 其他國家/地區	☐₃ （Please indicate the country/region 請注明：_____）	☐₃ （Please indicate the country/region 請注明：_____）

25. In your family, who help(s) you with your study? (can tick more than one)
    在家裡, 誰輔導你的功課？（可選多於一項）
    - ☐₁ Father 父親
    - ☐₂ Mother 母親
    - ☐₃ Sister(s)/brother(s) 兄弟姐妹
    - ☐₄ Grandparent(s) 祖父母
    - ☐₅ Nobody 沒有人
    - ☐₆ Other 其他人 (Please state 請註明：_____)

26. How often **after school** do you do the following activities **for leisure** (Tick ONE each)
    在校外，你多久**為休閒**而進行下列活動？（請每一項選擇一個）

	Never or hardly ever （幾乎）從不	Once or twice a month 每月一兩次	Once or twice a week 每週一兩次	Everyday or almost everyday （幾乎）每天
a) Reading for enjoyment. 趣味閱讀.	☐₁	☐₂	☐₃	☐₄
b) Playing sports. 體育運動.	☐₁	☐₂	☐₃	☐₄
c) Playing music instruments. 演奏樂器.	☐₁	☐₂	☐₃	☐₄
d) (Window) shopping. 逛街/購物.	☐₁	☐₂	☐₃	☐₄
e) Playing computer games. 玩電腦遊戲.	☐₁	☐₂	☐₃	☐₄
f) Spending time with friends. 與朋友一起.	☐₁	☐₂	☐₃	☐₄

27. How often do your parent(s) or grandparent(s) take following activities with you? (Tick ONE each)
    你多久與你的**父母或祖父母**一起進行下列活動？（請每一項選擇一個）

	Never or hardly ever （幾乎）從不	Once or twice a month 每月一兩次	Once or twice a week 每週一兩次	Everyday or almost everyday （幾乎）每天
a) Discuss your school life. 討論你的學校生活.	☐₁	☐₂	☐₃	☐₄
b) Help you with your homework. 輔導你完成家庭作業.	☐₁	☐₂	☐₃	☐₄
c) Eat dinner with you. 與你一起進晚餐.	☐₁	☐₂	☐₃	☐₄
d) Discuss social issues or news. 與你探討社會問題或新聞.	☐₁	☐₂	☐₃	☐₄
e) Watch TV with you. 與你一起看電視.	☐₁	☐₂	☐₃	☐₄

28. How much allowance (pocket money) **on the average** do you receive from your parents **each month**? (Please Tick one) 你的家長**平均每月給**你的零用錢金額為（請選擇一個）:
    - ☐₁ 0
    - ☐₂ HK$1-100
    - ☐₃ HK$101-250
    - ☐₄ HK$251-500
    - ☐₅ HK$501-1000
    - ☐₆ HK$1001-2000
    - ☐₇ HK$2001-5000
    - ☐₈ >HK$5000 (Please state 請註明金額: HK$_____)

29. Do you have a part-time job? 你有做兼職工作嗎？
    - ☐₁ Yes 是 (please state the job 請註明：_____)
    - ☐₀ No 否, **because** 因為:

    because 因為:
    - ☐₁ Support the family's needs. 補貼家用.
    - ☐₂ Gain pocket money. 賺取零用錢.
    - ☐₃ Gain job experience. 獲得工作經驗.
    - ☐₄ Others 其他 (Please state 請註明：_____)

    - ☐₁ Family income is sufficient. 家庭收入已足夠.
    - ☐₂ Parents want me to focus on studying. 家長希望我集中精力學習.
    - ☐₃ I want to focus on studying. 我想集中精力學習.
    - ☐₄ Others 其他 (Please state 請註明：_____)

Thank you for completing this survey. 問卷結束，謝謝！

Appendix 8.2: Interview Questions for Students

Questions for interviewing students **WITH** tutoring

I.   Facts about private tutoring

1. We are interested to learn about private tutoring.
   - Can you tell me when you first started to take private tutoring? On what subject?
   - What happened at the time that made you feel you need to take private tutoring?
   - Who suggested it?
   - Did you go to a tutoring center (or small group or one-on-one tutoring)?
   - Do you remember how it went?

2. So since then, you have kept taking private tutoring?
   - Can you tell me more about your later experience in private tutoring?
   - Still the same subjects?
   - When was the time that you took most private tutoring (in terms of subjects or time)?
   - What a typical day at that time looked like? How did you feel during that period?

3. (If multiple types of tutoring, center, one-on-one, small group, video, online, etc.) How are different types of tutoring different in your opinion?
   - What about their costs?
   - Is the tutoring cost a financial burden to your family?

4. For each subject, what in specific do you feel you need to strengthen through private tutoring?
   - Can you turn to your school teachers for help?
   - Can your parents help you out?
   - What about your classmates and friends?
   - Do you feel that the private tutoring is helpful to meet your needs in these subject areas?

II.   Learning

5. What do your tutors teach?
   - Do they follow the school curriculum? Do they tailor to your individual problems?
   - Do you get homework from tutors? How much?
   - Do you usually do it? If not, what would the tutors do? (if not) why do you still taking private tutoring?
   - Do you feel better when taking the extra courses?
   - More confident? Or else? In what ways? Why?

6. Are there any differences in the teaching styles of your school teachers and your tutors?
   - Can you please give some examples?
   - How would a typical school class go?
   - What about a tutoring class?
7. Are you interested in learning the school subjects?
   - Do you like taking the private tutoring classes?
   - Do your tutors help you to grow interests in the subject you are learning?
     - (Yes) How did he or she do that? Tell me more details please.
     - (No) If you don't like learning, why take all the troubles to attend extra courses?
   - Why are school grades so important? Why are exam results so important?
   - Do your parents scold you if you don't perform well?
   - What would they say and do if that happens?
   - Do you have the pressure from teachers and friends too? Like what?
8. Tutoring takes up some (or lot of) leisure time in your life.
   - Can you tell me how you spend your time after school?
   - Do you have any hobbies?
   - If you did not take the private tutoring classes, what would you spend the time on?

III. *Relationships*

9. In what ways does the tutoring shape your relationship with your teachers?
   - Do the teachers know that you receive tutoring? If so, what is their attitude?
   - Do the skills and perspectives that you gain in tutoring shape your responses in the classroom and therefore your relationships with teachers? If so, how?
10. In what ways does the tutoring shape your relationship with your peers?
    - Do different friendship groups arise as a result of tutoring?
    - Are there tensions because some students receive tutoring while others do not? If so, can you give an example?

IV. *Broad goals and family circumstances*

11. What do you want you to do in the future?
    - Going to university? Which university?
    - What occupation do your parents expect you to enter? What about yourself?
    - What do you want to study in university?
    - What kind of job or work do you want to do later? Why?
    - Will your private tutoring help you with these career goals? How?

12. What do your parents do?
    - Are they very busy with work?
    - Do they ask you what happened in school everyday?
    - What are the topics you usually talk about with your parents?
    - Do they check your homework?
    - Do you discuss your concerns and confusions with them?
    - Anybody else in your home can you turn to if you have a problem in study or in other aspects?

Questions for interviewing students **WITHOUT** tutoring

I.   Facts about private tutoring

1. We are interested to learn about learning strategies. We know that some students handle things by themselves, while other seek private tutors. We know that you are not receiving tutoring at this moment. Did you ever do so?
    - If yes, at what levels, in what subjects, and in what modes?
    - Why did you receive tutoring at that time, and why did you drop it?

II.   Learning

2. How do you feel about your academic performance in school?
    - And how do your teachers feel about your performance?
    - And your parents?
    - Do you feel pressure that your classmates are receiving tutoring and you are not? Can you give an example?

3. When you have difficulty in learning, to whom can you turn for help?
    - Do your school teachers help?
    - And your parents?
    - What about your classmates and friends?
    - Any other sources?

4. Are you interested in the school subjects?
    - Why or why not?
    - How does a typical class look like?
    - What activities do teachers ask you to do in class?
    - Do you like these activities?
    - What about tests and exams?
    - Do you feel pressure from teachers and friends? Like what?
    - Why are school grades and exam results so important?
    - Will anyone scold you if you do not perform well, and praise you when you do perform well? Who? And how do you respond?

5. How does a typical school day look like?

- Can you please tell me how you spend your time after school?
- Do you have any hobbies? What are they?

III. Relationships

6. In what ways does the fact that some people receive tutoring, but others do not, shape relationships with the teachers?
    - Do the teachers know who does and does not receive tutoring? If so, what is their attitude?
    - Do the skills and perspectives that classmates gain in tutoring shape their responses in the classroom and therefore their relationships with teachers? If so, how? What impact does it have on you?
7. In what ways does the tutoring shape your relationship with your peers?
    - Do different friendship groups arise as a result of tutoring?
    - Are there tensions because some students receive tutoring while others do not? If so, can you give an example?

IV. Broad goals and family circumstances

8. What do your parents want you to be in the future?
    - Going to university? Which university?
    - What occupation do they expect you to enter?
    - What about yourself? What do you want to study in university?
    - What kind of job or work do you want to do when you grow up? Why?
    - Do your teachers in school give you any guide for college studies and career choices?
    - How about your classmates and friends?
    - What do they want to do in the future?
    - Do you talk about this when you are together?
9. What do your parents do?
    - Are they very busy with work?
    - Do they ask you what happened in school everyday?
    - What topics do you usually talk about with your parents?
    - Do they check your homework?
    - Do you discuss your concerns and confusions with them?
    - Who else in your home can you ask if you have a problem in study or in other aspects?

Appendix 8.3: Questionnaire for Teachers

> This survey solicits teachers' opinions about the relationship between school learning and private tutoring in academic subjects (Chinese, Economics/Business, English, Humanities, Liberal Studies, Mathematics, and Sciences). The survey focuses on private tutoring which *takes place outside of normal school hours* and is *received in exchange for payment*.
>
> Please tick the boxes below or write the most suitable answers.
>
> Thank you for your help.

1. What is your gender? ☐₁ Male   ☐₀ Female

2. In what year were you born? 19_____

3. For how many years have you been employed as a full-time teacher? _____ years

4. What is the highest degree you obtained?
   ☐₁ Sub-degree ☐₂ Undergraduate ☐₃ Postgraduate Certificate or Diploma (e.g. PGDE or PGCE)
   ☐₄ Master ☐₅ Doctor ☐₆ Other (Please state: _____)

5. What subject(s) did you teach in the 2011/12 academic year? (Tick all that apply)
   ☐₁ Chinese ☐₂ Economics/Business ☐₃ English ☐₄ Humanities (e.g. History)
   ☐₅ Liberal Studies ☐₆ Mathematics ☐₇ Sciences (e.g. Biology, Chemistry, Physics)
   ☐₈ Other (Please state: _____)

6. Did you teach students in (either of) the following grades in the 2011/12 academic year?

	Yes	No
Form 3	☐₁	☐₀
Form 6	☐₁	☐₀

7. Please estimate the percentage of students in your class(es) who have taken private tutoring in the last 12 Months:

	0%	1-20%	21-40%	41-60%	61-80%	81-100%	I don't know
Form 3	☐₁	☐₂	☐₃	☐₄	☐₅	☐₆	☐₇
Form 6	☐₁	☐₂	☐₃	☐₄	☐₅	☐₆	☐₇

8. To what extent do you agree with the following statements about yourself as a teacher? (Tick ONE each)

	Strongly Disagree	Disagree	Agree	Strongly Agree
a. I am making a positive educational difference in the lives of my students.	1	2	3	4
b. I am able to help even the most unmotivated students learn.	1	2	3	4
c. I am successful in helping the students in my class learn.	1	2	3	4
d. I am able to make students follow my instructions.	1	2	3	4

9. Concerning tutoring in large classes by companies (including Queens and Kings), how often do you think the following things happen? (Tick ONE each)

	Never	Seldom	Sometimes	Often	Always
a. Tutoring helps students to raise exam scores.	1	2	3	4	5
b. Tutoring improves students' ability.	1	2	3	4	5
c. Tutoring focuses on exams.	1	2	3	4	5
d. Tutoring provides exam tips.	1	2	3	4	5
e. Tutoring provides exam drills.	1	2	3	4	5
f. Tutoring helps to build students' confidence.	1	2	3	4	5
g. Tutoring helps students to develop learning strategies.	1	2	3	4	5
h. Tutoring promotes students' critical thinking.	1	2	3	4	5
j. Tutoring helps students to cover material which is not covered in class.	1	2	3	4	5

10. In your opinion, how effective are the following types of private tutoring? (Tick ONE each)

	No Effect	Small Effect	Medium Effect	Large Effect
a. Private one-to-one	1	2	3	4
b. Small group	1	2	3	4
c. Lecture by tutors (live)	1	2	3	4
d. Lecture (video recording)	1	2	3	4
e. Internet tutoring	1	2	3	4

11. How often do the following things happen? (Tick ONE each)

	Never	Seldom	Sometimes	Often	Always
a. Students are willing to ask me when they have difficulties in learning.	☐1	☐2	☐3	☐4	☐5
b. When students are not able to catch up, I am willing to provide free after-class lessons.	☐1	☐2	☐3	☐4	☐5
c. For students who are interested in the subject I am teaching, I am willing to provide free after-class lessons.	☐1	☐2	☐3	☐4	☐5

12. What is your view on the following statements about provision of private tutoring? (Tick ONE each)

	Strongly Disagree	Disagree	Agree	Strongly Agree
a. Teaching is easier when many of my students attend private tutoring.	☐1	☐2	☐3	☐4
b. High-achieving children should receive private tutoring.	☐1	☐2	☐3	☐4
c. Low-achieving children should receive private tutoring.	☐1	☐2	☐3	☐4
d. Government should subsidize tutoring for students in need of extra learning support.	☐1	☐2	☐3	☐4
e. Government should reduce emphasis on exams as a means for allocation of education opportunities.	☐1	☐2	☐3	☐4
f. Government should regulate who are qualified to be private tutors for students.	☐1	☐2	☐3	☐4

13. Were you ever employed as a private tutor before you became a full-time school teacher?

☐1 Yes   ☐0 No

14. Have you ever been employed at the same time *both* as a private tutor *and* as a full-time school teacher?

☐1 Yes (If yes, please go to Q15)

☐0 No (If no, it is the end of the survey)

15. When did you conduct private tutoring? (Tick all that apply)

☐1 Weekdays during the school year   ☐2 Weekends during the school year

☐3 Holidays (e.g. Summer holidays, Christmas holidays)   ☐4 Other time (Please indicate: _____)

Thank you for completing this survey.

Appendix 8.4: Interview Questions for Teachers

1. *Scale and nature of private tutoring*
   [This initial set of questions sets the focus and acts as a warm up.]

   We are chiefly interested in extra tutoring received by students in Secondary 3 and 6. Could you tell me what you know about the scale of this tutoring?

   - Do some, many or most students receive it?
   - Which subjects are particularly popular?
   - What sorts of tutoring are dominant? Is it tutoring by the 'Kings and Queens'? Or by smaller companies? Or individual tutors working on an informal basis?

2. *Why the students go for tutoring*
   - What is your understanding of why the students go for tutoring?
   - What do the students get from the tutoring that they do not get from schooling?
   - How effective is private tutoring in increasing students' learning? Are some kinds more effective than others?
   - Are there differences between low-achievers and high-achievers?
   - Are there differences between boys and girls?

3. *Your attitude and responses as a teacher*
   - How do you feel about the students receiving tutoring in the subjects that you teach?
   - In what ways does the tutoring received by the students change your teaching? For example, does it make your work more difficult? Or does it make your work easier? Can you give some examples?
   - What signals do you send to the students about whether they should receive tutoring, and what type of tutoring?

4. *The impact on students*
   - Does tutoring work, in the sense of improving students' academic grades?
   - And does it increase students' interest in learning?
   - Do tensions arise in class because some students receive tutoring while others do not? Can you tell me about them?
   - How does tutoring affect other dimensions of their school life, such as relationships with peers and teachers?
   - Do you feel that tutoring impacts on the students' family lives?

5. *Teacher as tutor*
   - Have you yourself ever worked as a tutor?
     - If so,

- Can you tell me about the arrangements? Were you self-employed, or did you work for a company?
- At what stage of your career did you work as a tutor?
- And what sorts of students did you serve?
- Can you tell me what you felt about the experience?
  - If not,
    - Have you ever been asked to provide tutoring? Have you considered providing tutoring? Could you tell me the circumstances?

6. *The school in which the teacher works*
   - Does the school itself provide any tutoring? If so, who covers the costs? Can you tell me how it works? Are the students keen to use the service? What effect does it have on out-of-school tutoring?
   - In what ways would you say that your school is similar to or different from other schools in the extent and nature of private tutoring received by the students?

7. *Directions for society*
   - What do you feel about the impact of tutoring on the wider society? Do you feel that it is something to be encouraged or discouraged? Can you tell me why?
   - And in the future, do you expect tutoring to change in scale and nature? If so, what changes do you predict and/or desire?

Wrapping up
- Is there anything else that you feel I should know about this phenomenon?

9

Constraints and Possibilities in Small-Scale Research: A Mixed-Methods Study in West Bengal, India

Sulata MAHESHWARI

Introduction

This chapter presents the methods and some findings of a small-scale empirical study of private tutoring in West Bengal, India. It begins with background on West Bengal and patterns of private tutoring. It then elaborates on the methods employed, noting strengths and limitations and highlighting some ethical challenges. The next section presents some findings including participation rates, popular subjects, determinants of demand, inequalities, costs, and students' perceptions of tutors. The final section concludes and summarises on both methods and findings.

West Bengal has one of the highest educational participation rates among Indian states, as well as high per household expenditures on education (National Sample Survey Office 2010, p.A-304). Among the items of expenditure are private tutoring. However, little research has focused on the phenomenon. The study reported in this chapter collected data from seven schools, and focused on five research questions:

- What is the participation rate in private tutoring among students of Class VIII and Class X in West Bengal?
- Why do these students take private tutoring?

Bray, Mark; Kwo, Ora & Jokić, Boris (eds.) (2015): *Researching Private Supplementary Tutoring: Methodological Lessons from Diverse Cultures.* Hong Kong: Comparative Education Research Centre (CERC), The University of Hong Kong, and Dordrecht: Springer. © CERC

- What do students perceive to be the consequences or impact of private tutoring?
- How much do students or their families spend on private tutoring?
- Does private tutoring exacerbate inequalities in education and, if so, how?

The findings show a participation rate of 97.3% among sampled students with an annual per student private tutoring expenditure of 6,569 rupees (US$110) and an average 16.5 hours of tutoring per week.[2] Students seek private tutoring to increase examination scores and to learn subjects better due to issues of class size, ineffective classroom teaching, and lack of domestic help with homework. The study also found exacerbation of inequalities at various levels.

Background: West Bengal and Private Tutoring

A far-reaching policy experiment shaped, though did not initiate, the history of private tutoring in West Bengal. In 1983, the government removed English as a subject from the primary curriculum in order to enhance enrolment rates in the rural areas, support low-income families, and promote learning of the Bengali language (Scrase 2002). The policy did raise the enrolment rates of the targeted populations, but had the unintended fallout of increased private tutoring (Roy 2010). Since parents perceived knowledge of English to have strong links with the job market and broader life chances, they sought to supplement school education. The reintroduction of English later did not significantly reduce the consumption of private tutoring because by then the habit had become entrenched, and interests groups had already formed.

Nevertheless, the West Bengal government has been seriously concerned about the matter. In 2001 it banned teachers in government and aided schools from providing private supplementary tutoring; and in 2010 the ban was extended to all teachers (*Times of India* 2010). Private tutoring was also part of the investigation by a government-appointed Committee of Experts in 2011. One of the Terms of Reference for the Committee was: "To examine as to how the present menace and dependence on private tuition can be eliminated with emphasis on the sys-

---

[2] These figures apply only to the schools surveyed, and are not representative of the whole state. However, the participation rate was close to that reported by an earlier and more extensive survey (SCERT 2009).

tem of instructions at the classrooms" (West Bengal 2011, p.3). The use of words like "menace" and "ban" in public documents indicates strong feelings about the spread of private tutoring.

Methodology
Research design
Shadow education is a complex phenomenon that involves multiple stakeholders. A quantitative research instrument, though powerful and efficient in getting a broad picture of behaviour, is unable to capture every nuance of a complex subject. The study therefore used a mixed-methods design of both quantitative and qualitative approaches. This arrangement permitted some cross validation and triangulation of data.

The survey was initially designed for random selection of 25 students from each Class VIII and X. A random sample size of 25 from an expected class size of 45-50 was considered sufficiently representative of the population. However, random selection of 25 students from a class would have posed logistical problems for the schools. It would have required the non-selected students to wait somewhere while the selected students were completing the survey. To avoid this problem, cluster sampling of the whole class was adopted.

The initial design for interviews envisaged samples of male/female and tutored/non-tutored students in each class leading to 32 interviews in four schools with each interview for approximately 20 minutes in Bengali, Hindi or English as per the comfort level of the students. However, as some classes (especially Class X) had no non-tutored students, the sampling had to be modified. Further, some institutions were only-girls or only-boys schools.

Different sampling methods were used for different purposes.

- *Choosing seven schools*: Convenience sampling was used.
- *Questionnaire survey*: Cluster sampling was followed, i.e. all students in selected classes of Class VIII and Class X were given the questionnaire.
- *Interviews*: As far as possible, purposive sampling was used, e.g. for mixed schools the interview sample was constructed of male/female and tutored/non-tutored in each class. For only-boys and only-girls schools, the interview sample was primarily tutored/non-tutored in each class. The few interviews of parents, ex-

teachers, tutors and principals were based on availability of the individuals, and as such convenience sampling was used.

Research participants

The researcher contacted 10 schools. One school refused to participate when the principal saw the passive consent letter for parents. The refusal came on the day that the letter was to have been sent out. Another principal felt that private tutoring was politically sensitive due to the government ban. The principal indicated that the school did not want to invite trouble, perceiving the study as an action against the government. The refusal came at the first meeting when the letter of invitation was given. In another school, only interviews could be carried out due to ongoing examinations during the survey period.

The questionnaire survey was thus carried out in seven schools either for all students of Class VIII and Class X in the school or for all students in selected sections of Class VIII and Class X. The interviews were conducted in eight schools. School 1 had 40 students and School 5 had only 32 students in both classes, so all students were surveyed. By contrast, School 4 had over 200 students in three sections of each year group, so cluster sampling of only one or two sections was undertaken. The total number of students surveyed was 649, among which 633 provided usable data (Table 9.1).

Table 9.1: Distribution of Students with Usable Survey Data, West Bengal

School	Class VIII		Class X		Total
	Girls	Boys	Girls	Boys	
1	10	14	7	9	40
2		40	21	31	92
3	34	34	20	36	124
4		95		35	130
5	10		22		32
6		30		45	75
7		51		89	140
Total	54	264	70	245	633

For the qualitative data, 30 students from eight schools were interviewed (Table 9.2). In addition, three parents were interviewed: one each from rural, urban and semi-urban areas. Two ex-teachers-cum-tutors, one each from rural and urban areas, were also interviewed; and four current teachers were interviewed with a mix of rural, urban and semi-urban. Finally, six students from a coaching centre were interviewed. The interview recordings totalled approximately 19 hours, with an average of around 30 minutes per interview.

Table 9.2: Distribution of Interview Sample, West Bengal

School	Class VIII				Class X				Parent	Teacher
	Girls		Boys		Girls		Boys			
	Tutored	Non-tutored	Tutored	Non-tutored	Tutored	Non-tutored	Tutored	Non-tutored		
1	1	1	1		1		1			1
2			1	1	1		1	1	1	1
3			1		2		1			
4			1	1			1	1	1	1
5	1	1			1	2				
6			1				1			
7			1	1			1	1	1	1
8					1		1			
Coach	2						4			1 (Tutor)
Home										1 (Tutor)
Total	4	2	6	3	6	2	10	3	3	6

Demography and school profiles
The seven schools had a mix of:

- *location*: rural, urban and semi-urban;
- *gender*: only boys, only girls, mixed;
- *medium of instruction*: Bengali, English;
- *curriculum*: some taking the West Bengal (Madhyamik) examinations and others with the curriculum leading to the Indian Certificate of Secondary Education (ICSE);
- *type*: government, government-aided, private;
- *size*: large, medium, small; and
- *socio-economic status of students*: low-income, middle-income, high-income.

These features are summarised in Tables 9.3 and 9.4.

Table 9.3: Demographic Profile of Sampled Schools, West Bengal

School	Location	Class Size (approx.)	Year size (approx.)	Socio-economic status	Students
1	Urban	20	20	Low-income	Mixed
2	Rural	75-77	160	Mixed income	Only boys till Class VIII
3	Rural	90	270	Mixed income	Mixed
4	Semi-urban	70	200	Medium income	Boys
5	Semi-urban	15	15	Very low income	Girls
6	Semi-urban	40	100	Low income	Boys
7	Semi-urban	60	150	Medium income	Boys

Table 9.4: Administrative/Curricular Profile of Sampled Schools, West Bengal

School	Size	Medium of Instruction	Examinations Board	Type	Annual Fees (Rupees)	Band*
1	Small	English	West Bengal (Madhyamik)	Private/ Anglo-Indian	6,000	3
2	Large	Bengali	West Bengal	Government	Free	1
3	Medium	Bengali	West Bengal	Government	Free	2
4	Large	Bengali	West Bengal	Aided	350	1
5	Small	Bengali	West Bengal	Aided	550	3
6	Medium	Bengali	West Bengal	Aided	565	2
7	Large	English	ICSE	Private/ Anglo-Indian	15,600	1

* West Bengal does not have a Band system, but the author found this Hong Kong concept an easy way to communicate multiple levels of data regarding the schools, including student composition, socio-economic background, and academic status. Band 1 has high achievers, and Band 3 has low achievers.

The students were mostly aged 13-15. The family background was mixed, with some from poor and others from middle income range. No elite schools or students from very high income groups were included in the dataset.

Procedures
The study was initiated by giving a letter of invitation for participation from the University of Hong Kong to each school head. The letterhead was the Comparative Education Research Centre (CERC), with the re-

searcher as the undersigned. Upon agreement, passive parent consent letters were handed out and questionnaire surveys and interviews were administered.

The questionnaire survey was done in the classrooms of each class. The questionnaires were distributed, following which the researcher explained the questions and cleared doubts. The process of filling the questionnaires took 10-15 minutes.

Once the survey of each Class VIII and Class X had been completed, interview sampling was undertaken. Most interviews were conducted in separate rooms assigned to the interviewer. In a few schools, to minimise disruption of the school schedule and to accommodate the participants' time constraints, interviews were held on another day. Most interviews were in Bengali or English, with a few in Hindi.

Instruments

The questionnaire chosen for the survey was a modified version of the instrument used in the survey of Hong Kong schools considered elsewhere in this book (see Chapter 8). In the first stage, around 10 adaptations were done on leisure activities, tutoring expenditures, income ranges, subject groupings, etc.. Most changes were adaptations to a different demographic and cultural setting. For example, "window shopping" was removed as a leisure activity as it would not have been understood by most West Bengal students. Curriculum-related adaptations included removal of the Liberal Studies and Business subjects. Other adaptations were more system-driven, such as change of currency units.

Once the questionnaire had been finalised, a validity check was done. It was sent for feedback to a mix of friends, relatives, ex-teachers and some students whom the researcher knew in West Bengal. Commentators suggested that the questionnaire was too long and that if students became impatient they might refuse to complete it or would do so insincerely. The questionnaire was then shortened and adapted further.

After finalization of the English questionnaire, it was couriered to West Bengal for translation along with explanations of the purpose of the study and other details. The translation was checked through back translation, and once found satisfactory the final version was sent for typing, printing and photocopying.

The interview guide for the semi-structured interviews was also taken from the Hong Kong study. The Hong Kong guide was divided into two sets, one for students receiving tutoring and the other for students not receiving tutoring. The questions were in the categories of facts about private tutoring, learning (both in school and tutoring classes), relationships (both with teachers and tutors, in school and in tutoring classes), broad goals, and family circumstances.

The guide was sufficiently generic to allow for adaptation with minimal changes. The researcher added a question about students' future plans which was specific to the West Bengal context, viz. if they were already preparing for engineering, medical or any other entrance examinations which are normally taken after higher secondary examinations. The semi-structured nature of the interviews with open-ended questions allowed the researcher flexibility to follow interesting development in the interview process while at the same time adhering to exploration of the fundamental themes. The interview guide was translated into Bengali and Hindi for the interviews which had to be conducted in those languages.

Ethics and politics of the study
Some difficulties were faced in carrying out the study within the limits of ethical clearance required by the researcher's university,[3] due to local conditions, mistrust, and what seemed like fear of a politically sensitive topic. Four instances deserve specific mention.

First, as mentioned earlier, one principal was not comfortable with the passive parent consent letter, and the researcher had to withdraw from this school. Approximately 160 participants were missed as a result.

Another school authority was suspicious of the research intentions, despite an earlier meeting and the letter from the University of Hong Kong disclosing the research purpose. The authority wished to listen to the confidential interview recording as a condition to let the researcher continue. The authority expressed fear that the researcher, belonging to a different religious sect than the one to which the school was affiliated, might bring harm and disrepute to the school. Fortunately, after lengthy dialogue the authority decided not to pursue the wish to listen to the interview. The researcher provided details of her educational background and her current residence outside India, implying lower probability of her nexus to any religious sect within the country. The researcher also assured that the study could be stopped any time the school wished, and

---

[3] All researchers doing research under the auspices of the University of Hong Kong need to undergo ethical clearance which assures that no harm comes to research participants and that their privacy is protected.

reiterated the ethical policies of the University of Hong Kong for research studies. Finally, the authority was convinced that the researcher had no harmful intentions, and helped to complete the study.

The principal of another school insisted on the interviews being held in front of him at his office. The researcher agreed to the process with the hope that some useful information might still be forthcoming. As the interview progressed and one of the interviewees spoke frequently about the interviewee's mother, it was possible for the researcher to suggest that she visit the student's house. At the house, the researcher could interview not only the student but also the parent. Unsurprisingly, the independent interview had more important and relevant findings. The interview in front of the principal was not fully candid but still gave some useful information such as long commute durations for students taking tutoring.

Finally, in one semi-urban school where the principal had given written permission to the researcher to enter the classes for the survey, one teacher refused entry on the grounds of disturbance to the class. When the researcher repeated her request, showing him the permission slip, he was upset and told the researcher to leave. It was later revealed that he was one of the teachers who tutored his own students.

Limitations

Because the survey was small and used convenience sampling to select schools and cluster sampling for selecting students, generalization from the findings must be limited. However, the mix of schools in terms of location, socio-economic background, medium of instruction, curriculum, and public/private does provide an overview of commonality and diversity. Additionally, the qualitative data reveal many aspects of private tutoring which had not been previously analysed in West Bengal. Nevertheless, the study is context-specific, and the situation in West Bengal may not match every part of the country.

Other limitations arose from the instrument. For example, Question 1 is reproduced below. Many students needed clarification, asking: "What is small group - what size, how many students?". In the written responses, one student answered 70, another 50, and 10 answered 25.

Further, students typically attended more than one "small group". In the first three schools, where the students did not ask for clarification and were not specifically told to write the number of students for each of the 'groups they attended, the students responded with only one number for

"The number of students in your group is:___", though the interview data sometimes contradicted these numbers.

Question 1:

1. Have you received the following types of private tutoring in the past **12 months**? (can tick more than one)

   a Private one-to-one ☐   b Internet tutoring (including Skype) ☐

   c Small group ☐   d Lecture style by tutors (live) ☐
   the number of students in your group is:___
   e Lecture style (video recording) ☐

   f Others (Please state: _____) ☐   g None of the above ☐

Question 3, reproduced below, was about hours per week for tutoring. Students had difficulty answering as the groups of subjects for which they received tutoring varied from the options provided. The variations included from students going for just one subject, to "Maths and Science" as a combination, and "all subjects" taught in one tutoring group. A more parameterized question would have given the right flexibility and more detailed results for this section.

Question 3:

3. How many hours **per week** do you receive private tutoring in the following subjects? (If you do not receive any tutoring in some subjects, please write "0" [zero].)

Subject(s)	During the ordinary term-time per week (hours)	During test/exam periods per week (hours)	During holidays/vacation periods per week (hours)
Bengali/Hindi language/literature			
English language/literature			
Mathematics			
Arts (History, Geography, etc.)			
Sciences			
Others (please state)_____			

Question 6 was problematic because it assumed that 'teachers' and 'tutors' were separate people. In practice, many teachers were also tutors despite the government ban. The question was appropriate for Hong Kong, but did not fit in West Bengal.

Question 6:

6. To what extent do you agree with the following comparison about your school teachers and your tutors? (Tick ONE each)

	Strongly Disagree	Disagree	Agree	Strongly Agree	No opinion
a. My tutors are more knowledgeable	☐ 1	☐ 2	☐ 3	☐ 4	☐ 0
b. My tutors are less inspiring in teaching	☐ 1	☐ 2	☐ 3	☐ 4	☐ 0
c. I have more interaction with my tutor(s)	☐ 1	☐ 2	☐ 3	☐ 4	☐ 0

Note: Only some of the choices are shown in the above extract.

Question 12 was also widely misunderstood. It needed multiple explanations and yet it is clear from some responses that misunderstandings had persisted. Consequently, the data from this question were not valid for further analysis.

Question 12

12. Did you receive private tutoring earlier in your schooling? If yes, which grades? (If no, please write "0" [zero].)

    e.g. Secondary: __VIII, IX, X__

    Kindergarten: K. _____; Primary: P. _____; Secondary: S. _____

The question would have been better phrased as:

12. Did you receive private tutoring earlier in your schooling? If yes, which grades? (Please tick the grades)

Kinder-garten	Class I	Class II	Class III	Class IV	Class V	Class VI	Class VII	Class VIII	Class IX	Class X
☐	☐	☐	☐	☐	☐	☐	☐	☐	☐	☐

Finally, one significant translation issue arose in the questionnaire. It concerned Question 20, which in Bengali was:

20. তোমার বাড়ীতে কে তোমাকে পড়াশোনা দেখানোর সাহায্য করে ? ....

☐ 1 বাবা ☐ 2 মা ☑ 3 বোন / ভাই

☐ 4 ঠাকুরদা / ঠাকুরমা ☐ 5 কেউ নয় ☐ 6 অন্য কেউ উল্লেখ কর।

In English, the third choice is "Sister/Brother", which was rightly translated as "Bon/Bhai" in Bengali. Even in back translation, it was translated correctly as Sister/Brother. However, the words specifically stood for younger siblings and not older ones. For older brother and older sister, the words are "Dada/Didi". A few students ticked "others" and elaborated.

The issues and limitations faced with instrument validation reiterate the multi-stage nature of adaptation necessary in any cross-cultural study. In spite of over 15 categorically different adaptations made to the original questionnaire, the problems listed above show the challenges that context and language may bring. Harkness (2010) suggests that needs for adaptation of questionnaire appear at any stage of the study, and that it is not possible to identify a single stage. Certainly the experience in this project highlighted the need for constant vigilance and multiple revisions.

Gap reduction
In 2009, the School Education Department of the Government of West Bengal directed a detailed study through its research wing, the State Council of Educational Research and Training (SCERT), entitled *The Implications of Private Tutoring in West Bengal*. A more recent study analysed student, teacher and parent opinions about private tutoring in Burdwan District (Nandi et al. 2014). Other studies in West Bengal have wider foci but include findings on private tutoring (e.g. Pratichi 2006; Pratichi 2009; Jalan & Panda 2010). Surveys by the National Council of Educational Research and Training (NCERT), Pratham and the National Sample Survey Office also have important information.

The researcher found very few studies about secondary school students. Most existing data focused on primary schooling, particularly in rural areas. At the secondary level, studies at the Class X level were not found. There is also lack of data on key parameters including number of hours that students spend on private tutoring, and per student private tutoring expenditures at the secondary level compared with school fees. Also few qualitative studies had been undertaken.

Through its choice of methods and participants, this study tried to reduce the knowledge gaps. It addressed aspects of private tutoring which were not analysed previously including:

- intensity of tutoring;
- perceptions of students about tutoring types, teachers, and tutors; and
- comparative analysis of rural/urban, private/public and male/female dimensions.

This study thus attempts to improve understanding of the demand side by adding qualitative research outcomes and wider aspects of private tutoring to the existing literature. For the full study, readers are referred to Maheshwari (2013).

Findings and Analysis

Although the main focus of this chapter is on methodology, some findings are presented in this section. Information is provided on participation rates, subjects in which tutoring was received, factors underlying demand, social inequalities, costs, and students' perceptions of tutors.

Participation rates
The overall participation rate as reported by the sampled students was 97.3 per cent. This was even higher than the 90 per cent participation rate for secondary school students recorded by the SCERT (2009). The high participation rate created challenges for the intended sampling of both tutored and non-tutored students. Three schools had none or just one non-tutored student in the whole sampled population (Table 9.5). In Class X, four of the seven schools surveyed had no non-tutored students.

The pattern displayed a small but clear demographic variation. The two schools with participation rates below 90 per cent were small and had students from very low socio-economic status families. The interviews substantiated the data with a sense of inevitability:

"Right now [private] tutoring has increased much more in the last few years. Thirty years back, one student took one tutoring – not more than that. The big *change has been, now in every subject the student takes tutoring."* [Ex-teacher-cum-tutor, semi-urban area]

Table 9.5: Percentages of Students Enrolled in Private Tutoring by School

School	Total surveyed	Non-tutored	Tutored	%
1	40	5	35	87.5
2	92	2	90	97.8
3	124	1	123	99.1
4	130	0	130	100.0
5	32	4	28	87.5
6	75	1	74	98.7
7	140	4	136	97.1
Average	633	17	616	97.3

"The parents who do not send their children for private tutoring are doing grave injustice to the children. They cannot cope in studies. The ones who do not send are those who cannot afford." [Ex-teacher-cum-tutor, rural area]

"English and maths tutoring is a must." [Student, Class X, rural area]

"Where can we get non-tutoring students in Class X? I do not think, you will get them in any school." School Clerk, rural area, when the researcher asked for a sample of non-tutoring students.

In the minds of all, private tutoring was intricately woven into the fabric of the society. The voices lend credibility to the quantitative findings.

Subjects for private tutoring
Mathematics was the most popular subject for tutoring, followed by science and then English (Table 9.6). However, the two rural schools (Schools 2 and 3) showed near equal participation in English and mathematics. Since in a rural setting out-of-school exposure to English is very limited and English proficiency is considered key to future prospects, this finding is not surprising.

Student perceptions are illustrated by the following quotation:

"Maths is the toughest subject because you cannot just memorise it like history and geography. You need to understand it, so I feel I really need to take tutoring in maths, not in anything else." [Student, urban school]

Table 9.6: Percentages of Students Receiving Tutoring by Subject

Subject	School 1	School 2	School 3	School 4	School 5	School 6	School 7	Average
Maths	91	97	99	95	39	72	91	**90**
Science	74	91	86	93	36	64	89	**83**
English	63	100	98	93	14	62	72	**81**

N: Number of students taking tutoring = 616. Top subjects for tutoring are shaded.

The same viewpoint was presented by another student:

> "Maths I cannot learn by rote. So I need to go for tutoring." [Student, rural school]

Mathematics is also essential for examinations to careers in engineering, medicine and administrative services, for example.

Determinants of demand

When asked why they received tutoring, the top reason reported by the students was "I want to learn subjects better" (Table 9.7). This may mean an intrinsic love of learning or may indicate underlying factors in the school learning environment.

Table 9.7: Students' Indications of the Reasons for Receiving Private Tutoring

I took some [private tutoring] because: ...	Top responses
I want to learn subjects better	82%
I want to improve my exam scores	71%
My parents chose it for me	38%

N = 616 students receiving taking tutoring

The interview data helped to reveal some of the layers hidden inside the responses. The first issue was class sizes in school of 70-90 students. In a related finding, the SCERT (2009, p.38) had observed that one of the top reasons parents chose private tutoring was: "There is dearth of teachers in school". The study reported class sizes of 85 in upper primary schooling (SCERT 2009, p.166). However, one of students interviewed for the present study attended an English tutoring class of 60 students. Thus, students or parents sometimes choose large tutoring classes and yet complain that school class size obstructs proper learning.

A related matter concerned classroom teaching and learning practices (Box 9.1). Shortcomings included lack of class discipline, late arrival of teachers, and tired teachers due to long commute or long hours of private tutoring. One student reported favouritism by teachers for students whom they tutored outside school. While teacher favouritism of any kind is undesirable, this kind is arguably particularly pernicious and is a corrupting effect of private tutoring.

Box 9.1: Ineffective Teaching and Learning at School

Class X boy, receiving tutoring but not from school teacher: "Now ... well...., the teachers who teach in school, all of them individually provide private tutoring. So I think, they, whom they teach in tutoring, [teachers/tutors] give [students] more importance in class ... not [to] the others."

Another Class X boy, receiving tutoring: "Now, every class is 40 minutes or 30 minutes. In this, sirs [teachers] anyway come 10-15 minutes late to class. But not all sirs, some sirs. After that the time that remains ... in class there are many different types of boys, among them some are not well behaved. For them, there is a thing of keeping them quiet. In this case, I don't find it is sir's fault. If there is chaos in class, then how will the sirs teach? So sirs have to spend some time removing that noise. As a result the time that remains for teaching, that is very less."

Teacher in semi-urban area: "[A teacher] is not a machine that he will continuously go at the same rate. If he takes private tutoring for five hours after school, he has to rest in school."

Parent in rural area: "The School Service Commission (SSC) ... is centralized, so teacher appointment is not as per where [the teachers] stay. In our times, school teachers stayed nearby. Now the teachers are getting out of home at 7 am. Suppose they have to come from Kolkata to here, they get out at 7 am, then bus journey, after which train journey, so they become exhausted. They are automatically quite a bit tired [when they reach school, say at 10.30 am]. So they have lethargy [during class time].... I think this is also a big reason [for increase in tutoring]."

Interview data added that increased prosperity, smaller families and heightened parental aspirations drove the growth of demand for private tutoring:

"Average life standard has increased, they have more money. Ambitions of parents have increased. The student getting 85%, their parents want 95%,

so they send them for tutoring." [Tutor, semi-urban area]

"Parents don't have time. They have money – both parents are working – so they send the child to tutors.... Competition is another reason.... All parents have one or two kids and they want their kids to be the best. So to stay in this competition, if that child gets more marks by going to Tutor A, I also have to send my child to Tutor A." [Teacher, semi-urban area]

"Parents are busy. They do not have time. Otherwise no private tutor can support the child better than parents." [Parent, rural area]

These remarks match earlier comparative literature which connected demography and economic growth: "[H]ousehold resources will combine with aspirations for a smaller number of children and anxiety about ways to stay ahead in a global economy. This could offer all the ingredients for a dramatic expansion of shadow education" (Bray & Lykins 2012, pp.28-29).

Inequalities

The study showed that several levels of inequality are perpetuated through private tutoring. First is affordability, with many students (47% of non-tutoring takers; N = 17) responding that money was a factor why they could not afford private tutoring, as well as data showing lower participation rates in low-income schools. Poor students also spent less on private tutoring: average annual tutoring expenditure was 2,821 rupees in School 5, compared with 15,773 rupees in School 7. Statements in the interviews included:

"I have never taken tutoring but I want to take in maths. I find it difficult."

"Have you told your parents?"

"Yes ma'am, but my father says if I need any help I should take from my brothers and sisters. It is because of money that I cannot take." [Muslim minority student, urban area]

"Tutoring spend is a big proportion of education expenditure – almost 50%. Many cannot because they cannot afford, else they would have spent." [Parent, rural area]

The second issue is access to types of tutoring. The study found that 61% of students in a low income school and almost none from higher income groups received "All Subjects" tutoring (Table 9.8). Such tutoring is a compromise for students who cannot afford individual subject tutors. Students go to one private tutor who helps them in all academic subjects taught in school. The fees are sometimes as low as 75 rupees per month. The private tutors are not subject specialists. One interviewee mentioned that the private tutor was a student of Bachelor of Arts who teaches them "all subjects", while another mentioned that the tutor was not a teacher but just "private tutor", which may mean unemployed person.[4] The stratification thus happens not only among the 'haves' and the 'have-nots' of private tutoring (Sen 2010; Majumdar 2014), but also, as has been noted elsewhere, among the 'haves' where "less established social classes tend to engage cheaper and more affordable versions" (Mazawi et al. 2013, p.210).

Table 9.8: Proportions of Students Receiving 'All Subjects' Tutoring

Subject	School 5	School 6	School 7
All subjects	61%	26%	1%

Number of students taking tutoring = 616. Top subjects in which most students go for tutoring are shaded.

The third means through which inequalities are exacerbated concerns the impact on education as a public good. Student and ex-teacher interviews revealed the deterioration of public schools as most parents opt for private schools and teachers do not deliver.

> "Parents prefer private schools.... It is mainly because [government] teachers are not sincere. They are fond of tuitions. They can earn more money if they collect some students and teach them after school. If they teach well in school, then no need." [Ex-teacher-cum-tutor, semi-urban area]

The costs of private tutoring

The annual per student costs of tutoring were calculated by multiplying the reported monthly costs by nine to allow for seasonal variation. The results showed a mean annual expenditures of 6,569 rupees. Though students did not accurately know parents' incomes, they showed confidence and accuracy in the knowledge of private tutoring fees, as often they were the ones passing the fees to the tutors. Thus, unlike data on

---

[4] This claim is substantiated by studies which found that the majority of private tutors (72.8%) were educated unemployed (SCERT 2009). The finding is also corroborated by Pratichi (2009, p.23).

parental incomes, data for this heading are relatively robust.

> **Box 9.2: "Education is the only weapon with which everything can be done"**
>
> Mena studies in Class X and is top of her class. Her father is sick. *"I don't know what disease, but he coughs a lot and is very sick now. He has fever",* she says in a matter of fact tone. He was a mason and built wells, but because of his health he had to stop work. Among her two older brothers, one stays in the village and takes care of his family. He cannot help Mena as he can only just about sustain his own family. The other, who is also married, dropped out of school in Class V due to the father's sickness and is the only earning member of the family. He has a bicycle repair shop ('gumti': small temporary setup) on a street corner. On some days he does not earn anything, so has to borrow money from a nearby shop so that the family can eat that day. Mena's mother tries to earns something by selling wood-cuts for fuel. Mena's elder sister is already married off. The implication in Mena's tone was that marriage could not be postponed.
>
> It was redundant to ask whether private tutoring was a financial burden, yet I did so. Mena replied: *"I don't know. My didibhai [tutor] takes very little for teaching me – just 75 to 100 rupees, and she never asks. She always asks: "Are you sure you can pay? Only then pay, or else it is fine for you to pay later." I don't pay her every month. I pay her sometimes once in 4-5 months. She is very good, she never asks..."* Mena may have ticked 'no opinion' or 'disagree' for the question in the survey, as according to her "the tutor never asks or puts burden".
>
> Mena feels very grateful to her family for allowing her to continue studying. She feels she <u>has</u> to study because, as she says, *"Education is the only weapon with which everything can be done."*

The survey responses to the statement that "private tutoring is a financial burden" showed that 55% of the students strongly disagreed or disagreed, with only 24% agreeing or strongly agreeing, and 16% ticking 'no opinion'. However in interviews, 15 out of 30 students reported mild to great financial pressure, to the extent of borrowing money to meet daily expenses. The contrast is perhaps puzzling as it might be expected that students would hesitate to admit financial difficulty face to face rather than on an anonymous survey sheet. The result can be interpreted as students' lack of knowledge of parents' income and hence understanding of financial pressure; or it may be due to misinterpretation or misjudgement of the question by students. One interview in School 5 (very low income) is an example of the latter (Box 9.2). It was interesting to see how the answer on financial pressure may be better captured by an interview than a questionnaire.

Students' perceptions of tutors

The data on 'tutors are more knowledgeable' show near equal responses of 'agree', 'disagree' or 'no opinion'. This is because, in many cases, teachers were the tutors,[5] which was revealed in student interviews as below:

> *"I don't find any difference between my tutor and teacher because my class teacher teaches me in tutoring. So there is no difference."* [Student, urban]

> *"The same teacher teaches in class and tutoring, but he teaches better in tutoring. We are only five in that class."* [Student, rural]

So the question was not answerable. However, in spite of the identity mix, a majority (68%) of students think they have "more interaction with tutors". In other words, though the two entities were same, in many cases the students had more interaction with one form of the entity than the other. This emphasises the issue of class size (hence limited interaction between student and "teacher") which surfaced in the responses of all categories of stakeholders interviewed, viz. students, teachers, parents, and tutors.

Conclusions

This chapter has given a glimpse into the features of private tutoring in West Bengal through the study of different parameters across seven diverse schools. The methodological dimensions illustrate challenges faced by researchers, especially when they are working as individuals rather than within teams. Even when appropriate methods and processes have been chosen, power relations between authorities and researchers and the ensuing negotiation can shape the outcome of a research study. Nevertheless the findings, though restricted to a small number of schools, have validity. Some findings echo earlier studies while others deepen understanding.

The study may also provoke discussion on the extent to which the attempt to make education free of charge has been achieved. All schools visited had the words Sarva Shikshya Abhiyan[6] (Education for All) etched above, and in much bigger size than, the names of the schools (Figure 9.1). In doing so, the schools made a statement of the importance

---

[5] This is also common in other countries such as Cambodia (Brehm & Silova 2014) and Bangladesh (Nath 2008), though perhaps not in the same scale.

[6] Sarva Shikshya Abhiyan (SSA) is the Government of India's flagship programme for ensuring Education for All.

of free education to the government, to the schools as institutions, and to the society. Is the promise actually delivered?

Figures 9.1: School Buildings, West Bengal

With 97.3% of the student population receiving private tutoring, which by definition is not free, the students are making a statement too. This statement showed that they understand the importance of education and are keen to secure it even if they have to buy it outside the institutions where it was promised for free. The stratifying effect of education and social class reproduction that government policies and international educational bodies have been trying to mitigate in classrooms, is exacerbated in private tutoring classes. The implications are enormous. Government understanding of the impact of private tutoring, and then introduction of measures to regulate and preferably to reduce it, is thus as important as the steps to introduce free education for all. Such action will help not only those who cannot afford private tutoring, but also the even more hapless ones who borrow money to pay for it in the hope that one day at least the one whom they fed by starving the others can lift them out of the trap of poverty.

References

Bray, Mark & Lykins, Chad (2012): *Shadow Education: Private Supplementary Tutoring and Its Implications for Policy Makers in Asia*. Hong Kong: Comparative Education Research Centre, The University of Hong Kong, and Mandaluyong City: Asian Development Bank.

Brehm, William C. & Silova, Iveta (2014): 'Hidden Privatization of Public Education in Cambodia: Equity Implications of Private Tutoring'. *Journal for Educational Research Online*, Vol.6, No.1, pp.94-116.

Harkness, Janet (2010): 'Cross-cultural survey guidelines'. University of Michigan. Available online at: http://ccsg.isr.umich.edu/pdf/07AdaptationNov2010.pdf.

Jalan, Jyotsna & Panda, Jharna (2010): *Low Mean and High Variance: Quality of Primary Education in West Bengal*. Kolkata: Center for Studies in Social Sciences.

Maheshwari, Sulata (2013): *Private Tuition in West Bengal, India: Nature, Participation, Determinants of Demand and Equity Issues in Secondary Schools*. MEd dissertation, The University of Hong Kong.

Majumdar, Manabi (2014): *The Shadow School System and New Class Divisions in India*. London: German Historical Institute, Max Weber Stiftung.

Mazawi, André E.; Sultana, Ronald G. & Bray, Mark (2013): 'Beyond Shadows: Equity, Diversity, and Private Tutoring', in Bray, Mark; Mazawi, André E. & Sultana, Ronald G. (eds.), *Private Tutoring across the Mediterranean: Power Dynamics and Implications for Learning and Equity*. Rotterdam: Sense, pp. 205-216.

Nandi, Srikanta; Paul, Pankaj K. & Baskey, Sunil K. (2014): 'Private Tutoring and Academic Achievement of Students: A Cross Sectional Study with Reference to Burdwan District in West Bengal, India'. *Journal of Radix International Educational and Research Consortium*, Vol.3, No.5, pp.1-11.

Nath, Samir R. (2008): 'Private Supplementary Tutoring among Primary Students in Bangladesh'. *Educational Studies*, Vol.34, No.1, pp.55-72.

National Sample Survey Office (2010): *Education in India: 2007-08 Participation and Expenditure*. NSS Report No. 532 (64/25.2/1). New Delhi: Ministry of Statistics and Programme Implementation, Government of India.

Pratichi (2006): *Public Delivery of Primary Education in Kolkata: A Study*. Kolkata: Pratichi (India) Trust in association with Sarva Siksha Mission, Birbhum and District Primary School Council.

Pratichi (2009): *The Pratichi Education Report II: Primary Education in West Bengal – Changes and Challenges*. New Delhi: The Pratichi (India) Trust.

Roy, Joydeep (2010): 'Can Changing Academic Standards Affect Educational Outcomes? Evidence from a Policy Experiment in India'. Washington DC: Georgetown University.

SCERT (2009): *Implications of Private Tutoring in West Bengal: A Report*. Kolkata: State Council of Educational Research & Training (SCERT).

Scrase, Timothy J. (2002): 'Globalisation and the Cultural Politics of Educational Change: The Controversy over the Teaching of English in West Bengal, India'. *International Review of Education*, Vol.48, No.5, pp.361-375.

Sen, Amartya (2010): 'Primary Schooling in West Bengal'. *Prospects: Quarterly Review of Comparative Education*, Vol.40, No.3, pp.311-320.

Times of India (2010): 'All Teachers now under Private Tutoring Ban'. 28 December.

West Bengal, Government of (2011): Circular No.849-SE(S)/ES/S/10M-64/11. Kolkata: School Education Department, Secondary Branch. http://www.wbsed.gov.in/wbsed/readwrite/notifications/120113121404001.pdf, accessed 11 June 2015.

10

A Mixed-Methods Study of Extra Lessons in Jamaica: Methodological Experiences and Reflections

Saran STEWART

Introduction

This chapter focuses on the methodological decisions made in a study of extra lessons in Jamaica, and comments on choices and dilemmas during the research process. It begins with the research questions, and continues to the mixed-methods design. Subsequent sections focus on lessons learned in the instrument design, sampling, data collection, the stage of interface, disconfirming findings, and other methodological challenges.

The term 'extra lessons' is found not only in Jamaica but also in other parts of the Caribbean (see e.g. Brunton 2000). In Trinidad and Tobago, Lochan and Barrow (2008, p.46) defined extra lessons as: "all teaching/learning activities outside of the normal school timetable that attempt to cover the formal school curriculum at a cost to the student or parent". This was explicitly designed to fit the definition of shadow education employed by Bray (2006). In Jamaica, Spencer-Rowe (2000, p.4) also highlighted the private dimension as follows:

Bray, Mark; Kwo, Ora & Jokić, Boris (eds.) (2015): *Researching Private Supplementary Tutoring: Methodological Lessons from Diverse Cultures.* Hong Kong: Comparative Education Research Centre (CERC), The University of Hong Kong, and Dordrecht: Springer. © CERC

For several years the public formal education system has coexisted peaceably with an informal system known as "extra lessons." Born out of a real or perceived need to supplement the formal system, this form of private tuition is as pervasive as it is exclusive, catering primarily to those parents who anxiously desire the "best" of the system for their children.

However, some respondents in the research reported in this chapter included free-of-charge provision in their understanding of extra lessons. This was among the challenges of the research, creating an ambiguity that had to be negotiated. Much of the literature on shadow education focuses on fee-based support that supplements regular schooling (e.g. Bray 1999, 2009), but sometimes fee-free education is included in the focus (e.g. Baker et al. 2001). Difficulties may arise when the two categories are mixed, because the driving forces and the implications may be rather different.

Research Questions

The primary question for the study on which this chapter draws (Stewart 2013) was:

> From a postcolonial theoretical perspective, how if at all, might extra lessons improve educational outcomes for students at the secondary level in Jamaica?

From this question flowed three micro-level sub-questions:

- What is the relationship between extra lessons and students' academic achievement at the secondary level?
- What aspects of a critical-inclusive pedagogical framework can be aligned with the teaching and learning practices in extra lessons?
- How do teachers, students, parents and key government officials describe their experiences with and the impact of extra lessons on students' overall educational outcomes in three of Jamaica's six education regions?

The research also had two macro-level sub-questions:

- What is the social history of education in Jamaica, and how does it influence the current state of the education system?

- What are the scope and prevalence of the practice of extra lessons at the secondary level in Jamaica?

I collected quantitative data from 1,654 Grade 11 students in 62 schools across the country and qualitative data from 62 students, parents and teachers in three regions of the country. The survey indicated that 90.3% of the sample received extra lessons. Extra lessons were offered, primarily in the form of small classes, by the students' subject teachers, by other teachers in the schools, and by tutors within and outside the schools. The data showed that extra lessons form a pervasive, parallel education system that is especially driven by students' needs to perform in the assessments of the Caribbean Examination Council (CXC).

The Mixed-Methods Design

Given the research questions and the conceptual and methodological gaps in research on extra lessons in the Caribbean, I decided that a mixed methods approach would be best for the study. Following Greene et al. (1989) and Bryman (2006), I addressed each sub-question with quantitative and/or qualitative methods for data collection and analysis (Table 10.1).

I employed a transformative mixed-methods design as outlined by Creswell and Plano Clark (2011). I collected the data sequentially, and employed an interactive approach between the quantitative and qualitative strands so that each strand constantly informed the other. In the sequential phasing, I started with the quantitative strand and ended with the qualitative strand. The design allowed for equal priority to both strands. The point of interaction began with the research question, and continued through the data collection, analysis and interpretation. In doing so, I developed both the quantitative and qualitative procedures using four construct areas: (a) scope and prevalence, (b) educational outcomes, (c) critical-inclusive pedagogical tenets, and (d) socioeconomic indicators. Table 10.2 shows the quantitative construct and content areas.

To address the research questions, I undertook two phases of data collection and analysis, with three stages of interface. The first phase of quantitative data collection and analysis used a student questionnaire that had been piloted and administered on a multi-stage stratified sampling frame (Fowler 2009). Descriptive statistics and a two-level Hierarchical Linear Model (HLM) were used to examine interaction effects between student-level and school-level factors.

Table 10.1: Rationale for Selecting Mixed Methods Design

Rationale	Description
Triangulation	Triangulation seeks mutual corroboration from both qualitative and quantitative methods. Accordingly, I triangulated the results of the qualitative data with the quantitative data to answer the primary research question.
Complementarities	Clarification of findings may be gained through the insights of different approaches. The quantitative data were illuminated by data from the interviews, focus groups and observations.
Initiation	Questions may be reconstructed from one method with questions or results from another method. The analysis of this study was grounded on a postcolonial theoretical framework, which conceptually stands in great contrast to quantitative techniques such as Hierarchical Linear Modelling (used in the study). Using a postcolonial theoretical perspective, I initiated a new composite of knowledge construction.
Offset	Quantitative and qualitative methods have their own strengths and weaknesses. The combination of both permits researchers to offset their weaknesses and draw on the strengths of both. In this study, the quantitative results were better explained through deeper understanding of the qualitative results.
Completeness	Mixed methods can deliver more comprehensive accounts. As this was among the first studies of extra lessons in Jamaica, I wanted a thorough analysis of the phenomenon.
Different research questions	Each research question may be best answered individually or in combination with both research methods. The primary research question and the sub-questions called for both individual and mixed approaches.
Credibility	The integrity and credibility of findings may be enhanced by a combination of methods.
Context	Qualitative research commonly provides greater texturing of context, while quantitative research permits generalisations. Because this study was based on a postcolonial theoretical perspective, it was by nature qualitative; but the possible relationships uncovered through a survey instrument made for more generalisable findings.

Table 10.2: Construct Areas for the Student Questionnaire

Construct Area	Content
Prevalence and scope of extra lessons	Cost per month Activities in extra lessons Average hours spent per week Type of extra lessons Location of extra lessons
Education outcomes	Students' perceived academic achievement Self-efficacy outcomes: motivation, confidence level, and social identity development
Critical inclusive pedagogical framework	Tenet 1: Faculty-student (tutor-students and teacher-student) interaction Tenet 2: Sharing power Tenet 3: Dialogical teacher-student interaction Tenet 4: Activation of student voice Tenet 5: Utilization of personal narratives
Socioeconomic Implications	Average household monthly income Education level of parents/guardians Occupation of parents/guardians Number of rooms in home Number of children in home

The first stage of interface was introduced within the design of the instrument, which quantified the qualitative tenets of Tuitt's (2003) inclusive pedagogy using a five-point Likert scale. The second stage occurred within the selection of participants for Phase 2 data collection and analysis, as well as in the qualitative design protocol. Based on the descriptive statistics from Phase 1, I selected three education regions to comprise the holistic multi-case study in Phase 2. I then selected three sample populations for Phase 2: a sub-sample of students who completed the survey and their parents from three of the six regions; a convenience sample of students' extra-lessons teachers; and a convenience sample of government officials. The second phase of qualitative data collection and analysis included:

- stratified purposeful sampling (Fowler 2009; Hodgkin 2008) to select students, extra-lessons teachers, and parents according to region, as well as confirming/disconfirming sampling to bound the three cases;
- in-depth 90-minutes focus groups and interviews in each of the three regions;

- three two-hour observations of extra-lessons classes in two of the three education regions as well as documentary analysis of curricula, syllabuses and student class-work papers; and
- three 60-minutes, one-on-one interviews with administrators in the Ministry of Education.

The final stage of interface fitted the aims for the interpretation stage to (a) build a comprehensive picture of the status of extra lessons in Jamaica and the accompanying micro and macro factors, (b) explore financing tutoring programmes as a flexible means of educating disadvantaged children, and (c) challenge inequities of secondary education. As recommended by Creswell and Plano Clark (2011), the interpretation stage of the transformative design included theoretical analysis of the findings.

Lesson One: Instrument Design

The instrument was piloted to test its psychometric properties, including content validity, construct validity, and reliability. Regarding the original 34 items, participants were asked primarily to respond to statements such as "To what extent do you agree or disagree that extra lessons or private tutoring has improved CSEC (CXC) examination grades?", and "How would you respond to the following statement about your mathematics extra-lessons teachers?", using a five-point Likert scale. Other items placed on a five-point Likert scale pertained to critical-inclusive pedagogy, such as "I am encouraged to respectfully challenge my extra lessons [teacher's] style of teaching". The scale endpoints were "Strongly disagree" and "Strongly agree", with "Neither agree nor disagree" as the midpoint. The scale included numbers.

One of the constructs, *Education Outcomes*, was measured using 10 items to examine the effects of extra lessons such as increased motivation and confidence as well as belief in passing examinations and improving grades. The questionnaire also had several multiple-choice questions, such as one that asked students to indicate the types of extra lessons or private tutoring that they attended (e.g. private one-to-one, internet tutoring, lecture style, and in-class by teacher). Open-answered items pertained to socioeconomic levels, such as "Please state the numbers of the following rooms in your home: living room, dining room, bedroom, and so on." The demographic-type items identified ages, genders, and parishes in which the students lived and went to school.

Most questionnaire items were adapted from an instrument used to survey students in Hong Kong (see Chapter 8 of this book; also Bray 2013; Zhan et al. 2014). To improve content validity, I sought feedback on the pilot and final instrument from five experts in the field. Face validity is similar to content validity in that it appears to be a good measure of the test. I obtained face validity through the review of the instrument by content and statistics experts.

Because the instrument used for this study was an adaptation of a newly-constructed instrument, it was not tested for construct validity against similarly related instruments. Among the adaptations was that the survey was designed to be conducted online. However due to the lack of internet access in many schools, most questionnaires were answered by hand and the responses then entered manually into a computer. As such, there could have been uncorrected data-entry errors. Other limitations were found in the level-2 school variables. Within the initial construction of the instrument, school-level data were not a major part of the questionnaire. As a result, I did not have enough school-level variables to support the analysis. Future considerations would include variables such as total number of students in the school, total number of teachers who teach extra lessons in school, and student-teacher ratio.

Lesson Two: Sampling and Participant Selection

When sampling and selecting participants, researchers have to decide a) whether to select the same or different participants in the quantitative and qualitative methods, and b) how to choose appropriate sample sizes. As noted by Creswell et al. (2008), the decisions should be guided by the intent of the study. For this particular study the second phase (qualitative) was designed to elaborate on the first phase (quantitative), and therefore I selected a sub-sample of the students who participated in the quantitative phase. I intended to have a large sample for the quantitative phase to permit generalisation and produce an effect size large enough to make inferences on the population. For the qualitative phase, I purposely selected a smaller sub-sample of participants to triangulate varying sources of data. More specifically, my initial proposal to my university's Institutional Review Board (IRB) was a sample of 3,758 Grade 11 students, representing 10 per cent of the student population. However, given the lack of resources and responses, I concluded the data collection process with a smaller sample (Tables 10.3 and 10.4).

Table 10.3: Sample of Student and School Populations in Each Region

Region	Parish	Proposed Sample		Actual Sample	
		Students	Schools	Students	Schools
Kingston	Kingston St. Andrew	987	39	486	17
Port Antonio	St. Thomas Portland St. Mary	494	19	214	10
Brown's Town	St. Ann Trelawny	342	14	132	5
Montego Bay	St. James Hanover Westmoreland	550	22	248	8
Mandeville	St. Elizabeth Manchester	550	22	242	10
Old Harbour	Clarendon St. Catherine	835	33	332	12
Total		3,758	149	1,654	62

Table 10.4: School Sample in Terms of Gender and Location

	Gender		Location		Total
	Same-Sex	Co-Ed	Urban	Rural	
All secondary schools in Jamaica	22	127	111	38	149
Schools in study	14	48	51	11	62
Percentage	63.6	37.8	45.9	28.9	41.6

Within most high schools, a sample of randomly-selected students was chosen from within randomly-chosen classes, though in some schools all students in the classroom were sampled proportionate to size. On average, 27 students per school were sampled with a range from 20 to 32. The initial plan was to collect data from more students at each school, but principals and teachers did not want their scheduled lessons to be disrupted.

Lastly, as a result of unexpected costs, lack of time, and unanticipated resource limitations such as transportation to and from regional locations, I was unable to conduct observations and the proposed number of focus groups in the rural region. As a result, the sample of extra-lessons classrooms observed was not sufficiently representative of the population to permit inferences or generalisations. However, indicative statements were made from the other two regions observed.

Lesson Three: Data Collection Procedures

Within mixed methods studies, the questions in data collection procedures include when to collect and what data to use. Whether it is better to collect the qualitative or quantitative data first depends on several factors including the context and circumstances of the study, availability and access to data, resources to collect the data, and the purpose of the data in the study. In the study described here, I first collected the quantitative data and then the qualitative data. The Jamaican Ministry of Education gave permission to conduct the research, and provided contact information for the schools. At the outset, I sent two e-mails to each of the 149 schools, and discovered that one was no longer operational. Among the remaining 148 schools, 72 agreed to participate, four did not agree, and 72 never responded. Finally I collected data from 62 schools representing 41.6% of the total secondary school sample. Data collection was time-intensive, because I had to visit each school, sometimes on multiple occasions. The lack of internet connection in some schools obstructed scheduling of visits.

Students from five of the 62 schools completed the survey online in the schools' computer laboratories. For the others, paper copies of the surveys were printed and distributed to each student. I found that students who completed the surveys online usually took less time than students who completed the survey by hand. This could be due to the fact that the online survey had automated forwarding of questions that were response driven.

To protect the anonymity of each student, I received from the IRB a waiver of signature for the consent forms for students completing the surveys. Prior to the distribution of surveys in the classrooms, I explained the purpose of the study, the data collection procedures, the time needed to complete the study, and the benefits and drawbacks of participation. After receiving verbal consent from each student, I handed out the consent forms attached to each printed survey and asked the students to read and agree prior to starting the survey. The same measures were taken with students who completed the survey in the computer laboratories. When students did not agree to take the survey, they were excused with permission from the teacher to work quietly on their own while the other students completed the survey. All paper-copy questionnaires were collected on the days of the visits, sealed in envelopes, and identified by school names. Data collection took 13 weeks. A total of 1,681 questionnaires were administered, of which 1,654 (98.39%) were completed and collected.

Lesson Four: Stage of Interface

After the data were collected from student questionnaires, I completed preliminary analysis using descriptive and inferential statistical procedures. The last part of the questionnaire had an open-ended question requesting participation in focus groups. Students who agreed to participate left their contact information for me. The qualitative scale that was quantified in the student instrument (critical-inclusive pedagogy tenets) was rephrased in the focus group protocol. I used the preliminary case study protocols to conduct semi-structured interviews, but the survey data raised additional questions. Furthermore, following the transformative-emancipatory paradigm, I asked students, their parents, and extra-lessons teachers who agreed to participate in the focus groups to shape the case study protocol, review the research questions, and member-check the transcripts.

I used the sampling strategy of confirming and disconfirming cases in which the purpose is to elaborate on initial analysis and seek exceptions that look for variations (Miles & Huberman 1994, p.28). I bounded the cases according to the Ministry of Education's six education regions. Each region had two or three parishes, and I selected three regions as individual cases or replications within the multiple-case design (Yin 2009), which represented seven parishes out of 14.

The regions were partly selected based on students' participation responses in paid extra lessons, but also to demonstrate diversity. Three education regions were selected, namely Regions 1, 2 and 6. Region 1 was an urban centre with the capital city (Kingston) and the highest participation rates in extra lessons. Region 2 comprised mainly rural communities with the lowest participation rate in extra lessons, while Region 6 had both urban and rural areas with the second highest participation rate in extra lessons. This form of cluster purposive sampling was used to select, from each of the three regions, a sample of students and their respective parents. Extra-lessons teachers were selected through snowballing in which students suggested teachers, and convenience sampling in which a school administrator or I selected teachers. I conducted a total of seven focus groups and four one-to-one interviews across the three regions. Each of the 62 participants was asked to read and, if agreeing to participate, to sign a consent form.

Lesson Five: Dis/Confirming Findings

When having inconclusive, contradictory or disconfirming findings in a sequential mixed methods design, the researcher has to decide whether to discuss conflicting results, introduce an additional phase to the study, or use the data from one phase to explain and expand on the findings from another phase. In this study, the quantitative data had some contradictory and inconclusive findings.

One interesting finding from the quantitative data was that most students reported receiving free extra lessons or did not know the cost of tutoring. Many students did not answer the question: "What is the amount of money you/your parent(s)/your guardian(s) spend on extra lessons or private tutoring on average per month in JA$?" The response rate for the question was 39.9% (n = 660), with a reported average cost per month for extra lessons of JA$6,193 (US$55). Among the 60.1% with missing values, one third wrote "free" or "$0", and the remainder did not respond or wrote "I don't know". These data were unexpected, because the literature in the field typically uses a cost analysis to predict for academic achievement (e.g. Dang & Rogers 2008; Zhang 2011). Therefore my findings called for further research not previously anticipated. This represents a dimension of extra lessons not investigated within the scope of this study, namely government subsidies and other costs related to free tutoring. As a result, I decided only to select participants in the qualitative phase who reported paying for extra lessons, so that I could gain insight on private tutoring in Jamaica. Also, the inferential statistics were calculated using data from students who reported receiving fee-paying extra lessons.

Inconclusive findings were revealed in the HLM analysis. After testing and comparing four models, the second random-coefficients model was selected as the best fit on parsimonious grounds. Based on the random-coefficients regression model, the variables extra lessons hours, household monthly incomes and critical-inclusive pedagogical tenets were significant predictors of students' perceived academic achievement. Yet although the data revealed statistically significant predictors, those predictors were not centred on the mean and could not be interpreted beyond statistical significance. The level-2 variables were centred on the mean but were statistically non-significant. Given these inconclusive findings, I moved on to the qualitative phase to explore how these statistically significant predictors could be explained better.

Throughout the qualitative data, my role as the researcher was inextricably linked to the participants and the data. I made sure to transcribe and re-present information that was respectful and accountable to my participants. I presented the data in three-formats (composite narrative, descriptive cases, and thematic constructs) that I believed would best represent the emergent data to answer the research questions and expand on the inconclusive quantitative data. In selecting descriptive case studies, I followed the advice of Creswell (2007), Stake (2005) and Yin (2009, 2012) to provide rich illustrations and deep contexts.

Following the case descriptions, the data revealed a model representing what I termed the *Ecology of Extra Lessons*. The model illustrated the macro- and micro-level systems that interact internally and with each other to produce educational outcomes at the core of the model. Fundamental to that core, the answer to the research question and transcendent between the quantitative and qualitative data is the occurrence of conditions for learning in which lies the critical-inclusive pedagogical framework. Toward this end, within pockets of excellence, where extra lessons teachers provide conditions for learning and engage in critical discourse and critical-inclusive pedagogy, students believed that extra lessons considerably improved educational outcomes.

An application of the study's findings, based on both the quantitative and qualitative data gathered from the student questionnaires, one-to-one and focus-group interviews, direct observations, and documentation, has its limitations despite the protocols that have been put in place. However, using both phases to complement and explain the other helped to provide a holistic picture of the perceived impact of extra lessons on students' education outcomes.

Lesson Six: Final Decisions

Other challenges concerned decision-making on appropriate methods, sequencing of methods, and integration of results. Initially I had planned to conduct an econometric design using data from the Jamaica Survey on Living Conditions (JSLC), but due to lack of second-hand data I decided to switch methods. Additionally, still wanting to use portions of the JSLC for the proposed parish-level data, I designed and piloted the student survey based on that assumption. As such, the HLM analysis did not have all the school-level variables needed to test the hypotheses properly.

In addition, violation of homogeneity was a limitation in the empirical analysis, because it was related to model misspecification where one or more level-1 predictors were not used in the model. Further, the presence of heterogeneous residual variance could be due to the presence of outliers from data entry errors, because data were entered by hand for each of the surveys collected. I attempted to correct for the violations by creating two separate heterogeneous variance models with variables not otherwise used in the model, *hours spent on homework per week* and *gender*. Separately, I tested the variables by running a simple regression and looked at the differences between the residual sum of squares. Both variables seemed to be good predictor candidates. However, when included in the heterogeneous variance model, the homogeneity *p*-value was significant.

In hindsight, I considered whether in the sequencing of methods I should have started with the qualitative methods in order to develop a better instrument to assess the scope and prevalence of extra lessons. Had I done so, data collected from the qualitative phase could have been used to develop items and scales for the instrument.

The integration of results from one phase to another can be challenging in sequential mixed methods designs. One strategy may be to select initial results to expand upon in later phases. In the study, results gathered on students' perceived academic outcomes in the quantitative phase needed to be described further in the qualitative phase. In the quantitative phase, students in Grade 11 were asked to recall their Grade 10 end-of-year grade average that had been released at the end of July or start of August. Given the data collection time period, there was a gap of three to six months, which could result in some unreliable data due to memory and maturation of age between receipt of reported grades and data collection. Students selected in the qualitative phase (as a purposive sub-sample of the quantitative phase) were asked again about their academic achievement due to participation in extra lessons. Some students were able to provide evidence of academic achievement in the form of reported CXC distinctions in mathematics, and I also collected academic reports from extra lessons teachers of students interviewed in the qualitative phase. The students who reported distinctions took the CXC examination in Grade 10 rather than the standard Grade 11 sitting, and registered to take the examination with the extra lessons institute rather than with their school.

Methodologically, one challenge lay in use of a transformative mixed methods approach when the very quantification meant that the first phase rested in a positivistic approach to research. The same issues arose when mixing the data and engaging in the processes of interpreting the mixed findings.

Conclusion

This chapter has provided an overview of the sequential mixed-methods design. The study (Stewart 2013) provided data not previously available, but greater rigour in the collection of quantitative data would have permitted stronger generalisation. Methodologically, extra lessons as a unit of analysis is challenging in that the constructs need to be defined clearly to be measurable across sample populations and understood in comparative contexts, both nationally and internationally. The qualitative portion of the study is a step towards an instrument that is culturally and contextually relevant to the Caribbean.

As commonly recommended in mixed methods (e.g. Johnson & Turner 2003), the study utilized both intramethod and intermethod mixing techniques. An example of intramethod mixing was the concurrent use in the constructs of the student questionnaire of both open- and closed-ended items. An example of intermethod mixing was the use of direct observations. The coupling of techniques provided varying levels of interaction between the quantitative and qualitative strands, and allowed more rigorous cross-over mixed analysis (Onwuegbuzie et al. 2009). The analysis included the visual presentation of both the qualitative and quantitative data in the same display as well as deduction of meta-inferences from both sets of data.

On the matter of definitions, the study was intended to examine paid private tutoring. However, some students in the quantitative portion of the study reported receiving free extra lessons. This brought the definition of extra lessons into question and highlighted the need for further deliberation. The students selected for the qualitative data collection were all fee-paying.

A further dimension concerned the relationships between the researcher and the host society. Although Jamaican, I was based in the USA. I found that my study was met with initial distrust, but I was not deterred because I realised that in Jamaica the term 'research' often carried negative connotations. These connotations were often due to researchers' lack of cultural sensitivity, as well as participants not being provided with the findings. As such, I had to develop trust and rapport with gatekeepers of data who would facilitate the process. This required numerous visits to site locations and many pre- and post-conversations with participants. Additionally, the constant need to bracket my biases, prejudgments, and an outsider-saviour mentality proved challenging. The research from start to finish revealed much psychosocial re-imagining of a 'foreign' homeland – one that I had never learned about during my high schooling in Jamaica. As such, my unlearning of the normative narrative had to begin with my unlearning of my utopian predispositions of 'home'. To manage the process I wrote about and video-documented the journey, and endeavoured to engage meaningfully with participants through teaching and workshops.

Conducting research in developing countries can be physically draining and require allowance for unanticipated demands. In highly violent or garrison communities, I travelled with a research assistant who knew the areas well. This increased my personal safety, which was critical for a female researcher. Many incidences of violence outside of the scope of this study reinforced the environmental barriers to learning in schools and the drive for learning in extra lessons. Being able to communicate the research to my participants in a way that was empowering was crucial to achieve the desired level of meaningful discussions.

Although this chapter has highlighted complexities in using mixed methods, it is not exhaustive of the tensions and possibilities of this research design. Further exploration of dimensions is very desirable, and I hope that the chapter will expand discussions and interrogation of approaches in this evolving topic of research.

References

Baker, David; Akiba, Motoko; LeTendre, Gerald & Wiseman, Alexander W. (2001): 'Worldwide Shadow Education: Outside-school Learning, Institutional Quality of Schooling, and Cross-national Mathematics Achievement'. *Educational Evaluation and Policy Analysis*, Vol.23, No.1, pp.1-17.

Bray, Mark (1999): *The Shadow Education System: Private Tutoring and its Implications for Planners*. Paris: UNESCO International Institute for Educational Planning (IIEP).

Bray, Mark (2006): 'Private Supplementary Tutoring: Comparative Perspectives on Patterns and Implications'. *Compare: A Journal of Comparative and International Education*, Vol.36, No.4, pp.515-530.

Bray, Mark (2009): *Confronting the Shadow Education System: What Government Policies for What Private Tutoring?*. Paris: UNESCO International Institute for Educational Planning (IIEP).

Bray, Mark (2013): 'Benefits and Tensions of Shadow Education: Comparative Perspectives on the Roles and Impact of Private Supplementary Tutoring in the Lives of Hong Kong Students'. *Journal of International and Comparative Education*, Vol.2, No.1, pp.18-30.

Brunton, Ronald (2000): 'Extra-lessons in Trinidad and Tobago: Qualification, Inflation and Equality of Educational Opportunity'. *Caribbean Curriculum*, Vol.7, No.2, pp.1-17.

Bryman, Alan (2006): 'Integrating Quantitative and Qualitative Research: How is it Done?'. *Qualitative Research*, Vol.6, No.1, pp.97-113.

Creswell, John (2007): *Qualitative Inquiry and Research Design: Choosing Among Five Approaches*. 2nd edition, Thousand Oaks: Sage.

Creswell, John & Plano Clark, Vicki (2011): *Designing and Conducting Mixed Methods Research*. 2nd edition, Thousand Oaks: Sage.

Creswell, John W.; Plano Clark, Vicki & Garret, Amanda L. (2008): 'Methodological Issues in Conducting Mixed Methods Research Designs', in Bergman, Manfred Max (ed.), *Advances in Mixed Methods Research: Theories and Applications*. Los Angeles: Sage, pp.66-83.

Dang, Hai-Anh & Rogers, F. Halsey. (2008): *How to Interpret the Growing Phenomenon of Private Tutoring: Human Capital Deepening, Inequality, or Waste of Resources?* Policy Research Working Paper WPS 4530, Washington, DC: The World Bank.

Fowler, Floyd (2009): *Survey Research Methods*. 4th edition, Thousand Oaks: Sage.

Greene, Jennifer C.; Caracelli, Valerie J. & Graham, Wendy F. (1989): 'Toward a Conceptual Framework for Mixed-Method Evaluation Designs'. *Educational Evaluation and Policy Analysis*, Vol.11, No.3, pp.255-274.

Hodgkin, Suzanne (2008): 'Telling it All: A Story of Women's Social Capital using a Mixed Methods Approach'. *Journal of Mixed Methods Research*, Vol.2, No.3, pp.296-316.

Johnson, R. Burke & Turner, Lisa A. (2003): 'Data Collection Strategies in Mixed Methods Research', in Tashakkori, Abbas & Teddlie, Charles (eds.), *Handbook of Mixed Methods in Social and Behavioral Research*. Thousand Oaks: Sage, pp.297-320.

Lochan, Samuel N. & Barrow, Dorian A. (2008): 'Extra-lessons: A Comparison between "Different Sides of the Track" in Trinidad and Tobago'. *Caribbean Curriculum*, Vol.15, pp.45-69.

Miles, Matthew & Huberman, A. (1994): *Qualitative Data Analysis: A Sourcebook of New Methods*. 2nd edition, Thousand Oaks: Sage.

Onwuegbuzie, Anthony J.; Johnson, R. Burke & Collins, Kathleen M. (2009): 'A Call for Mixed Analysis: A Philosophical Framework for Combining Qualitative and Quantitative'. *International Journal of Multiple Research Approaches*, Vol.3, No.2, pp.114-139.

Spencer-Rowe, Joan (2000): *An Investigation of the Practice of Extra Lessons in Schools at the Primary Level of the Jamaican Education System: A Report*. Kingston: Planning Institute of Jamaica/Ministry of Education and Culture.

Stake, Robert E. (2005): 'Qualitative Case Studies', in Denzin, Norman, K. & Lincoln, Yvonna S. (eds.), *The Sage Handbook of Qualitative Research*. 3rd edition, Thousand Oaks: Sage, pp.443-466.

Stewart, Saran (2013): *Everything in di Dark Muss Come to Light: A Postcolonial Examination of the Practice of Extra Lessons at the Secondary Level in Jamaica's Education System*. PhD Dissertation, University of Denver.

Tuitt, Frank A. (2003): 'Afterword: Realizing a More Inclusive Pedagogy', in Howell, Annie & Tuitt, Frank (eds.), *Race and Higher Education: Rethinking Pedagogy in Diverse College Classrooms* Cambridge: Harvard Educational Review, pp.243-268.

Yin, Robert K. (2009): *Case Study Research: Design and Methods*. 4th edition, Thousand Oaks: Sage.

Yin, Robert K. (2012): *Applications of Case Study Research*, 3rd edition, Thousand Oaks: Sage.

Zhan, Shengli; Bray, Mark; Wang, Dan; Lykins, Chad & Kwo, Ora (2013): 'The Effectiveness of Private Tutoring: Students' Perceptions in Comparison with Mainstream Schooling in Hong Kong'. *Asia Pacific Education Review*, Vol.14, No.4, pp.495-509.

Zhang, Yu (2011): *The Determinants of National College Entrance Exam Performance in China – With an Analysis of Private Tutoring*. PhD Dissertation, Columbia University.

11

Researching Private Supplementary Tutoring in Cambodia: Contexts, Instruments and Approaches

Mark BRAY, Wei ZHANG,
Magda Nutsa KOBAKHIDZE & Junyan LIU

Introduction

Cambodia is widely known as a country with a long history exemplified by the Angkor Wat temple, that greatly suffered in the 1970s under the Khmer Rouge regime led by Pol Pot, and that has since developed at remarkable albeit unsteady speed as a member of the Association of Southeast Asian Nations (ASEAN). The context for private supplementary tutoring is rather different from that in most other countries addressed in this book. In particular, much private tutoring is provided by regular teachers, often on school premises. Although the façade of the education system states that schooling is free of charge, families commonly feel pressed to receive such tutoring. As such, the provision and receipt of private supplementary lessons alongside government classes are widely viewed by families as a matter of daily life.

The chapter partly builds on research on household costs, including those associated with private supplementary tutoring, conducted during the 1990s and again during the following decade (Bray 1996, 1999; Bray &

Bray, Mark; Kwo, Ora & Jokić, Boris (eds.) (2015): *Researching Private Supplementary Tutoring: Methodological Lessons from Diverse Cultures.* Hong Kong: Comparative Education Research Centre (CERC), The University of Hong Kong, and Dordrecht: Springer. © CERC

Bunly 2004). This work was undertaken in partnership with government personnel and with support in different phases from UNESCO, UNICEF and the World Bank. In 2014/15, new research was embarked upon by a team at the University of Hong Kong (HKU) in partnership with a Non-Governmental Organisation (NGO) called This Life Cambodia (TLC). The work focused on the perspectives and experiences of students and teachers in secondary schools in Siem Reap Province. This chapter examines methodological issues relating to research on private supplementary tutoring in Cambodia, drawing particularly on experiences in the Siem Reap project.

The chapter begins with the context, first of Cambodia's society and economy, and second in the structure of the education system and the place of private tutoring. The next section explains the objectives and design of the Siem Reap project, and is followed by remarks on methodological challenges and achievements during implementation. The final section comments with wider perspectives on the lessons learned.

The Context

Society and economy

Cambodia has a population of approximately 14.7 million. It had an estimated per capita Gross Domestic Product (GDP) of US$1,100 in 2014 (Cambodia, Ministry of Planning 2014, p.ii). With this level, Cambodia is classified by the United Nations as a Least Developed Country, but it achieved significant economic growth in the 2000s and early 2010s. The economy is dominated by agriculture, and 78.6 per cent of the 2013 population was classified as resident in rural areas. Phnom Penh, the capital, is the largest urban area. Cambodian integration into the ASEAN economic community has permitted enhanced regional flows of labour and capital.

In recent decades the government's development policy has moved through several phases. The emphasis since the early 1990s has been reconstruction "from a state of near total destruction" during the civil war associated with the Pol Pot regime (Cambodia, Ministry of Planning 2014, p.1). During the 1990s the priority was rebuilding the society, economy and infrastructure; and during the 2000s the government pursued planned development in a market framework. Aspirations for the 2010s and beyond include transition to an upper-middle-income country (Cambodia, Ministry of Planning 2014, p.4).

Administratively, the country is divided into 24 provinces. Siem Reap Province has a population of approximately 1.0 million (Cambodia, Ministry of Planning 2013), accounting for 6.7 per cent of the total national population. Within the province, Siem Reap town is the country's most important tourist hub, adjacent to Angkor Wat which generates considerable foreign exchange. Beyond the town, Siem Reap is a low-income province (Cambodia, Ministry of Planning 2014, p.8).

The education system and its shadow
Cambodia's education system was destroyed by the Pol Pot regime alongside most other social institutions, and thus was a major focus for reconstruction in the 1980s and particularly from the early 1990s (Ayres 2003; Chhinh & Dy 2009).

The three priorities named by the Ministry of Education, Youth and Sport (MoEYS) in its *Education Strategic Plan 2009-2013* were ensuring equitable access to education services; improving the quality and efficiency of education services; and institutional and personnel development for decentralisation (Cambodia, MoEYS 2010, p.2). These priorities were recalled in the sequel *Education Strategic Plan 2014-2018* (Cambodia, MoEYS 2014, p.1). Cambodia has a 6+3+3 structure of schooling, i.e. six years of primary followed by three years of lower secondary and three years of upper secondary schooling. Net enrolment rates in 2012/13 were said to be 97.0 per cent in primary, 37.8 per cent in lower secondary, and 18.1 per cent in upper secondary schooling (Cambodia, MoEYS 2014, p.2), though some alternative estimates were lower (Brehm & Edwards 2014, p.51).

During the 1990s and 2000s, private contributions to public schooling in Cambodia were high, in some years representing over half of total educational expenditures and consuming up to 20% of non-food household spending (Bray 1999; Bray & Bunly 2005; NGO Education Partnership 2007; UNDP 2014). Household expenditures cover many of the hidden costs of attending schools, including pencils, notebooks, uniforms, transportation, and school meals. Households that can afford it also pay for tutoring, often directly to the teachers who hold additional classes after the end of the official school day. These classes are commonly held in the same classrooms as the official classes (Dawson 2009; Brehm & Silova 2014; Brehm 2015). Tutorial centres as free-standing commercial enterprises do exist, especially in Phnom Penh and other urban areas (Brehm et al. 2012, p.16). However, tutoring by regular classroom teachers is much more common.

Many Cambodian teachers who have to support families on single salaries live near or below the poverty line (Benveniste et al. 2008, p.52; Engel 2011, p.15; Tandon & Fukao 2015, p.24). Low-paid teachers have a stronger incentive to drive up demand for private tutoring by limiting the depth and breadth of instruction during the official school day (c.f. Jayachandran 2014). Students have reported that those who do not receive private tutoring have significantly lower chances of scoring well on examinations (Brehm & Silova 2014, p.110). Thus, reliance on private tutoring may have consequences for both equity and quality in the mainstream school system.

Design of a Mixed-Methods Study

The project on which this chapter particularly reports was designed to focus on relationships between education policy and participation in private supplementary tutoring at the Grades 9 and 12 transition points. The project was especially interested in eight components of policy influences on private supplementary tutoring:

1. *Teachers' incomes*. Teachers' salaries have long been low (Geeves & Bredenberg 2005, p.12; Benveniste et al. 2008, p.52; Engel 2011, p.15). Dawson (2009, p.63) argued that the inadequacy of these salaries led to "forced corruption", as teachers had to rely on tutoring income in order to survive.
2. *Instructional time*. Many schools operate double shifts, with one group of students using classrooms in the mornings and another group using the classrooms in the afternoons. The single-shift schools may not take advantage of the possibility of afternoon classes, and commonly provide instruction only in the mornings. The shortness of the school day constrains the amount of instruction that can be delivered, thus increasing demand for extra lessons (Cambodia, MoEYS 2010, p.96; see also Bray 2008, p.48).
3. *Pedagogy*. The government advocates 'child friendly' teaching methods (Cambodia, MoEYS 2007). Some teachers consider these methods more time-consuming, making it difficult to cover the full curriculum.
4. *Class size*. In large classes, teachers commonly focus strongly on maintaining an orderly environment (Blatchford 2003; Blatchford

et al. 2007). Smaller classes permit greater attention to individual students. The fact that private tutorial classes are generally (though not always) smaller than regular classes makes the tutorial classes attractive to students.

5. *Curricular breadth*. The difficulties of the shorter school day are compounded by the breadth of the curriculum. Teachers are encouraged to promote 'whole-person' education, rather than simply academic learning (Cambodia, MoEYS 2004, p.4; 2010, p.26; Brehm et al. 2012, p.25). Many teachers find it impossible to cover the range of material using the prescribed pedagogical styles within the normative time-frame. This leaves much material to be consumed in after-school tutorials.

6. *School governance*. The government has devolved some responsibilities from the Ministry to the school level while retaining control over curriculum, assessment, and teachers' salaries (Cambodia, MoEYS 2010, p.17). Changes in the locus of control may shape teachers' opportunities and incentives to provide supplementary private tutoring.

7. *Examination structure*. The national examination has high stakes insofar as students must pass in order to gain entrance to university. Prior to a clampdown in 2014 (Ponniah 2014), passing rates exceeded 70% due to the fact that students could purchase answers and bribe the invigilators. Yet to be able to sit for these examinations, students had first to pass their school-based assessments in which teachers had considerable discretion. This discretion strengthened the teachers' ability to extract fees in exchange for tips on the examinations that they themselves set (Brehm et al. 2012, p.10).

8. *University admission rates*. Private tutoring can be used to increase individuals' success in gaining entrance into university. Changes in the percentages of students enrolling in university may influence participation in private tutoring, but the direction of this influence is unclear. On the one hand, if there is a general sense of increased opportunity, students may redouble their participation in private tutoring. On the other hand, if university admission seems 'easier', students may back away from the extra effort involved in private tutoring.

Data on these matters were secured through questionnaires and semi-structured interviews of students and teachers. The research was conducted in six schools in Siem Reap Province, selected through stratified sampling as indicated in Table 11.1. The HKU team set the broad criteria, and was given a list of potential schools from which to select. The TLC team then secured government approval and approached the schools. The final list resulted from negotiation between TLC and the schools. Three were high schools, i.e. having grades 7-12, while the other three were lower secondary schools with grades 7-9. Two of the lower secondary schools also had primary sections.

Table 11.1: Characteristics of Sampled Schools, Siem Reap Province, Cambodia

School	Type	Location	No. of Grade 9 students	No. of Grade 12 students	No. of teachers
1	High	Urban	327	291	93
2	High	Rural	224	246	95
3	High	Rural	122	135	48
4	Lower secondary	Urban	130	0	20
5	Lower secondary	Semi-urban	91	0	15
6	Lower secondary	Remote	60	0	10
Total			954	672	281

Table 11.2: Sample of Students and Teachers, Siem Reap Province, Cambodia

School	Grade 9 students sampled (questionnaire)		Grade 12 students sampled (questionnaire)		Grade 9 students interviewed	Grade 12 students interviewed	Teachers sampled (questionnaire)		Teachers interviewed
	No.	%	No.	%	No.	No.	No.	%	No.
1	214	65.4	270	92.8	4	4	16	17.2	2 (Grade 9) 2 (Grade 12)
2	166	74.1	218	88.6	4	4	23	24.2	2 (Grade 9) 2 (Grade 12)
3	106	86.9	124	91.9	4	4	13	27.1	2 (Grade 9) 2 (Grade 12)
4	80	61.5	--		8	-	8	40.0	4 (Grade 9)
5	42	46.2	--		8	-	8	53.3	4 (Grade 9)
6	54	90.0	--		8	-	4	40.0	4 (Grade 9)
Total	662	69.4	612	91.1	36	12	72	25.6	24

Within the schools, questionnaires were administered to students in Grades 9 and 12. A separate questionnaire and interview guide was devised for teachers (Table 11.2). The HKU team secured ethical approval from the relevant committee in HKU, and the TLC team carefully followed the requirements albeit meeting some cultural and contextual obstacles as explained below.

Implementing the Project

This section focuses on several dimensions. It begins with the motives for undertaking the research in a cross-national partnership. It then turns to procedures for ethical clearance, and reflects on the design and translation of the instruments. A further section focuses on the administration of the instruments.

Cross-national partnership
As indicated by other chapters in this book, the academic staff and students at HKU focusing on shadow education have many nationalities and explicit interest in comparative analysis. Cambodia was chosen as the location for this project in part because key individuals already had acquaintance with the country including previous research, and partly because it fitted aspirations to collect data in a setting that contrasted with Hong Kong, Mainland China and other locations.

Nevertheless, the Hong Kong researchers could not undertake research on their own. They had neither the linguistic competence nor the necessary connections to secure official approval and to gain entry to schools. They therefore needed a partner, and were glad to be introduced to TLC who in turn welcomed collaboration with HKU.

TLC's core mission is to listen to, engage with and advocate alongside communities in Cambodia as they define and act on their own solutions. TLC's Community Research and Consultancy Program (CRCP) conducts local research, monitoring and evaluation of development interventions in order to inform policy and good practices in sustainable development. TLC's work includes community-led school development, and the organisation actively engages in education policy discussions through NGO networks at provincial and national level. As such TLC has an active interest in issues relating to the right to education in Cambodia. Senior members of the TLC team had previous experience researching private tutoring and other education issues in Cambodia. Some data collectors on the team were recruited from other TLC community development programs. As such, although they may have lacked specific experience in research on education issues, their perspectives on the study were framed by their work at TLC.

The value of this partnership, bringing outsider and insider perspectives, will be evident in subsequent parts of this chapter. Throughout the whole project, the teams learned a great deal from each other. As noted, Cambodia was still in the process of developing its human capacity following the legacy of the Khmer Rouge regime, and the TLC team contained some members who had limited experience of research of this kind. By corollary, the HKU team included doctoral students who were developing their research skills and had much to learn from and about the context since they were visiting Cambodia for the first time. Yet even the experienced researchers also benefited from the insights generated in the cross-national collaboration.

Ethical clearance and related procedures
Other chapters in this book have referred to bureaucratic processes of ethical clearance which became widespread during the initial decades of the present century. As noted by McTaggart (2013), these processes were to a large extent driven by applied sciences rather than social sciences, and by contexts in North America and Western Europe rather than other parts of the world. HKU is rightly concerned with ethics. Nevertheless, elements of the standard procedures cannot fit Cambodia as easily as they can fit Hong Kong itself and the North American and Western European contexts from which they were imported. For example because Cambodia has high rates of illiteracy, requests to approve procedures explained in written documents may not be as valid as they would be elsewhere. Moreover, the legacy of Cambodia's political history has made many adults cautious about signing official papers. With such considerations in mind, the research team had to be sure to work within the HKU requirements but also to recognise limitations. Written documents were accompanied as far as possible by the spoken word.

In addition, TLC had its own requirements which again reflected the context. Cambodia has suffered from much child abuse, and TLC has a firm and far-reaching policy on the matter (TLC 2010). Before proceeding to the schools with TLC personnel, each member of the HKU team was required to sign a statement to recognise having read and been committed to comply with the TLC Child Protection Policy.

Design and translation
At the outset, the questionnaires and interview guides for both students and teachers were prepared in English and translated into Khmer by the

HKU team.[1] The principal objective was to identify the strength of policy levers which could be built into a quantified theoretical model. The instruments were then transmitted to Siem Reap, and were the focus of a training workshop with the TLC team.[2] The workshop focused first on the wording of the instruments in both English and Khmer, and then on ways in which the instruments would be administered.

One issue in the wording of instruments concerned the use of US dollars as well as Cambodian riels. It is common in Cambodia to cite prices in dollars, which circulate widely in urban areas. Reasons for working in dollars include that the unit is smaller,[3] and that the currency is less subject to inflation. However, use of both currencies led to confusion since the research team could not know what exchange rate had been used. Further confusion when asking about teachers' salaries arose because respondents could have been unclear whether various allowances were included.

Translation was also difficult in some cases, not only because of vocabulary but also because of concepts. Thus the question about class size was initially translated by the HKU team in terms of area (square metres) rather than number of students.

Administration of instruments

The HKU team much appreciated the systematic approach of the TLC team in the administration of instruments. The TLC personnel first explained the ethical procedures to the sampled schools, and sought help to obtain consent from parents. Negotiations were then undertaken to secure times for the surveys and interviews.

For the student surveys, in each classroom the data collectors took about five minutes to explain the study and procedures, identified students whose parents had not opted out in the passive-consent form, and

---

[1] Chad Lykins was at this stage the Principal Investigator of the HKU project. He designed the instruments which were then translated into Khmer by Suon Raksmey, a Master of Education (MEd) student.

[2] On the HKU side, members were Mark Bray and William Brehm. The TLC team was led by Tuot Mono and included Ngam Kimsorn and Seab Sophon, with several additional TLC staff members participating as data collectors. Subsequently Robin McNaughton played a lead role. Sen Se, Deputy Director, and Billy Gorter, Executive Director, provided additional guidance to the TLC team and knowledge of the local policy context.

[3] At the time of the workshop, the official exchange rate for one US dollar was 3,600 riels. Thus even small purchases had many zeros.

asked these students to sign the active-consent forms to indicate their own willingness. Then team members spent another five to 10 minutes explaining each question, answering further queries as the process moved along. In general, the student interviews were conducted immediately after the survey. The survey and interview of teachers followed a similar procedure, but of course did not require parental consent.

Sampled schools differed in the extent of cooperation and physical accessibility. School 1 was the most cooperative and accessible, partly because a former TLC staff taught there. The school was also close to the TLC office. As a result, when supplementary information was required the team could easily make follow-up visits. In contrast, collaboration with School 3, which was four hours by road from the TLC office, was more difficult. Due to miscommunications, the school was not ready for data collection when the TLC team arrived. The principal, who initially was off the premises, recognised the authorisation from the provincial education office but was reluctant to assist. After some discussion, he did assign a teacher to call the Grade 9 students for the survey but arrangements still did not work smoothly.

Elaborating, when the assigned teacher in School 3 called the Grade 9 students, they had already finished government lessons and the classrooms were occupied by students sitting monthly examinations or receiving private tutoring. As a result, the survey had to be conducted under trees with the students asked to sit on the ground. Many students were unwilling to stay for the survey, so when the TLC team commenced by asking for the parental consent form that had been distributed previously, some students decided to tick "I do not want my child to participate" (i.e. indicating that the forms had not actually been taken to their parents, and/or that they were answering on behalf of the parents). Then when the TLC team explained that the students themselves could decline to participate, many more did so. Eventually, only 13 out of 122 students in the class remained.

While these 13 students were completing the questionnaires, the HKU team talked with the teacher in charge with the help of an American volunteer teacher who spoke Khmer and was a good friend of the teacher. The teacher in charge was able to learn about the research agenda, and to see that it would not harm his school. The conversation increased understanding about teachers' tutoring practices in the school. It also helped to build trust, and improved the relationship between the research team and the teacher. The researchers felt that the group of 13 students was likely to comprise only the obedient and diligent students, and as such would have been biased. In order to achieve a representative sample, the researchers decided to abandon the data and the TLC team made arrangements for a return visit one month later. With help from the teacher, and now with much greater assistance from the principal who had perhaps understood from the teacher more about the research and its purpose, the Grade 9 survey was conducted again under more encouraging conditions. This time, 106 students completed the questionnaires.

For this repeat of the survey, the arrangements were very different. The principal and teacher had asked the students to come to school at 7.00 am, i.e. before the official commencement of their school day. This school operated double shifts, with Grades 10-12 in the morning and Grades 7-9 in the afternoon. The students were evidently willing to come at that time, and the school ensured that four classrooms were available for conduct of the survey. This experience has been presented in detail to exemplify unexpected circumstances but also to show ways in which obstacles can be overcome.

Other challenges, which again could have been ameliorated through improved testing of draft instruments, arose from translations and time management. Despite the effort devoted to translation, the questionnaires had long sentences in Khmer which were difficult for some students and even a few teachers to comprehend. A related challenge was that the participants' literacy levels were low compared to that of counterparts elsewhere who had responded to instruments of similar length (see Chapter 12). As a result, the surveys usually took 40-60 minutes instead of the 20-30 minutes anticipated. This made some schools uncomfortable since they were under pressure from higher authorities to use class time efficiently. This was especially the case in the later parts of data collection, since the Minister of Education had recently issued a policy directive on the use of class time (Robbins 2015).

A more important implication relates to data quality. Even when the survey duration exceeded 40 minutes, some participants seemed to need more time. The teams noticed that some students did not seek guidance when they had difficulty understanding the questionnaire. This matched remarks from some interviewed teachers that students were afraid to ask questions at school. Data collectors endeavoured to identify such students and offer help. However, data collectors administering surveys to 40-60 students under pressure to complete as soon as possible could not identify and address the queries of every participant. Under these circumstances, a few students just looked at and followed their neighbours' answers. When the HKU team found several pairs having the same answers for most questions, the team could discard one from each pair; but the situation seemed negatively to impact the reliability of the data.

Concerning the interviews, first there was a minor flaw in the recruitment of participants. The data collectors categorised students' consent forms into four groups, i.e. male students with or without tutoring, and female students with or without tutoring, with the intention of selecting one of each per grade (or two of each in lower secondary schools). However, some students whose names were drawn then decided not to participate and had to be replaced by volunteers. The final list of student interviewees had 31 females but only 17 males, and failed to keep the balance between students who received (39) or did not receive tutoring (9). Nevertheless, these balances did to some extent fit the overall picture identified by the quantitative data.

Another complexity arose from the fact that schools had limited infrastructure and supplementary tutoring occupied some classrooms. Most interviews were therefore conducted in common areas and under trees, and some interviews were disturbed by classmates making noise and playing around. When the interviewees were distracted, the interviewers found themselves disciplining the students in addition to asking questions. Since few interviewers had specific experience in such matters, issues that could have been explored further in the interviews were omitted.

In general, the teacher survey went more smoothly since the teachers understood the questions better and the survey could be administered in staff rooms or similar locations. However, the sample of teachers in the rural lower secondary school appeared biased by teacher absenteeism. In this school, which had required the team to travel for half a day, six teachers were absent and only three teachers and the teacher-librarian were present. These four may have been more committed than the others, and the sample may not have been sufficiently representative of teachers in rural schools.

One Project, Two Phases
An interactive model of two phases
The instruments were developed jointly by the TLC and HKU teams, benefiting from the experience of the HKU team in preparing and adapt-

ing instruments on shadow education (see Chapter 12). The instruments were refined through discussions and role plays. The division of the implementation into two phases enabled some issues picked up in Phase 1, which covered the first three schools, to be addressed in Phase 2 (Figure 11.1). The TLC team collected data from the Phase 1 schools independently, while the HKU team was involved in fieldwork for two of the three Phase 2 schools in order to monitor processes and gain deeper understanding of the context.

Figure 11.1: Flowchart of the Two-phase Project

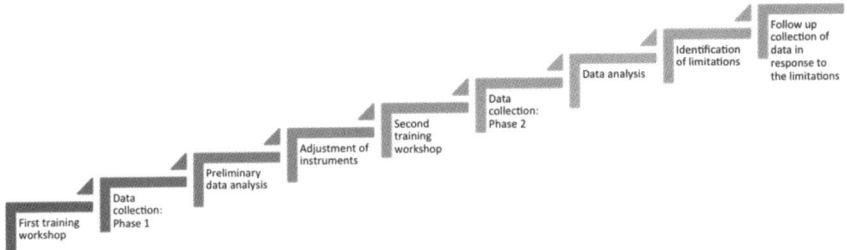

The TLC team inputted the data for analysis by the HKU team using the Statistical Package for the Social Sciences (SPSS); and the TLC team similarly prepared transcripts in English of the interviews which could be analysed by the HKU team using NVivo 10 software. Analysis of the quantitative data commenced with descriptive statistics and then moved to regressions to identify relationships between variables. Analysis of the qualitative data commenced with coding of interview responses according to categories and broad themes. An inductive approach to coding helped the research team to discover topics that were not part of the interview questions. For more elaborated analysis, classification sheets were created for each individual case through the software that later permitted comparison and contrast between different categories of teachers and students.

These procedures strengthened data analysis, and also exposed some inconsistencies in the data collection methods. The HKU and TLC teams discussed preliminary findings while noting potential shortcomings, and then made follow-up visits to three schools to confirm pictures and collect 'remedial' information. These three schools were ones in which the HKU team had not previously been involved in data collection, and the discussions greatly assisted understanding by both HKU and TLC teams.

This strategy reflected the approach underlying the model for data analysis presented by Miles and Huberman (Figure 11.2). As expressed by those authors (1994, p.12), data collection and analysis is an interactive, cyclical process: "The researcher steadily moves among these four 'nodes' during data collection and then shuttles among reduction, display, and conclusion drawing/verification for the remainder of the study". The model has been widely adopted for qualitative research, which is distinguished by the "merging of analysis and interpretation and often by the merging of data collection with data analysis" (Cohen et al. 2011, p.537). Quantitative research is often regarded as a linear process, but in a mixed-methods study having two phases the model can be equally applied to the quantitative component.

Figure 11.2: An Interactive Model of Data Analysis Components

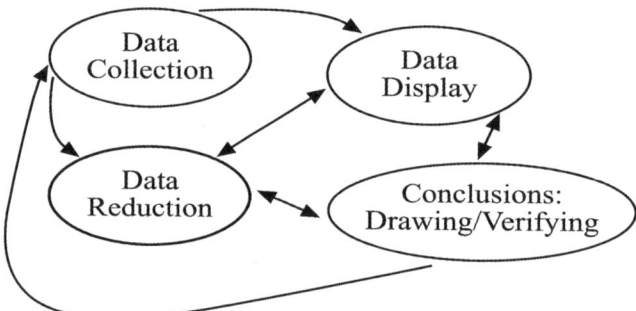

Source: Miles & Huberman 1994, p.12.

Phase 1 started with data collection, and was followed by preliminary data analysis. Then Phase 2 began with modification of instruments and more training on interview skills, and moved to another round of data collection. Following Phase 2, data from the whole study were analysed by means of data reduction and display. The return visits to the three schools after preliminary conclusions had been drawn could perhaps be called a third round of data collection albeit a restricted one. In two schools the visits focused on extended interviews with vice principals plus, in one of these schools, more superficial discussions with students. In the third school the chief focus was a group interview with four teachers.

Modification of instruments and implications for analysis
The initial design omitted some important information from the student survey. One key question was about providers of tutoring, in particular to learn about the roles of the students' own teachers and appropriate policy levers that might be applied. The item on providers was added to the questionnaire for Phase 2.

Overall, 89.8 per cent of sampled Grade 12 students and 74.7 per cent of sampled Grade 9 students stated that they received tutoring. Since the question about providers was only added in Phase 2, data on this item were missing for the sampled 506 students in Schools 2, 4 and 5 but available for the others. Among the 768 students who responded to this question, 600 (78.3%) stated that they were receiving tutoring. As shown in Table 11.3, 47.5 per cent of these indicated that they were tutored by their own teachers, while 33.7 per cent reported receiving tutoring from other teachers in their schools. These findings cannot be generalised to the whole population, but at least provide some evidence for the widespread practice of teachers tutoring their own students or other students from their schools.

Table 11.3: Providers of Private Tutoring

	No.	%
My own teacher	285	47.5
Another teacher in my school	202	33.7
A teacher from a different school	6	1.0
A university student or other self-employed person	1	0.2
A company	0	0

Changes were also made in the interview guide, since initially some questions were not articulated in a way that could fully serve the research objectives. For instance, the original interview guide asked students to report on their participation in tutoring as follows:

Do you receive normal private tutoring (*rien kuo*)?
- For what subjects?
- How much time do you spend in normal private tutoring for each subject?
- If the government school day (*rien rot*) was longer, would you still take normal private tutoring?

Since the research design could not link the interviewees to their anonymous survey responses, the information gathered from these questions was not complete for understanding the participation in tutoring and the motives of the interviewees who received tutoring. Furthermore, no items explored why some students in the same school did not receive tutoring. The following modifications were therefore made for the second round of interviews:

Do you receive normal private tutoring (*rien kuo*)?

If the student receives:
- For what subjects? When and Where? Who are the tutors? Who are your classmates in the tutoring class, e.g. own classmates at school or from other schools?
- How much time do you spend in normal private tutoring for each subject?
- Why do you attend the extra classes?
- Why do you think teachers provide tutoring? Do you feel pressed to attend extra lessons by your own teacher? If so, in what ways?
- If the government school day (*rien rot*) was longer, would you still take normal private tutoring?

If the student does not receive:
- Why do you not receive tutoring? Why do you think teachers provide tutoring?
- Do your teachers treat you differently from classmates who attend the teachers' tutoring classes?
- Does the fact that you are not attending extra classes by your own teachers affect your examination performance? If so, how?
- Have you ever been pressed to take tutoring? If so, by whom?

The initial version of the teacher interview guide also had limitations. Because it focused on the eight policy components in the proposed theoretical framework, it only asked about teachers' views on each component in relation to the tutoring practice. However, teachers may provide tutoring for other reasons, and other important variables might not have been included in the proposed framework. More importantly, the eight components would not have had equal influence on teachers' decisions to provide tutoring. Therefore, before moving to the eight components in the researchers' hypothesis, during Phase 2 the teachers were asked why they did or did not provide tutoring so that the answers came from the teachers rather than having been assumed in advance by the interviewers. Also, in Phase 2 items were added on how and why teachers provided tutoring:

Do you teach extra classes?
- If yes, to how many students?
- Where?
- Why do you provide normal private tutoring?
- When and how much time do you spend teaching normal private tutoring per day? (existing item in the first version)

Practices that could be viewed as forms of corruption were a key issue related to tutoring, but since the topic was sensitive the first version of the interview guide omitted questions about it. In order to obtain such data in a skilful manner, the following items were added with guidance to interviewers for Phase 2:

- *Enrolments*: How do you recruit students to your tutoring classes? Are they all your own students? If some are not, who are they? [Possible answer might be: students/parents request. Then the interviewer can ask: Do you also advise?]
- *Relationships*: How do you address the gap between the students who receive tutoring and who do not in your formal class? [Do you treat the tutees differently? How?] Is your relationship with the students who attend your extra classes different from those who do not?

The added items helped to explore issues of corruption related to school governance and teacher favouritism. Most teachers stated that they treated both tutored and non-tutored students equally, but four of the 24 teachers noted that relationships between teachers and students were better in private tutoring classes. The teachers indicated that they had more interaction with the students, both because the tutoring classes were smaller and because the students who attended the tutoring classes were likely to be more active. This raised a question for the researchers whether to pay more attention to the responses of the four teachers or to the 20. Because of the sensitivity of the matter, teachers may have responded with their 'outer voice' (guarded public voice) rather than their 'inner voice' (Seidman 1998, p.63) to protect their schools and themselves. The researchers recognised the responses of the 20 teachers while also valuing the responses of the four teachers who may have been providing a more complete picture.

Similarly, when the students were asked during interviews whether teachers treated students receiving and not receiving tutoring differently, some hesitated and asked whether their teachers would know their answers. The interviewers stressed the confidentiality of the data but still felt that some students answered with an 'outer voice'. Ultimately, seven of the 48 students indicated cases of discrimination against students without tutoring, which seemed to be a valuable 'inner voice'. The interviewers also sought answers to sensitive questions by asking more than once but with different phrasing and sometimes at different stages of the interview, in the process enhancing the reliability of the data and in some cases exploring the 'inner voice'.

Granting higher marks to tutored students was another sub-theme that emerged when four teachers commented about relationships and treatment of different students in class (which was also mentioned by some students). One teacher said:

> Usually the students who attend the private tutoring are given high scores even if their [real] score is not good. But the students who don't study in the private tutoring don't get the scores. So the student can file a complaint against the teachers, and this is a disadvantage for the teachers.

Because the teachers' involvement in tutoring could be considered problematic, teachers may instinctively protect themselves with the 'outer voice' by hiding some information. The interview guide had a question on instructional time as follows: "Do you ever use normal private tutoring (*rien kuo*) to finish things that you could not finish during government school (*rien rot*)?" Teachers commonly answered "No", and the interviewers moved to the next question. To strengthen understanding of the reliability of the answers, in Phase 2 a follow-up question was added: "If not, what do you teach in the tutoring class?" The responses indicated that many teachers saw private tutoring as a place for doing exercises. Ten teachers reported that usually they did exercises in tutoring class and explained general lessons in government class.

A new question that emerged during the data collection was about free tutoring for disadvantaged students. To learn more, two questions were added in Phase 2 on the cost of tutoring: "How do you charge?", and "Do you charge differently according to their situations such as family financial status?"

Interviewers as Instruments

In the above commentary, the authors recognise that the qualitative researcher is "a central figure who influences, if not actively constructs, the collection, selection and interpretation of data" (Finlay 2002, p.212). In other words, the data collectors and analysts in both HKU and TLC teams were all instruments. Of course the point is also to some extent valid in quantitative research, though perhaps to a lesser extent. To avoid self-indulgence, the researchers in this project were constantly reflexive about their own cultures and research practices, and about the effects on the course of the design, collection and interpretation of data (see also Hardy et al. 2001; Finlay 2002).

For Phase 2 the interviewers were reminded to ask follow-up questions, especially digging deeper on the phenomenon of teachers providing tutoring and its implications. The modifications were made not only because the initial instruments needed improvement, but also because the interviewers were not experienced researchers on the topic and were insiders who may have taken tutoring by teachers for granted.

In turn, this raises questions about the roles of insiders and outsiders. In most circumstances, ideally project designers should also collect data since they know what they are seeking; and rigour can be enhanced when researchers are insiders who share the respondents' language and culture. However, the designers of this project were outsiders who did not speak the local language and had limited knowledge of the local culture. Since the data collectors were all Cambodians and native speakers of Khmer, in this regard they were more suitable as interviewers than the designers. Yet because they had grown up in the society where tutoring by teachers was widespread and corruption in the public system was common, they may have been blind to some aspects of the situation. The training workshops enabled both the HKU and TLC teams to reflexively think about the impact of their own experience, thinking and pre-understandings on the research processes (Hardy et al. 2001; Alvesson & Skoldberg, 2009). For the HKU team, the sharing from the TLC team on their personal experiences and knowledge about schooling and tutoring facilitated understanding of the Cambodian contextual and cultural traits and real-life circumstances of various stakeholders. In turn, data collectors became more aware and critical about issues related to teachers providing tutoring.

Analysis of the Phase 1 interview transcripts showed that some interviewers did not comprehend well the background and objectives of the project. This was understandable, since TLC to some extent viewed the project as a form of capacity development and brought in some colleagues who had not been involved at the outset. Many interviewers followed the interview guide mechanically and literally rather than thinking actively about the implications of interviewees' responses, and few interviewers asked probing questions to seek details, elaboration and clarification. For example:

> *Interviewer*: This is important information that you can share something. What do you think about student-centred teaching compared to the old method we call teacher-centred?
>
> *Teacher*: We can accept the student-centred around 80 per cent. Students are active to learn with the student-centred method. Students can work in their groups. They are very active, and have a lot of work to do during their session.

The interviewer moved immediately to the next question, but the research aimed to explore the influence of pedagogy on tutoring. It might have been preferable for the interviewer then to have asked how the pattern was related to the participation in tutoring. For example, the interviewer might have asked: "Is tutoring student-centred or teacher-centred? If the pedagogy is good, why do some students receive tutoring?" It might have been useful to have increased the training on these matters during the first workshop. In any case, HKU team did expand awareness during the training session prior to Phase 2, and the interviewers matured in their skills as they interviewed more people.

Close examination of interview transcripts and flow in NVivo identified some other areas that indicated weaknesses in interviewers' research skills, such as asking leading questions (pointing interviewees' answers to a certain direction) and two-in-one questions (asking about two different matters in one question). Fortunately, others in the interview team had stronger skills, and indeed some appropriately asked the same question twice in different contexts to crosscheck accuracy of the initial reports. The latter approach generated particularly interesting findings with teacher data on the sensitive topic of splitting the national curriculum content between government classes and tutoring.

The idea of researchers as instruments also implies that researchers bring their own identities, personalities and biases into research process. This project included multiple interviewers with different interviewing styles and knowledge of other research methods. When research is conducted through cross-national partnerships, project designers commonly have limited information about possible personal biases of interviewers. In this case the HKU team received the quantitative and qualitative data and embarked on analysis with general knowledge of the context and with long experience of research on shadow education in other settings. They found that they needed more contextual information on each school and extensive discussion with the TLC team. This was achieved in the follow-up after Phase 2, with the sharing of preliminary findings and the visits to the three schools for verification and deepening of insights.

Conclusions

Research into supplementary tutoring in Cambodia has great value not only for the education authorities and families in that country but also more widely. Patterns of provision provide an instructive contrast to those in Hong Kong, for example, in particular because teachers are the main providers and commonly provide tutoring to their own students in their own classrooms. This provides a significant model for conceptual analysis. Research is also desirable for practical reasons. The Cambodian government has long been aware of the issues, and research can identify levers for policy making.

The Siem Reap project which is the principal focus of this chapter complements and updates previous research in Cambodia, some of which has used quantitative or mixed methods (e.g. Bray & Bunly 2005; UNDP 2014), and some of which has used qualitative methods (e.g. Brehm 2015). Focusing on just six schools, the research cannot claim statistical representation even for Siem Reap Province let alone for the whole country. Nevertheless, the research has provided illustrative findings from urban, semi-urban and rural settings, and the quantitative and qualitative data have complemented each other in meaningful ways.

Research collaboration between universities and NGOs has increased in recent years across the globe (see e.g. Aniekwe et al. 2012), and this project was an example of partnership operating on a cross-national basis. The outsiders from HKU were able to raise issues, provide a more critical understanding of shadow education in other national contexts, and bring elements of research expertise. At the same time the insiders brought local knowledge and linguistic competence without which the research would have been impossible. Relationships with some schools were better than with others, but even the problematic cases were managed effectively – in one case through a return visit after discarding a set of survey data from Grade 9.

While many factors favour research collaboration, the chapter has highlighted challenges. Outsiders may not always have sufficient understanding of local cultures and administrative practices at the school level for design of instruments and implementation procedures, and insiders may not always grasp the nuances which the outsiders have in mind but do not fully articulate. This particular project was funded by the outsiders and involved a contractual relationship in which the insiders were respectful of the expressed intentions and designs of the outsiders. If the project had been reversed, e.g. with initiation by the TLC team and with HKU being brought in just for advice and technical expertise, the balances and perhaps the details of design would have been different. Fortunately, the work was indeed perceived as a partnership from both sides, and the atmosphere of mutual respect and collaboration permitted significant learning and capacity development for both teams.

On one specific, because the project was funded from Hong Kong and managed through HKU, it had to follow the ethical procedures required by that university. These were not all appropriate to the Cambodian context, in which high levels of adult illiteracy prevail. This is another domain for consideration in cross-cultural analyses which will be addressed in the final chapter of the present book. The TLC team was able to handle the matter by supplementing the written requirements with spoken notifications in a way that was appreciated by the HKU team.

The partnership was also beneficial in permitting the research to reach different audiences. The HKU team, operating as a group of academics, was primarily concerned with conceptualisation and contribution to the international literature on private supplementary tutoring. The TLC team, by contrast, aimed to serve the local society and contribute to national development. The project design permitted both types of audience to be served. This chapter is itself an example of the work reaching an international audience through the medium of English. In parallel, TLC was committed to feed the research findings into the NGO and government channels through Khmer as well as English so that they could be useful to the Cambodian society.

Finally, the research indeed built on existing literature with insights into policy levers for addressing private supplementary tutoring. The research cannot lead to a mathematical model demonstrating the impact of pulling one lever by a certain amount and comparing it with the impact of pulling another lever by a comparable amount. This is chiefly because the variables are interrelated in complex ways, and partly because efforts to shape human behaviour can rarely lead to precise outcomes. Nevertheless, the research did explore some policy variables. It recorded teachers' views on the pressure to secure income from tutoring in the context of low salaries and, by implication, the extent to which they would be less inclined to offer tutoring if salaries were higher. It also shed light on the implications of curriculum content and examination structure compared with available hours of instructional time. The research noted the backwash of tutoring on regular classes, providing insights not only for Cambodia but also internationally; and the comparisons of schools showed the significance of school cultures and policies as well as national ones.

Acknowledgements: The research reported in this chapter was funded by the General Research Fund (GRF) of the Hong Kong Research Grants Council (RGC), project 747113H. The authors thank Robin McNaughton, Sen Se and Billy Gorter at TLC and William Brehm at HKU for comments on a draft.

References

Alvesson, Mats & Skoldberg, Kaj (2009): *Reflexive Methodology: New Vistas for Qualitative Research*. 2nd edition. London: Sage.

Aniekwe, Chika C.; Hayman, Rachel & Mdee, Anna (2012): *Academic- NGO Collaboration in International Development Research: A Reflection on the Issues*. London: Development Studies Association. www.intrac.org/data/files/resources/750/Academic-NGO-Collaboration-in-International-Development_September-2012.pdf

Ayres, David (2003): *Anatomy of a Crisis: Education, Development, and the State in Cambodia, 1953-1998*. Chiang Mai: Silkworm Books.

Beneviste, Luis; Marshall, Jeffery & Araujo, M. Caridad (2008): *Teaching in Cambodia*. Washington DC: Human Development Sector, East Asia and Pacific Region, The World Bank.

Blatchford, Peter (2003): 'A Systematic Observational Study of Teachers' and Pupils' Behaviour in Large and Small Classes'. *Learning and Instruction*, Vol.13, No.6, pp.569-595.

Blatchford, Peter; Russell, Anthony; Bassett, Paul; Brown, Penelope & Martin, Clare (2007): 'The Effect of Class Size on the Teaching of Pupils aged 7-11 Years'. *School Effectiveness and School Improvement: An International Journal of Research, Policy and Practice*, Vol.18, No.2, pp.147-172.

Bray, Mark (1996): *Counting the Full Cost: Household and Community Financing of Education in East Asia*. Washington DC: The World Bank in collaboration with UNICEF.

Bray, Mark (1999): *The Private Costs of Public Schooling: Household and Community Financing of Primary Education in Cambodia*. Paris: UNESCO International Institute for Educational Planning (IIEP) in collaboration with UNICEF.

Bray, Mark (2008): *Double-Shift Schooling: Design and Operation for School Effectiveness*. 3rd edition. Paris: UNESCO International Institute for Educational Planning (IIEP).

Bray, Mark & Bunly, Seng (2005): *Balancing the Books: Household Financing of Basic Education in Cambodia*. Hong Kong: Comparative Education Research Centre, The University of Hong Kong and Washington DC: The World Bank.

Brehm, William C. (2015): *Enacting Educational Spaces: A Landscape Portrait of Privatization in Cambodia*. PhD thesis, The University of Hong Kong.

Brehm, William C. & Edwards, D. Brent (2014): 'The Many Spaces of Learning: Private Tutoring and Education for All'. *Norrag News*, Vol.50, pp.49-51. http://www.norrag.org/de/publications/norrag-news/online-version/the-global-politics-of-teaching-and-learning-the-real-story-of-educational-cultures-and-contexts-june-2014/detail/the-many-spaces-of-learning-private-tutoring-and-post-2015-education-for-all.html

Brehm, William C. & Silova, Iveta (2014): 'Hidden Privatization of Public Education in Cambodia: Equity Implications of Private Tutoring'. *Journal of Educational Research Online*, Vol.6, No.1, pp.94-116.

Brehm, William C.; Silova, Iveta & Tuot, Mono (2012): *The Public-Private Education System in Cambodia: The Impact and Implications of Complementary Tutoring*. Budapest: Education Support Program, Open Society Foundations.

Cambodia, Ministry of Planning (2013): *Economic Census of Cambodia 2011: Provincial Report – 17 Siem Reap Province*. Phnom Penh: National Institute of Statistics, Ministry of Planning. http://www.stat.go.jp/info/meetings/cambodia/pdf/ec_pr17.pdf

Cambodia, Ministry of Planning (2014): *National Strategic Development Plan 2014-2018*. Phnom Penh: Ministry of Planning.

Cambodia, MoEYS (2004): *Policy for Curriculum Development 2005-2009*. Phnom Penh: Ministry of Education, Youth & Sport.

Cambodia, MoEYS (2007): *Child Friendly Schools Policy*. Phnom Penh: Ministry of Education, Youth & Sport. http://www.moeys.gov.kh/en/policies-and-strategies/child-friendly-school-policy.html#.VSIQpIeIp9A

Cambodia, MoEYS (2010): *Education Strategic Plan 2009-2013*. Phnom Penh: Ministry of Education, Youth & Sport. http://planipolis.iiep.unesco.org/upload/Cambodia/Cambodia_Education_Strategic_Plan_2009-2013.pdf

Cambodia, MoEYS (2014): *Education Strategic Plan 2014-2018*. Phnom Penh: Ministry of Education, Youth & Sport. http://planipolis.iiep.unesco.org/upload/Cambodia/Cambodia_Education_Strategic_Plan_2014-2018.pdf

Chhinh, Sitha & Dy, Sideth S. (2009): 'Education Reform Context and Process in Cambodia', in Hirosato, Yasushi & Kitamura, Yuto (eds.), *The Political Economy of Educational Reforms and Capacity Development in Southeast Asia: Cases of Cambodia, Laos and Vietnam*. Dordrecht: Springer, pp.113-129.

Cohen, Louis, Manion, Lawrence & Morrison, Keith (2011): *'Research Methods in Education'*. 7th edition. Abingdon, Oxon; New York: Routledge.

Dawson, Walter (2009): 'The Tricks of the Teacher: Shadow Education and Corruption in Cambodia', in Heyneman, Stephen P. (ed.), *Buying Your Way into Heaven: Education and Corruption in International Perspective*. Rotterdam: Sense, pp.51-74.

Dawson, Walter (2010): 'Private Tutoring and Mass Schooling in East Asia: Reflections of Inequality in Japan, South Korea, and Cambodia'. *Asia Pacific Education Review*, Vol.11, No.1, pp.14-24.

Engel, Jakob (2011): *Rebuilding Basic Education in Cambodia: Establishing a More Effective Development Partnership*. London: Overseas Development Institute.

Finlay, Linda (2002): 'Negotiating the Swamp: The Opportunity and Challenge of Reflexivity in Research Practice'. *Qualitative Research*, Vol.2, No.2, pp.209-230.

Geeves, Richard & Bredenberg, Kurt (2005): *Contract Teachers in Cambodia*. Paris: UNESCO International Institute for Educational Planning (IIEP).

Hardy, Cynthia; Phillips, Nelson & Clegg, Stewart (2001): 'Reflexivity in Organization and Management Theory: A Study of the Production of the Research 'Subject''. *Human Relations*, Vol.54, No.4, pp.531-560.

Jayachandran, Seema (2014): 'Incentives to Teach Badly: After-school Tutoring in Developing Countries'. *Journal of Development Economics*, Vol.108, May, pp. 190-205.

McTaggart, Robin (2013): 'Evolving Ethics in Educational Research', in Reid, Alan D.; Hart, E. Paul & Peters, Michael A. (eds.), *A Companion to Research in Education*. Dordrecht: Springer, pp.457-469.

Miles, Matthew & Huberman, Michael A. (1994): *'Qualitative data analysis: An expanded source book'*. 2nd edition. Thousand Oakes, CA: Sage.

NGO Education Partnership (2007): *The Impact of Informal School Fees on Family Expenditure*. Phnom Penh: NGO Education Partnership.

Ponniah, Kevin (2014). 'Cambodia Crackdown on Corruption in Schools Scores Low with Exam Cheats'. *The Guardian*, 2 September. http://www.theguardian.com/global-development/2014/sep/02/cambodia-corruption-crackdown-exam-cheats

Robbins, Jill (2015): 'New Minister Cleans up Cambodia's Education System'. *Voice of America*, 30 January. http://learningenglish.voanews.com/content/cambodia-education-system-cleanup/2599977.html

Seidman, Irving (1998): *Interviewing as Qualitative Research: A Guide for Researchers in Education and the Social Sciences*. 2nd edition. New York: Teachers College Press.

Tandon, Prateek & Fukao, Tsuyoshi (2015): *Educating the Next Generation: Improving Teacher Quality in Cambodia*. Directions in Development, Washington DC:

The World Bank.
TLC (2010): *Child Protection Policy*. Siem Reap: This Life Cambodia. http://www.thislifecambodia.org/wp-content/uploads/2011/10/TLC_2013_ChildProtectionPolicyEnglish.pdf
UNDP (2014): *Curbing Private Tutoring and Informal Fees in Cambodia's Basic Education*. Phnom Penh: United Nations Development Programme (UNDP).

Learning and Comparing

12

How a Research Instrument Changed in Different Settings: Methodological Lessons from Adaptation and Adjustment

Junyan LIU

Introduction

Chapter 8 of this book has described a study of shadow education in Hong Kong, including the instruments used. Other chapters, namely those on Malaysia (Chapter 2), Iran (Chapter 7), India (Chapter 9), and Jamaica (Chapter 10) have indicated ways in which the questionnaire for students was adapted for use in those countries. The questionnaire has also been adapted for use in Chongqing, China (Zhang 2013) and Dubai (Naismith 2014). The present chapter considers the nature of the adaptations and the lessons that can be drawn from them.

Categories in the Hong Kong Questionnaire and its Adaptations

The Hong Kong student questionnaire (Appendix 7.1) had three preliminary (unnumbered) questions and then 29 numbered questions with 114 items. It was used to survey students in Grades 9 and 12. The questions may be grouped into nine areas:

- five questions to collect demographic information including students' genders, ages and nationalities;

Bray, Mark; Kwo, Ora & Jokić, Boris (eds.) (2015): *Researching Private Supplementary Tutoring: Methodological Lessons from Diverse Cultures*. Hong Kong: Comparative Education Research Centre (CERC), The University of Hong Kong, and Dordrecht: Springer. © CERC

- seven questions asking students whether they received private tutoring and, if so, the motivations, forms, intensities and durations;
- three questions about the students' perceptions of the effectiveness of private tutoring;
- one question about comparisons of teachers and tutors along nine dimensions;
- four questions about costs;
- nine questions about family socioeconomic status (SES);
- one question about students' self-assessed academic achievement compared to their peers;
- one question about family members who helped students with study; and
- one question about students' part-time jobs.

Table 12.1 compares the Hong Kong questionnaire and the adaptations in Jamaica, Malaysia, Chongqing, Iran, Dubai and India. The table shows some common interests among researchers in the different societies. The first is the prevalence and scope of private tutoring, which is a prerequisite for further study of the phenomenon. The questions aimed to identify the percentages of students receiving private tutoring, the subjects, durations, etc..

A second common theme was the perceived effectiveness of private tutoring. The researchers were interested not only in the perceived impact of private tutoring on academic performance, but also on students' confidence in school performance and on learning strategies.

A third common theme was the cost of tutoring. Researchers needed such information to examine social inequalities and to assess the extent to which the costs were a financial burden for families. In addition, some researchers wished to know about opportunity costs, i.e. the sacrifice of time for leisure and other activities.

A fourth common theme was family SES. Again this can be linked to issues of equity. Parents are usually the chief decision-makers on whether to seek private tutoring, so indicators on their educational levels and other variables are important.

Finally, students' academic achievement levels are also important. Studies that aim to identify correlations between tutoring and students' academic achievement have to collect such data.

Table 12.1: Summary of Versions Derived from the Hong Kong Questionnaire

Hong Kong	Jamaica	Malaysia	Chongqing	Iran	Dubai	India
• General information (5 question)	• Keep 2 questions the same • Delete 3 questions • Add 4 questions	• Keep 3 questions the same • Modify 2 questions	• Keep 1 question the same • Delete 4 questions • Add 3 questions	• Keep 2 questions the same • Delete 3 questions • Add 2 questions	• Keep 2 questions the same • Modify 2 questions • Delete 1 question • Add 1 question	• Keep 3 questions the same • Delete other 2 questions
• Prevalence and scope of private tutoring (7 questions)	• Modify 5 questions • Delete 2 questions • Add 2 questions	• Keep 5 questions the same • Modify 2 questions	• Keep 1 question the same • Modify 5 questions • Delete 1 question • Add 5 questions	• Keep 4 questions the same • Modify 2 questions • Delete 1 question	• Keep 2 questions the same • Modify 4 questions • Delete 1 question • Add 6 questions	• Keep 4 questions the same • Modify 2 questions • Delete 1 question
• Perceived Effectiveness of private tutoring (3 questions)	• Modify 1 question • Delete 2 questions • Add 1 question	• Keep 3 questions the same	• Delete the 3 questions • Add 1 question	• Keep 2 questions the same • Modify 1 question	• Modify 2 questions • Delete 1 question	• Keep 2 questions the same • Modify 1 question
• Comparison between teachers and tutors (1 question)	• Modify this question	• Keep the question the same	• Delete this question	• Keep the question the same	• Keep the question the same	• Keep the question the same

Cost of private tutoring (4 questions)	• Keep 1 question the same • Modify 1 question • Delete 2 questions	• Keep 4 questions the same	• Modify 2 questions • Delete 2 questions • Add 1 question	• Keep 4 questions the same	• Keep 4 questions the same	• Keep 3 questions the same • Modify 1 question
Socioeconomic status (9 questions)	• Keep 1 question the same • Modify 3 questions • Delete 5 questions • Add 4 questions	• Keep 8 questions the same • Modify 1 question	• Keep 1 question the same • Modify 2 questions • Delete 6 questions	• Keep 6 question the same • Modify 3 questions	• Keep 1 question the same • Modify 4 questions • Delete 4 questions • Add 1 question	• Keep 6 questions the same • Delete 2 questions • Modify 1 question
Student's academic level (1 question)	• Modify this question	• Keep question the same	• Modify this question	• Keep question the same	• Modify this question	• Modify this question
Help with study (1 question)	• Delete this question	• Keep question the same	• Keep question the same	• Keep question the same	• Keep question the same • Add 2 questions	• Keep question the same
Student's part-time job (1 question)	• Delete this question	• Keep question the same	• Delete this question	• Keep question the same	• Delete this question	• Delete this question

How the Hong Kong Questionnaire was Adapted

The Hong Kong questionnaire was designed specifically for use in that territory according to the research interests of the team. Some questions would not be relevant elsewhere, and the instrument could not cover all possible issues related to private tutoring. Researchers designing their own instruments with reference to the Hong Kong questionnaire would have to make adaptations. As noted in the wider literature (e.g. Harkness 2008, 2010), adaptations may be made to the content, format, response options, and/or visual presentation of any part of a questionnaire. The following sections address some of these themes.

Adaptations for socio-cultural contexts
For Malaysia, Iran, Dubai and India, the questionnaire had to be translated into local languages. When translation is undertaken, some adjustment of concepts is usually needed – or may happen inadvertently. Yet adjustments may also be needed even when the questionnaire is retained in the original languages (in this case English and Chinese). For example, although private tutoring is common vocabulary in Hong Kong, in Jamaica it is called extra lessons. Likewise, in Hong Kong *buxi* (補習) is the dominant term whereas in Mainland China *kewai fudao* (课外辅导) is more common.

Another example of necessary adaptation from the Hong Kong context concerns the phenomenon of star tutors known as 'Tutorial Kings and Queens'. The pair of questions in the Hong Kong questionnaire may be not relevant in other settings, and the adapted versions in Chongqing, Dubai, Iran and Jamaica just deleted them.

Education in a particular socio-cultural context may also have special characteristics which researchers want to incorporate into study. For example, in Mainland China, the household registration (*hukou*) status is commonly correlated with students' education opportunity and demand for private tutoring. Urban *hukou* students usually have more educational opportunities and can enjoy better resources than rural *hukou* students, and several studies have found that urban *hukou* students are more likely than rural *hukou* students to receive private tutoring (e.g. Chu 2009; Zhang 2011). Zhang (2013) added a question about students' *hukou* status in the Chongqing questionnaire, and then included the *hukou* status as a variable in her analysis. In Malaysia, students from poor families may receive vouchers from the government for private tutoring. Kenayathulla (Chapter 2) included this issue in her research, asking students whether their families received such vouchers. In Iran, senior secondary students may be separated into different fields for arts or sciences, and Madandar Arani (Chapter 7) added one question about the field of study.

Further, since private tutoring in different socio-cultural contexts may have different features, questionnaires must be prepared with these features in mind. One example concerns the possibility that teachers also work as tutors. In Hong Kong, this is uncommon: the public recognises that teachers would encounter a conflict of interest if they privately tutored their own students; and since teachers are well paid, the profession would frown on them undertaking additional remunerated employment (Bray & Kwo 2014, p.9). Thus in Hong Kong teachers and tutors are separate categories, and it was meaningful for the Hong Kong questionnaire to include a comparison of teachers and tutors. However, Kenayathulla (Chapter 2) noted that Malaysian teachers are permitted to offer tutoring even to their existing students. This required adjustment to the comparison of teachers and tutors, since the roles overlapped.

The issue also arose for Zhang (2013) in Chongqing. Teachers there are explicitly forbidden to provide tutoring to their own students, but the rules are not always enforced. Zhang therefore adapted the questionnaire to ask students about the identities of the people from whom they received tutoring. The options included the students' own teachers in school, other teachers from their schools, teachers from other schools, and other categories of tutors. Then Zhang asked students to compare the effectiveness of tutoring provided by each category according to their experience.

Adaptations to meet specific research interests
A second reason for researchers to adjust the Hong Kong questionnaire was to match their specific research interests. For example Stewart (2013) aimed to find out how, if at all, private tutoring might improve the educational outcomes of secondary students in Jamaica, and planned to test the hypothesis that the practice of critical-inclusive pedagogy in private tutoring was related to academic achievement. When adapting the Hong Kong questionnaire, therefore, she added a question with 12 items about critical-inclusive pedagogical performance in private tutoring.

On a different dimension, Zhang (2013) was particularly interested in the study burden for Grade 9 students in Chongqing. She therefore designed two questions to collect data this matter. And the Dubai study had a specific comparison of the help from schools and the help from tutors. Asking about the support that students could gain from schools and individual class teachers, the Dubai questionnaire added two questions with the options: does not provide any support; free after-school classes; paid after-school classes; free remedial classes during schooling hours; and paid remedial classes during schooling hours.

Adaptations to fit the target respondents
The next theme concerns adaptations to fit the maturity levels of respondents. As noted, the Hong Kong questionnaire was designed for students in Grades 9 and 12. Researchers using the questionnaires for younger students would have to consider both language competence and the likelihood of younger students knowing the answers. Further, the maturity of Hong Kong students in Grades 9 and 12 may differ from that of counterparts in Grades 9 and 12 elsewhere.

A related matter concerns questions that require recall of events. Again, such recall is more difficult for younger students (De Leeuw 2011, p.14); and studies have showed that responses are especially likely to be unreliable if respondents are asked to recall events in which they have not been interested (Holaday & Turner-Henson 1989, p.249). The Hong Kong questionnaire had one question asking students to recall whether they had received private tutoring from kindergarten onwards, and to indicate the grades in which they had received private tutoring. Some of the adapted questionnaires also had this question. Secondary students may not easily recall activities so long ago. With this in mind, Zhang (2013) reduced the reference period to primary and secondary education. The change of course meant a sacrifice of some potentially interesting data, but avoided the issue of whether the data on kindergarten level would have been sufficiently accurate.

A different matter of accuracy arises in some other questions. The Hong Kong questionnaire had two questions about monthly expenditures on tutoring and whether the expenditures were a financial burden to students' families. Questions about the costs of tutoring may not yield reliable information from students because they may not know the details of payments made by their parents. Also, some students may not know the financial status of their families and therefore cannot easily answer the question about financial burden. The Hong Kong team did not survey parents, so could not ask them. However, Zhang (2013) did so. By asking parents rather than their children, Zhang is likely to have received more accurate responses.

Adaptations following piloting

Literature suggests that needs for adaptation of questionnaires may become apparent at any stage of the study (Harkness 2011), but that one of the most important stages for adjustment is after the pilot. Stewart (2013), for example, made several adjustments to the student questionnaire in Jamaica after her pilot study.

Stewart made one kind of modification to improve the reliability of data. The beginning part of the questionnaire originally had four questions to ask students whether they had received private tutoring, the main type of tutoring, and the motivation for receiving or not receiving tutoring. The reference period for these four questions was "during fourth and/or fifth form", which may be too long ago for some students to recall. Responses to questions about the current situation are likely to be more accurate than those about tutoring received in the past (Ireson 2007). After the pilot study, Stewart reduced the number of questions asking about recollection of experiences, and shortened the reference period to only "during fifth form".

Stewart also deleted several questions to make the questionnaire shorter. The student questionnaire for her pilot study had included questions adapted from the Hong Kong questionnaire about domestic helpers and the private cars owned by the students' families, and the allowances that students received from parents. These questions were considered helpful to analyse students' family socioeconomic status. But after looking into the data collected from pilot study, Stewart found that these three items were not essential for assessing the SES, and that she had other more relevant items.

Stewart modified one question in order to avoid confusion. One question in the pilot study asked: "How many children live in your household [whether brother(s), sister(s) or cousin(s)]?". Respondents might not know whether they should count themselves, and inconsistency would make the responses incomparable. Further, students who were the only children in families and did not number themselves may just leave this question blank, which could be interpreted as missing data. To handle this matter, Stewart rephrased this particular question as: "How many children including yourself live in your household including all brother(s), sister(s) and/ or cousin(s)?".

Methodological Lessons

The studies in Chongqing, Dubai, India, Iran, Jamaica and Malaysia treated the Hong Kong questionnaire as a template and adapted it for their own use. From their efforts and experiences, some methodological lessons may be identified for researchers planning to adapt either the Hong Kong questionnaire or other instruments.

First, researchers should think about the question format. In the Hong Kong questionnaire, the most common questions were closed items with limited sets of predefined answers. Other questions permitted respondents to answer in their own words, and some provided ratings in which respondents selected one position on an ordered scale of answer options. When adapting instruments for other settings, the match between format and the types of respondents should be considered. Usually the closed question format is the easiest for respondents, but sometimes in order to get more reliable data from younger students one could consider alternative formats. The Jamaican questionnaire had one question about parents' occupations using the closed format with categorised options, but students may not know clearly the categories of their parents' occupations. In this case, some students may choose the option "others" or "I don't know", which results in missing data. One possible solution is to adopt the open question format and ask students to write down their parents' occupations. With this kind of detailed data, researchers could then themselves categorise occupations.

Second, the questionnaire layout is important. Route instructions help to reduce the demands on students and, as pointed out by Bethlehem (2009, p.57), "irrelevant questions may irritate people, possibly resulting in refusal to continue". Figure 12.1 is an example of a route question in the Hong Kong questionnaire, indicating to respondents that they should answer on the left-hand side if they did receive private tutoring and on the right-hand side if they did not. On the whole, this worked well in Hong Kong, though Madandar Arani reported in Iran (Chapter 7) that many students in his pilot did not follow the instructions and responded in both columns. With this in mind, Madandar Arani decided to make two completely separate questions, and to ask the research assistants to stress the differences when administering the questionnaire. However, even this arrangement did not work smoothly, again emphasising the challenges of finding the best arrangement. Stewart (Chapter 10) was able to avoid the issue in her electronic version of the questionnaire, which automatically switched to appropriate follow-up questions and excluded irrelevant ones, but Stewart could only use the electronic version in a minority of schools so had to rely on a paper version for the majority.

Figure 12.1: A Routing Layout in the Hong Kong Questionnaire

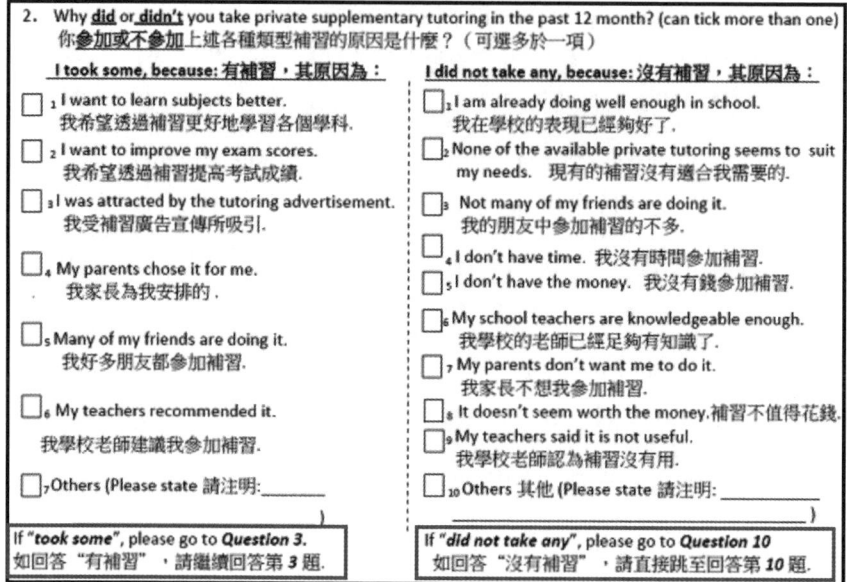

A further lesson is that pretesting is essential. Even questions previously used elsewhere must be tested for their suitability in new contexts. Pretesting can help to evaluate a questionnaire's capacity to collect the desired data, the capabilities of the selected mode of data collection, and the adequacy of the field procedures (Caspar & Peytcheva 2011). Various pretesting techniques include focus groups, cognitive testing, prototype studies, and pilot studies (Harkness et al. 2011). The researchers whose work is discussed in this chapter generally adopted the procedure of pilot study, but also learned lessons about the design of pilot studies. For example, Kenayathulla (Chapter 2) failed to collect data on ethnicity because she omitted this question when adapting the Hong Kong questionnaire and overlooked this problem even with her pilot study because the student body was relatively homogeneous in ethnicity. If she had pretested the questionnaire on a representative student sample covering ethnic diversity, she might have noticed this problem.

Finally, the procedures for administration may influence the quality and reliability of data. In all the countries covered by this chapter, the student questionnaires were delivered to sampled students in their classrooms. The regular teachers may play a positive role in the survey process. If the teachers try to explain the aim and the importance of the survey carefully, students would be more likely to cooperate and complete the work. However the roles of teachers may also be problematic. In the presence of their teachers, students may feel pressured. Thus the ideal may be for teachers to request serious cooperation from the students then leave the room while the researchers administer the instruments.

Discussion from the Perspective of Comparative Education

Researchers in the field of comparative education should pay careful attention to establish the basis for comparability in order to provide a foundation for meaningful interpretation of results (Bray et al. 2014). Bereday (1964) proposed a four-step method of comparative analysis, consisting of description, interpretation, juxtaposition, and simultaneous comparison. The data collected from survey using questionnaires adapted from the Hong Kong questionnaire could to some extent permit juxtaposition of the information on private tutoring in different countries and provide some basis for comparative research.

However, analysts should always keep in mind the complexities of obtaining systematically comparable data, owing to diversity between and within countries. Further, although standardised questionnaires may be appealing, researchers cannot easily ensure comparable samples, negotiate questions that fit different cultures, and achieve adequate translations across languages. Even the most influential cross-national surveys, the Trends in International Mathematics and Science Study (TIMSS) and the Programme for International Student Assessment (PISA) also faced the challenges of adaptation and translation (Bray & Kobakhidze 2014). One concept could be translated into different phrases even in same language within different social contexts. Different wordings can lead to divergent understandings and make the data substantially incomparable cross cultures. The same issues have arisen with the data on private tutoring gathering through the questionnaires adapted from the Hong Kong instrument. Perhaps this is a disappointing conclusion; but it stresses the need for caution rather than over-confidence in the goal of securing data that are truly meaningful and insightful.

References

Bereday, George Z.F. (1964): *Comparative Method in Education*. New York: Holt, Rinehart & Winston.

Bethlehem, Jelke (2009): *Applied Survey Methods: A Statistical Perspective*. London: John Wiley.

Bray, Mark; Adamson, Bob & Mason, Mark (2014): 'Different Models, Different Emphases, Different Insights', in Bray, Mark; Adamson, Bob & Mason, Mark (eds.), *Comparative Education Research: Approaches and Methods*. CERC Studies in Comparative Education 19, Hong Kong: Comparative Education Research Centre, The University of Hong Kong, and Dordrecht: Springer, pp.417-432.

Bray, Mark & Kobakhidze Magda (2014): 'Measurement Issues in Research on Shadow Education: Challenges and Pitfalls Encountered in TIMSS and PISA'. *Comparative Education Review*, Vol.58, No.4, pp.590-620.

Bray, Mark & Kwo, Ora (2014): *Regulating Private Tutoring for Public Good: Policy Options for Supplementary Education in Asia*. Hong Kong: Comparative Education Research Centre, The University of Hong Kong, and Bangkok: UNESCO.

Caspar, Rachel; Peytcheva, Emilia & Cibelli Kristen (2011): 'Pretesting', in *Guidelines for Best Practice in Cross-cultural Surveys*. Ann Arbor: Survey Research Centre, University of Michigan.

Chu, Hong-li (2009): 'The Impact of Family Background and Personal Characteristics on the Participation in Supplementary Education in Mainland China'. *Education Research Monthly*, 12, pp.22-27 [in Chinese].

De Leeuw, Edith (2011): 'Improving Data Quality when Surveying Children and Adolescents: Cognitive and Social Development and its Role in Questionnaire Construction and Pretesting', in *Public Health Challenges and Health and Welfare of Children and Young People*. Helsinki: Academy of Finland.

Harkness, Janet A. (2008): 'Comparative Survey Research: Goals and Challenges', in De Leeuw, Edith D. & Dillman Don A. (eds.), *International Handbook of Survey Methodology*. New York: Lawrence Erlbaum, pp.56-77.

Harkness, Janet A. (2011): 'Translation', in *Guidelines for Best Practice in Cross-cultural Surveys*. Ann Arbor: University of Michigan.

Harkness, Janet A.; Bligen, Ipek; Cazar, Analucia C.; Cibelli, Kristen; Huang Lei; Miller Debbie; Stange, Mathew & Villar, Ana (2011): 'Questionnaire Design' in *Guidelines for Best Practice in Cross-cultural Surveys*. Ann Arbor: University of Michigan.

Harkness, Janet A.; Villar, Ana & Edwards, Brad (2010): 'Translation, Adaptation, and Design', in Harkness, Janet A.; Braun, Michael; Edwards, Brad; Johnson, Timothy P.; Lyberg, Lars E.; Mohler, Peter; Pennell, Beth-Ellen & Smith, Tom

W. (eds.), *Survey Methods in Multinational, Multicultural and Multiregional Contexts*. Hoboken: John Wiley & Sons, pp.115-140.

Holaday, Bonnie & Anne Turner-Henson (1989): 'Response Effects in Surveys with School-age Children'. *Nursing Research*, Vol.38, No.4, pp.248-250.

Ireson, Judith (2007): 'Monitoring and Evaluating Private Tutoring: How and why should we do it?'. Paper presented at the IIEP Policy Forum on Confronting the shadow education system: what government policies for what private tutoring? Paris: UNESCO International Institute for Educational Planning.

Naismith, Luke (2014): 'Supplementary Private Tutoring in Dubai'. Unpublished report, Dubai: Knowledge and Human Development Authority.

Stewart, Saran (2013): *Everything in di dark muss come to light: A Postcolonial Investigation of the Practice of Extra Lessons at the Secondary Level in Jamaica's Education System*. PhD Dissertation, University of Denver.

Zhang, Wei (2013): *Private Supplementary Tutoring Received by Grade 9 Students in Chongqing, China: Determinants of Demand, and Policy Implications*. PhD thesis, The University of Hong Kong.

Zhang, Yu (2011): *The Determinants of National College Entrance Exam Performance in China – with an Analysis of Private Tutoring*. PhD Dissertation, Columbia University.

13

Organisational and Cross-Cultural Issues: Learning from Research Approaches

Mark BRAY & Ora KWO

Introduction

This concluding chapter pulls together some of the threads in this book. As mentioned in the Introduction, research on private supplementary tutoring is beginning to catch up with the scale of the phenomenon, but has far to go. As such, the contributors to this book are at the forefront of an emerging and very significant field. Insofar as shadow education mimics regular schooling, it may be argued that approaches to research should also mimic. This includes selection of instruments for quantitative, qualitative and mixed methods, and also includes lenses drawn from the disciplines of economics, philosophy, psychology, sociology, etc.. However shadow education does not simply mimic regular schooling, and in some respects research on shadow education requires particular types of approach to secure data and insights that may otherwise be difficult to obtain.

The chapter begins with implications of the volume of research in particular countries. While globally the research on the theme is limited, in a few countries it is relatively developed. The initial question is about the implications of this picture for researchers in countries of with relatively developed and severely undeveloped research.

Bray, Mark; Kwo, Ora & Jokić, Boris (eds.) (2015): *Researching Private Supplementary Tutoring: Methodological Lessons from Diverse Cultures*. Hong Kong: Comparative Education Research Centre (CERC), The University of Hong Kong, and Dordrecht: Springer. © CERC

The next section turns to the even more important matter of defining the focus of research. Private supplementary tutoring can be defined and understood in different ways by different people. It is essential for all researchers to have clear conceptions of their own definitions, and then to check whether their respondents have the same conceptions. Variations in definitions may be found not only across countries but also among different groups of actors. Similarly, variations may be found in the rigour of research practices.

From these observations the chapter makes some remarks about conceptual lenses, and then about the merits and limitations of quantitative, qualitative and mixed approaches as exemplified by the chapters in this book. The subsequent sections, also drawing on the chapters of the book, consider the roles of cultures at macro, meso and micro levels, and the nature and impact of ethical requirements of research institutions. The final section concludes not only the chapter but also the whole book.

Cross-national Variations in the Volume of Research

The opening pages of this book pointed out that private supplementary education is not a new phenomenon. The Introduction highlighted the existence of tutoring during the first half of the 20th century in Mauritius, Greece and Ceylon, and cited literature from the second half of the 20th century in such countries as Egypt, Sri Lanka, Japan and the Republic of Korea.

Among these countries, the research has been most voluminous in the Republic of Korea. Governments in that country have been actively concerned about private supplementary tutoring since the 1950s, and have taken multiple measures to shape the phenomenon in order to ameliorate its perceived negative effects (Seth 2002; Lee & Jang 2010). This official orientation, coupled with vigorous public concern, has encouraged research not only by universities but also by government bodies. For example the Korean Statistical Information Service (KOSIS) has produced annual data on household expenditures and the scale of tutoring received by students at different levels of education (e.g. KOSIS 2015).

For this book on methodology, the volume of Korean research is mentioned because for researchers in that country it sets a very different context from that experienced by counterparts elsewhere. Researchers in the Republic of Korea have extensive literature on which to draw (both in Korean and in other languages). The researchers can therefore construct research designs that take account of existing explorations with a range of quantitative, qualitative and mixed techniques. They may also experience more exacting standards because peer reviewers have detailed knowledge of methodological possibilities and constraints.

At the other end of the spectrum are countries in which almost no literature exists on the topic. These countries, taking examples from widely different regions of the world, include Central African Republic, Chile, Netherlands, and Papua New Guinea. Other countries have only one or two substantive studies, which in effect are candles in the darkness. Indeed two chapters in this book, again from widely different regions of the world, are extracted from studies which are pioneers in this respect. In the Maldives, Nazeer (2006) had made passing reference to private supplementary tutoring but Mariya's (2012) thesis was the first work to focus fully on the phenomenon. Similarly in Jamaica Spencer-Rowe (2000) had touched on the theme, but Stewart's (2013) thesis was the first extensive study. Related remarks can be made about other countries. For example Davis (2013) produced pioneering work in Australia, Wattar (2014) did so in Syria, and Addi-Raccah and Dana (2015) did so in Israel.

The question then is whether the volume of national research makes a methodological difference, or whether work in the Republic of Korea and elsewhere could provide an adequate framework and reference point for researchers in Chile, Central African Republic, Netherlands and Papua New Guinea – and/or in the Maldives, Jamaica, Australia, Syria and Israel. The answer is that certainly researchers in these countries should examine the Korean work for both its methodological lessons and its findings. However, the different contexts require different research approaches to fit education systems, government policies, economic forces, and social structures. Whereas the Korean authorities encourage research on tutoring, governments elsewhere may be neutral – or even discouraging if for example they feel that supplementary tutoring reflects poorly on the public system and is therefore better left hidden. Also, researchers wishing to investigate the roles of public teachers in private tutoring would find limited inspiration from Korean studies since very few if any Korean teachers provide such tutoring. Also, the Republic of Korea has levels of literacy and technology that permit investigation with web-based forms completed by respondents in ways that would be largely impossible in Central African Republic or Papua New Guinea, for example.

Moreover, the need for tailoring of approaches does not rest only at the national level. As research on the theme expands in volume and geographic coverage, it shows that different communities within countries behave in different ways. Thus the work in Israel (Addi-Raccah & Dana 2015) distinguished not only between schools serving high and low socioeconomic communities but also between schools serving Jewish and Arab communities. As noted in the Introduction to this book, work in the USA and Australia has similarly distinguished between the amounts and forms of tutoring received by various racial communities and shaped by the cultures of those communities (Zhou & Kim 2008; Sriprakash et al. 2015), and counterpart studies of different racial groups may be cited in such countries as Sri Lanka (Gunasekara 2009; Pallegedara 2011) and Vietnam (Ha & Harpham 2005; Dang 2007). Different methods and approaches may be needed to reach communities of different types, including ways to solicit information and vocabularies to do so.

Defining the Object of Study

Remarks about vocabularies in different communities are allied to ones about precisely what is being researched, and how it is understood by whom. Again linking back to the Introduction, private supplementary tutoring takes many forms and has diverse content. Indeed ambiguities may exist in each work of the phrase:

- *Private*: Does this mean fee-paying, or can it mean merely that the tutoring is conducted privately, i.e. in a home or similar location rather than in a public space, or even in a public space (such as a school or public library) but not as part of a regular class? If it does mean fee-paying, does it allow for payments in forms other than cash? How would cases be treated in which tutors normally charge fees but waive them for low-income individuals perhaps in the same classes as ones who do pay fees? And how would government-sponsored schemes that also charge fees be classified?
- *Supplementary*: The research under the label of shadow education focuses especially on extra classes on academic subjects that are already taught in regular schooling. However, supplementation can be additional content rather than just more of the same. Indeed this is a core objective for some providers of supplementary tutoring, who argue that their clients should receive more than schooling can pro-

vide. Moreover, the focus on academic subjects raises questions on precisely what those are and in what circumstances. Music, sports and religion, for example, may be studied for examinations as well as for more rounded development.
- *Tutoring*: For many people, this word implies instruction to individuals or possibly small groups. These people would not naturally consider large classes to be tutoring, especially when they are taught by regular teachers in regular classrooms as in Cambodia (see Chapter 11). Similar problems of vocabulary might apply to Hong Kong's multiple classrooms divided only by glass walls which in effect become large lecture theatres (Chan & Bray 2014; Koh 2014).

Going further, research is increasingly exposing forms of tutoring with blurred administrative boundaries (see e.g. Kodakos & Fragiskos 2015). Public schools may invite private enterprises into their premises, remunerating the enterprises with public funds and/or arranging for parents to make payments either through the schools or directly. Some of these enterprises may be for-profit bodies while others may be community or philanthropic organisations simply seeking to cover their costs.

Moreover, operations in private fee-charging schools may add to the complexities of classification. The Dubai study discussed in Chapter 12 of this book noted some private schools that operated with full packages providing students with both core teaching and supplementary lessons if needed, while other schools had a basic charge only for the core teaching and demanded extra for supplementary lessons provided either on or off the school premises by external operators. The question would be on what grounds the extra lessons in the latter group of schools would be classified as private supplementary tutoring but not those in the former group of schools.

In such circumstances, at least four demands arise. First, the researchers themselves must be clear about the variety of models and about their own definitions. Second, the researchers must structure their questions to include some types of operation but to exclude others. Third, the researchers must communicate the definitions and parameters to their respondents; and fourth, they must check whether in fact the respondents understood those communications and provided information in ways that fitted the desired categories. Much research on private supplementary tutoring does not reach adequate standards in one or more of these domains.

To illustrate the complexities it is useful to consider experiences in the Trends in International Mathematics and Science Study (TIMSS) operated by the International Association for the Study of Educational Assessment (IEA) and the Programme for International Student Achievement (PISA) operated by the Organisation for Economic Co-operation and Development (PISA). These bodies have organised regular cross-national surveys, dating from 1995 in the case of TIMSS and from 2000 in the case of PISA. The surveys have included questions which could variously be described as about extra lessons, private tutoring, and out-of-school support. Space in this chapter precludes detailed analysis of the questions, and readers are referred to Bray and Kobakhidze (2014) for commentary on ambiguities and inconsistencies in the phrasing of questions. Problems were exacerbated by translations in which original meanings from English text were changed and/or lost. Yet some analysts of the data (e.g. Southgate 2009; Song et al. 2013) have given insufficient attention to these matters, and have presented alleged findings that are not fully valid.

The challenges first of expressing meanings and then of securing reliable data were also evident in some studies reported in this book. For example, Stewart (Chapter 10) intended the focus of her questions in Jamaica to be on extra lessons received in exchange for a fee, but many respondents included fee-free lessons in their answers. Similarly, the Cambodian team found that some questions were rather long and not easily understood by students (Chapter 11). The Cambodian team was to some extent able to handle the matter through personal explanations when distributing questionnaires in the classrooms, but such actions have not been possible for teams in other countries. In general, when serious doubts might exist about the clarity and understandings of questions, interviews are a better tool because it is possible to check whether respondents indeed have the same understandings as researchers and to make adjustments as necessary.

Also pertinent in the choice of vocabulary and the phrasing of questions is the sensitivity of the topic. Thus shadow education, for example, may be increasingly common vocabulary among many researchers but is not in common usage among providers or recipients of private supplementary tutoring. Moreover, some people may feel that the term has a negative connotation, perhaps conveying an illegal motive. For such reasons it could be better to avoid the term in questionnaires and interviews, even if it is retained in subsequent reporting.

Related factors apply to political dimensions. The research team in Cambodia (Chapter 11) found that teachers were ready to talk about private supplementary tutoring (which some respondents, when speaking English called "part-time classes", perhaps providing vocabulary with greater clarity) since it was an obvious and long-accepted form of daily life. One member of the research team contrasted this pattern with her experience in Georgia, where teachers are much more cautious because such extra lessons are frowned upon and can be linked to corruption (Kobakhidze 2014). In the Georgian context more initial effort was needed by this researcher to establish trust between interviewer and interviewees, and even then questions had to be phrased indirectly and in different forms for probing. Elsewhere, Paviot (2015, p.90) was aware in Kenya of sensitivities in the context of government prohibition of types of private tutoring, and decided in her interviews to use the more positive and less politically-charged phrase "extra academic support".

Finally under the heading of defining the object of study, worthwhile comparative analysis may be conducted on which categories of people define private supplementary tutoring in different ways. Do Koreans tend to define it in different ways from Americans? Or Greeks from Egyptians? One might expect differences based on historical patterns of provision of tutoring and the cultures of the countries. And then within individual countries how different actors define it? Do companies define private supplementary tutoring differently from university students and other informal providers? And do governments define it differently from families? Again much scope exists for illuminating comparative analyses.

Conceptual Lenses

Manzon and Areepattamannil (2014, p.392) pointed out that multiple perspectives may be used to comprehend the shadow education phenomenon:

> These may be drawn from sociology, which examines the relationships between education – and shadow education – and society, and critical social theory. Psychological studies, which examine constructs such as student motivation, achievement, and self-concept, may be applied to shadow education. Likewise, historical, economic and philosophical lenses may be employed.

The chapters in this book are dominated by sociological lenses, but that is not the exclusive orientation. Yu Zhang, for example, framed her work by reference to education production functions, citing Cohn and Geske (1990) in the economics of education; Yung was especially concerned with learning styles, and in this respect drew on work in psychology such as that by Watkins and Biggs (1996); and Stewart, as elaborated in her full thesis (Stewart 2013), was concerned with the tenets of critical inclusive pedagogy as espoused by Tuitt (2003) and with dimensions of postcolonialism as espoused by Spivak (1988) and Smith (1999).

Of course many other frameworks could have been used, just as they are used in research about regular schooling, the wider field of educational studies, and the social sciences more broadly. Manzon and Areepattamannil (2014, p.395) stressed the need for "a wider range of disciplinary and interdisciplinary lenses", including more explanatory, experimental and intervention studies. The field does have a few quasi-experimental studies, such as those by Mischo and Haag (2002) and Guill and Bos (2014), but they are relatively rare. In a different orientation, Brehm (2015) developed he called landscape portraiture, noting in detail the ways in which six different actors (of whom he made individual portraits) enacted processes of privatization. Expansion of the repertoire of disciplinary lenses will provide a more comprehensive understanding of the phenomenon, challenging and enhancing research methods for construction and re-construction of knowledge and understanding. From such work will emerge more nuanced awareness of the implications for policy makers and administrators responsible for whole education systems, for institutional managers and teachers/tutors, and for families, community bodies and other stakeholders.

Quantitative, Qualitative and Mixed Approaches

The first three chapters in this book were grouped under the heading 'Employing Quantitative Instruments'. The instruments to which they referred were diverse. Kobakhidze focused on TIMSS and the Progress in International Reading Literacy Study (PIRLS), which were large cross-national research exercises. As Kobakhidze explained, TIMSS 2011 assessed students' achievements in 63 countries and 14 states or regions, while PIRLS 2011 assessed students' achievements in 49 countries and nine states or regions. Within Georgia, responses were collected from 9,362 students and 4,744 parents. Most TIMSS and PIRLS questions were common across participating countries, states and regions, but with translation as necessary to national languages. Kobakhidze's analysis was based on her own questions which were integrated with and placed in the format of the international questions.

By contrast, Kenayathulla collected data in Malaysia through a questionnaire that she had herself designed on the basis of the Hong Kong questionnaire (see Chapter 8). She piloted the questionnaire with 30 students in one school, and then arranged for administration of the questionnaire to 4,200 students in 10 schools.

Yu Zhang (Chapter 3) also designed her own questionnaire, which she used to survey 6,474 students in 25 schools in China. This sample permitted much statistical analysis, though like Kenayathulla she did not aspire to national representativeness. In contrast, Kobakhidze could claim national representativeness. She had a larger sample for a smaller country (population 4.5 million, compared with 29.7 million in Malaysia and 1,357.0 million in China). Nevertheless Yu Zhang could certainly make claims about patterns in the city in which she conducted her work, and Kenayathulla aspired similarly to be able to make claims about the state within Malaysia in which she conducted her work. These permit comparisons with other parts of their respective countries. Thus the work of Yu Zhang in Jilin may be contrasted with the work of Wei Zhang (2013) in Chongqing, China; and the work of Kenayathulla in Selangor State, Malaysia, may be contrasted with that of Jelani and Tan (2012). As more research is conducted in these and other countries, patterns of internal variations and similarities will become clearer.

Review of the chapters reveals some familiar strengths and limitations of quantitative analysis. The strengths, particularly evident in Yu Zhang's chapter, include the ability to conduct statistical analyses to identify the nature of relationships between variables. For example, she assessed the effects of private tutoring participation on achievements in the National College Entrance Examination in mathematics, Chinese and English using T-tests, Ordinary Least Squares, Instrumental Variables, and Propensity Score Matching. The weaknesses of the approach include the absence of case studies showing the types of decisions made by individual students and families according to their specific circumstances. In this respect, the work of Wei Zhang (2013) is a useful complement as well as a parallel from a different part of China.

Some additional constraints that became apparent to Kobakhidze, Kenayathulla and Yu Zhang during data analysis, and also to the team that reported on the Cambodian study in Chapter 11, arose because they as designers of the research (or in Kobakhidze's case, designer of her component of the research) did not themselves administer the questionnaires. The Georgian questionnaires were administered by teams managed by the Ministry of Education; the Malaysian questionnaires were administered by teachers who were at the end of a hierarchy of principals, district education officers and the State Department of Education; the Chinese questionnaires were administered by 20 graduate students working as research assistants (Zhang 2011, p.83); and the Cambodian questionnaires were administered by a Non-Governmental Organisation (NGO). Kobakhidze recognised that her supplementary questions had not been piloted and that problems with some questions emerged, and similarly Kenayathulla recognised that, despite piloting in one school, significant shortcomings of some questions later emerged. Had the designers of the research administered the questionnaires themselves, rectification during the process of implementation might have been possible. The researchers would also have known more about the circumstances in which the respondents answered the questions, which could have been pertinent to assessment of credibility and to interpretation of findings. Kenayathulla added that direct administration in Malaysia could have reduced the number of unfilled questionnaires. Yet no single individual can administer surveys on the scale undertaken in Georgia, and indeed it would be challenging to do so on the scale undertaken by Kenayathulla and Yu Zhang in Malaysia and China. In this respect researchers have to confront balances. They need the partnerships for large-scale researcher, but may lose dimensions of sensitivity in data collection.

In contrast to these large quantitative studies are smaller ones undertaken by individual researchers. Commonly they can be characterised as case-oriented rather than variable-oriented research (della Porta 2008). For example, Mariya's work in the Maldives (Chapter 6) was strongly grounded in her own history and identity. Especially in the atolls and also in Male', the capital, anonymity is difficult to achieve even if desired. With such considerations in mind, Mariya chose an ethnographic approach and "found data everywhere, including personal experiences, observations and conversations that are part of everyday life" (Mariya 2012, p.68). She took an insider's perspective, engaging in extensive communications with people in ways that demanded dynamic participation and self-examination. The participants were not just subjects from whom the researcher extracted information. Rather, Mariya stated (2012, p.224), "all participants enjoyed reflecting upon their practices and were keen to contribute to reform and change". Mariya did not claim national representativeness, but certainly secured insights that were pertinent to the whole country and indeed to the wider region.

The Cambodian project (Chapter 11), by contrast, had a combination of outsiders and insiders. The outsiders, based at the University of Hong Kong, had different nationalities and extensive international experience, but did not speak, read or write Khmer, the national language of Cambodia. The insiders were employees of a Cambodian NGO who undertook to implement the project with guidance and dialogue across national boundaries. Margaret Mead, the distinguished anthropologist, is alleged once to have remarked: "If a fish were to become an anthropologist, the last thing it would discover would be water" (Spindler & Spindler 1982, p.24). The outside viewers of the goldfish bowl could see the water which the insiders to some extent took for granted; but the insiders were able to secure data within their own environment for collaborative analysis and advancement of understanding.

Yung's work differed from the majority of studies reported in this book by focusing on learning in a single institution. For this he again chose a qualitative approach. He commenced with questionnaires to secure preliminary information about students' backgrounds, learning practices and beliefs about teaching and learning, and then conducted individual interviews of 19 students. Initially a slightly larger sample was selected, but three students dropped out and then one more followed. Yung asked the students to write reflective pieces about their English learning experiences, following which he engaged in a second round of interviews. In related components Yung observed lessons and interviewed tutors, and he conducted a final round of interviews with the students following release of their public examination results. The iterative process adopted by Yung secured deep knowledge of the students over a period of months.

Yung's approach also contrasted with the methods in Iran (Chapter 7), Hong Kong (Chapter 8), India (Chapter 9), Jamaica (Chapter 10), and Cambodia (Chapter 11) in which short one-off interviews complemented data collected through questionnaires. In the Hong Kong study, for example, 105 students and 48 teachers were interviewed. The arrangement allowed for larger numbers and therefore greater variation and/or evidence of consistency. However, the design clearly compromised on depth. Similar remarks are applicable to the studies in India, Jamaica and Cambodia.

Since many of the balances and compromises chosen by these researchers are similar to those required across the field of educational studies and indeed the social sciences more generally (see e.g. della Porta & Keating 2008; Johnson & Christensen 2012; Creswell 2014), they do not need much elaboration here. Nevertheless, insofar as research on private supplementary tutoring is at an early stage of development, it perhaps has needs which are less evident in other domains. Reflecting on his five-country study (see Chapter 4), Jokić observed that effective debate about private tutoring and exploration of its foundations would not have been possible without the quantitative data from a predecessor project in nine countries (Silova et al. 2006). At the same time, Jokić added that it would be impossible to fully understand the complexity of private tutoring without the rich descriptive data of the new project. Agreeing with Gorard and Taylor (2004), Jokić argued that quantitative research can provide answers to 'what' and 'how many' questions, while qualitative research should answer 'how' and 'why' questions.

Different Cultures, Different Strategies

Elaborating on earlier points and again taking the collection of chapters in this book as a group, a rich tapestry of cultural settings may be identified. Geographically, the collection includes work in East Asia (Hong Kong and Jinan in China), South Asia (West Bengal in India, Maldives), Southeast Asia (Cambodia, Malaysia), Western Asia (Azerbaijan, Iran), Eastern Europe (Bosnia & Herzegovina, Croatia, Estonia, Georgia), and the Caribbean (Jamaica). Some of these societies are urban (e.g. Hong Kong, Jinan), while others include rural areas (e.g. Maldives). The countries also have wide diversity in dominant religious practices, including Islam (especially Iran, Malaysia, Maldives), Christianity (especially Croatia, Jamaica, Georgia) and Buddhism (especially Cambodia). They also have a range of political systems.

The macro groupings presented above will be considered first in this section. Also important to researchers as they consider their strategies are factors at the meso and micro-level factors relating to institutions, families and individuals. They will be considered second.

Macro levels

The chapter with the most explicit reference to a combination of religion and politics focused on Iran, having the subtitle 'Methodological Experiences in an Islamic Republic' (Chapter 7). One major issue concerned gender segregation of schools since all schools in Iran are single-sex, even at primary level, in conformity with the authorities' views about appropriate arrangements in the context of Islamic beliefs and values. Researchers of the 'wrong' sex cannot easily visit schools serving the other sex. Madandar Arani describes some ways round the restrictions, but they are demanding. Islam is also the dominant religion in Malaysia and the Maldives. Researchers there should be appropriately sensitive in dress and behaviour – as indeed would be the case in all countries, regardless of the dominant religion – but the authorities in Malaysia and the Maldives are more flexible than their counterparts in Iran. This observation shows variations in ease of access to informants and the care required for preparing the ground for data collection.

Madandar Arani also referred to other dimensions of organisational culture in Iran. Approval to conduct research was required from the central authorities, who scrutinised instruments for sensitive content, and only questionnaires bearing official stamps on every page may be distributed to schools. Madandar Arani suggested that this procedure discourages researchers from having long questionnaires and large samples, and steers researchers towards interviews instead of questionnaires. In a related observation, Madandar Arani noted that relationships between researchers and the government authorities were distant, and that researchers "need to be strongly aware of political discourses, the overt and unspoken views of government officials, and the overall climate of schools".

Of course such considerations again apply to other contexts, albeit perhaps in less extreme form. Thus Kenayathulla's research in Malaysia required approval from the Educational Planning and Research Division of the Ministry of Education, and the application process demanded her proposal, questionnaires and a letter from her university. In addition, for work in the specific state, she required approval from that state's Department of Education. Having received the approval, distribution and collection of the questionnaires was undertaken by the state, district and school authorities. Kenayathulla indicated that it would have been possible to approach the schools directly, but it would have taken longer to secure consent from each principal and to manage collection of questionnaires from each school.

The government machinery was also pertinent to the research reported in other chapters. Thus the TIMSS and PIRLS research in Georgia was conducted by the Ministry of Education itself. In China, Yu Zhang was operating as an independent researcher but was assisted by the Jinan Education Bureau "who issued the approval letter for the survey and informed all the principals in the public schools ... asking them to provide assistance" (Zhang 2011, p.83); and in Jamaica, Stewart sought permission from the Ministry of Education which then assisted by providing contact information for the schools.

Researchers elsewhere may be able to work independently of the government authorities. For the Hong Kong study reported in Chapter 8, approval was needed at the school level but not from the government's Education Bureau. A similar remark applies to Maheshwari's research in West Bengal, India (Chapter 9), and to the work in the five Eurasian countries reported by Jokić (Chapter 4) even though some of the people interviewed in these five countries were government personnel. These differences show variations in the cultural contexts of research insofar as governments may desire and feel able to control investigations, perhaps encouraging certain orientations and discouraging others.

Also worth mentioning are ways in which instruments need to be adapted for work in different cultures. Madandar Arani (Chapter 7) indicated that he added the name of God at the beginning of his questionnaire in line with the common practice in Iran. Maheshwari (Chapter 9) indicated that when adapting the Hong Kong questionnaire she removed "window shopping" as a leisure activity because it would not have been understood by most of her respondents in West Bengal. Wei Zhang (2013), who also adapted the Hong Kong questionnaire for use in Chongqing, China, added questions about students' *hukou* residential status; and she adjusted the questions comparing teachers and tutors because in Chongqing some teachers also worked as tutors and therefore could not be compared as if they were separate people. These examples again highlight the need for attention to cultural contexts. Chapter 12 has highlighted some of the advantages of having instruments that can be adapted to different settings, but has also stressed some of the challenges.

Meso and micro levels
Even when researchers have secured central government permission,

they commonly need to negotiate access at the school level. Again in this regard a variety of perspectives emerge from the chapters. The Hong Kong team found that it was one thing to devise an ideal sample in the comfort of a university office but quite another to persuade the principals of the target schools to agree. Fortunately, the team had sufficient social capital through alumni and other connections to be able to replace the schools that declined to participate with others that were deemed sufficiently similar to retain the overall integrity of the project. Nevertheless, Madandar Arani noted that even in Iran – where the volume of research is much lower than in many other countries – schools are increasingly burdened by "researcher traffic".

Kenayathulla (Chapter 2) added insights by distinguishing between urban and rural communities. She indicated that urban schools are more likely to be overburdened, and therefore that it is commonly easier for researchers to access rural schools. For work on private supplementary tutoring, this creates a danger of biased sampling insofar as the phenomenon is generally greater in scale and impact in urban than rural areas. On the other hand, biases may arise in an opposite direction because rural areas are difficult to reach. Stewart (2013, pp.107, 122) explicitly noted this challenge in her Jamaican research. In her situation a further sampling consideration arose from her identity as a female travelling in high-incidence violent communities. She addressed this by hiring a male research assistant who also functioned as a driver.

Issues of researcher identity were also evident in Maheshwari's work in West Bengal (Chapter 9). Tension arose in one school when the principal realised that Maheshwari was from a different religious background than that of the school's sponsoring body. The principal was suspicious that Maheshwari might have ulterior motives for trying to find out about private supplementary tutoring, especially because government regulations prohibited teachers from providing tutoring. Eventually Maheshwari was able to convince the principal that she was a bona fide researcher with unthreatening intentions, but the incident exemplified the challenges that can arise at the meso level and the importance of sensitive and receptive effort to address tacit concerns.

Few chapters in this book report data from parents and other family members, partly because of logistic challenges in securing balanced samples. This domain may deserve special attention and effort from future researchers. Meanwhile, collection of data from schools is easier because they can be accessed as institutions in which students are used to being asked questions by adults.

However, researchers may still need to be mindful of biases arising from the act of collecting data in schools, and hence the ways that depth of data can be probed. Students, particularly young ones, may not be well informed on matters such as the costs of tutoring. Also, teachers may be sensitive about students providing information on shadow education, particularly when the tutoring is supplied by the teachers themselves. Students may be aware of this, and may adjust their responses on questionnaires and in interviews, particularly when their teachers are present. This constraint is less problematic in Hong Kong, where teachers rarely provide private supplementary tutoring to any students and certainly not to their own students. However, it is more problematic in countries where teachers do play these roles, such as India (Chapter 9), Cambodia (Chapter 11) and China (Zhang & Bray 2013, pp.80-81).

Yet while most chapters in this book report on data collected in schools, Yung's research (Chapter 5) was in a different category. As indicated above, his focus was on the strategies employed by students to learn English, and his sample was selected from a tutorial centre rather than a school. Again he had to be mindful of the culture of that centre, negotiating access and considering the implications of signals sent by the centre for the information provided by his informants. His pilot study initially gained limited response because the tutor asked his students to "think very carefully whether [they] really wanted to participate". Accordingly, Yung felt a need for the main study to secure a more positive atmosphere. He managed to achieve this goal, and subsequently reduced the institutional impact by conducting interviews outside the tutorial centre.

Ethical Approval and Requirements for Participants' Consent

Some aspects of research have become much more bureaucratised in recent decades. They include requirements for ethical approval and the consent of participants which feature in the majority of chapters. Some ethical guidelines and requirements in social sciences research have been imported from biomedical sciences with inadequate attention to relevance and sensitivity (Guillemin & Gulam 2004, p.262). Few researchers would deny the importance of attention to ethics in research, and many welcome the more systematic treatment that ethics now receive in universities and elsewhere. However, bureaucratic procedures may not be culturally neutral. As noted by Robinson-Pant and Singal (2013, p.443), procedures that fit one setting may not be appropriate for another and may even undermine some of the purposes of research (Wolcott 1994, p.403).

The studies reported in this book are instructive in this perspective since they were undertaken within a range of organisational frameworks as well as cultures. Most were led by researchers based in universities, albeit with partnerships of various kinds. The most obvious exceptions were the Georgian study reported in Chapter 1 which was undertaken by the Ministry of Education in conjunction with the IEA, and the five-country study reported in Chapter 4 which was led from an independent research institute and resourced by a Network of Policy Centres. Two of the universities in which chapter authors were based were located in the USA, one in New Zealand, and three in Asia (Hong Kong, Iran and Malaysia). These universities had their own perspectives on ethical matters and accompanying procedures.

Table 13.1 summarises the permissions sought and obtained by the researchers, in most cases accompanied by review from an ethical perspective, as reported in the chapters of this book and/or in more complete accounts such as the theses written by the authors. For the work conducted in Malaysia, China, Maldives, Iran, Jamaica and Cambodia, approval was secured from the government authorities. However, this was not a requirement for the Hong Kong research reported in Chapter 8: permission was required from the school principals but not from the government's Education Bureau. Nor was it required for the research reported in Chapter 5 which was routed through a tutorial centre rather than a school.

Robinson-Pant and Singal (2013) were especially concerned with ways in which the norms and bureaucratic requirements of UK and other 'Northern' universities might not fit cultures of the 'South' and particularly less developed countries in Asia and Africa. They cited the postcolonial perspectives of Smith (1999) and of White and Fitzgerald (2010), which include the notion that ethics should commence "with a dialogue not an ethics application" and "shift from a single moment to open and critical conversation" (White & Fitzgerald 2010, p.284 cited by Robinson-Pant & Singal 2013, p.448). Such perspectives were very pertinent to the Stewart's study in Jamaica (Chapter 10), but she was nevertheless obliged

Table 13.1: Ethical Approval and Consent Requirements from Participants

Chapter	Jurisdiction	Approval process and consent required
1	Georgia	Research conducted by Ministry of Education. No consent requested from parents or students responding to questionnaires.
2	Malaysia	Research conducted by university assistant professor with approval of national and state authorities. No consent requested from parents or students responding to questionnaires.
3	Jinan, China	Research conducted by doctoral student with approval of the city Education Bureau, following approval of instruments and procedures by IRB of the researcher's US university.
4	Five countries	Research conducted by teams in five countries. In some countries, ethical permission of the institution required and granted. Personal consent secured from all interviewed participants, and anonymity in reporting.
5	Hong Kong	Research conducted by doctoral student following approval by university committee. Informed consent required for head of tutorial company, tutors and students, and passive consent for parents of students aged below 18.
6	Maldives	Research conducted by doctoral student with approval from Ministry of Education and New Zealand university authorities. All data collected by interview and observation. The researcher states that participants received clear information through face-to-face meetings.
7	Iran	Research conducted by university assistant professor with approval from the education authorities. No consent requested from parents or students responding to questionnaires.
8	Hong Kong	Research conducted by university professoriate team following approval from institutional ethics committee. Passive consent required from parents of students, and active consent from students themselves. Active consent also required from teachers responding to questionnaires and interviews.
9	India	Research conducted by university master's student following approval from Hong Kong university ethics committee. Passive consent required from parents of students, and active consent from students themselves.
10	Jamaica	Research conducted by doctoral student following approval from Ministry of Education and US university's IRB. Active consent required for student, teacher and parent interviews. Prior to collection of questionnaire data, researcher gave spoken explanation in the classroom. IRB waived requirement for parental consent for data collection by questionnaire.
11	Cambodia	Research conducted by an NGO on behalf of Hong Kong university researchers and with approval from provincial authorities. University procedure required passive consent from parents and active consent from students from teachers.

to follow the bureaucratic requirements of her US university. By contrast, Madandar Arani's Iranian university and Kenayathulla's Malaysian university were evidently willing to leave such matters to the discretion of the researcher.

An intermediate position was taken by Mariya's New Zealand university. The Chairperson of the Human Ethics Committee in that university wrote an official letter (placed as an appendix in Mariya 2012, p.242) indicating that the project had been "evaluated by peer review and judged to be low risk". Accordingly, the letter indicated, the procedures were not evaluated by the Human Ethics Committee, and the researcher was permitted to proceed for a period of three years with her own judgement on ways to conduct the research in an ethically responsible manner.

The University of Hong Kong (HKU), by contrast, has more demanding requirements that seem to have been imported from 'Northern' cultures and that arguably, in the words of Robinson-Pant and Singal (2013, p.448), "are no longer just a response to limiting harm" and instead have become a process that "can itself shape what we think of as research". Chapter 8 records that the requirement for student approval led to variations in response rates to the questionnaire that would not have arisen had the Hong Kong researchers been permitted simply to administer the questionnaires in the ways that the Georgian researchers did (Chapter 1). Even more problematic were the experiences of the researchers in India and Cambodia who were governed by the requirements of HKU.

The experiences in India recounted by Maheshwari (Chapter 9) included the refusal of one principal to participate when he saw the passive consent letter for parents. Maheshwari did not elaborate on the reasons for the principal's reaction, but they may have been related not only to the labour required for such distribution but also to the relationships that the principal felt that he desired between the parents and his school. Official-looking forms may be intimidating to parents, particularly ones who have received little education and may even be illiterate, and in this respect parents in such locations as West Bengal may respond very differently from parents in Hong Kong, North America or Western Europe.

Similar reactions were encountered in Cambodia, where official forms are widely seen as intimidating. The experiences recounted in Chapter 11 echo the remarks of Robinson-Pant and Singal (2013), noting that respondents' unwillingness to sign consent forms can arise from fear of the unknown and fear of deceit and that in Pakistan, for example, a spoken promise may carry more weight than written consent (Qureshi 2010, p.86 cited by Robinson-Pant & Singal 2013, p.446). Illiteracy remains high in Cambodia, and cultures may respect individuals more than forms.

Going further, doubts may arise on the meaning of the consent even when it has been granted. Thus the Interview Consent form required by the University of Denver for Stewart's work in Jamaica consisted of a page and a half of single-spaced and uninviting text (Stewart 2013, pp.313-314). One paragraph stated that:

> Your responses will be identified by code number only and will be kept separately from information that could identify you. This is done to protect the confidentiality of your responses. Only the researcher will have access to your individual data and any reports generated as a result of this study will use only group averages and paraphrased wording. However, should any information contained in this study be the subject of a court order or lawful subpoena, the University of Denver might not be able to avoid compliance with the order or subpoena. Although no questions in this interview address it, we are required by law to tell you that if information is revealed concerning suicide, homicide, or child abuse and neglect, it is required by law that this be reported to the proper authorities. Lastly, while every effort will be made to keep responses confidential, they are not anonymous.

From this and other parts of the form, one might suspect that the procedure aimed more to protect the university than to protect the interviewee.

Since these matters are to some extent generic, i.e. not specific to research on private supplementary tutoring, they perhaps do not need further exploration here. Nevertheless, it is pertinent to stress that research traditions and requirements vary across cultures, and that bureaucratic procedures that may seem reasonable for the home societies in which universities are located may not always be optimal for other societies in which researchers from those universities collect data.

At the same time, the converse may apply. With reference to the research by the Ministry of Education in the Republic of Georgia reported in Chapter 1, Kobakhidze observed that sample consent forms had been made available by the IEA and were used in other countries. She felt that they should have been used in Georgia, and remarked that the lack of national regulations "is not an excuse for an international organisation to forego ethical requirements". The Georgian authorities should perhaps be encouraged to review their own procedures to ensure integrity regardless of the guidelines or requirements of the wider sponsoring body.

These points suggest that both requiring multiple clearance procedures (e.g. in Jamaica, Hong Kong and Cambodia) and the absence of ethical clearance procedures (Georgia) may raise concerns about fairness and integrity. These ethical issues also relate to matters of validity and reliability in research (Merriam 2009). As shown in this book, ethical and methodological issues overlap. Further attention is needed to ways in which ethical approval procedures can provide adequate protection to participants while not obstructing research processes. Allied to this are processes of reflexivity which relate to what Guillemin and Gillam (2004, p.261) described as "ethics in practice" in contrast to mere procedural ethics in which completion of the forms required by institutions is viewed as "a formality, a hurdle to surmount to get on and do the research". Matters may be as complex in the domain of private supplementary tutoring as in other domains.

Conclusion

Private supplementary tutoring has become a multifaceted phenomenon across the globe with far-reaching implications for the lives of students and their families and for the shape of whole societies. A major feature of the 20th century was the spread and globalisation of mass formal education. Wiseman (2013, p.xi) has suggested that during the 21st century the expansion and institutionalization of supplementary education promise "to usurp mass education" in this position. At the same time, Wiseman rightly noted that supplementary education remains "among the least understood" education phenomena. The database has expanded, but major gaps are evident in both knowledge and understanding. Some of these gaps are geographic, i.e. in countries and parts of countries where little or no research has been conducted. Other gaps are in specific themes, e.g. on the curricula in private supplementary tutoring for particular subjects, age groups and social groups. Yet other gaps are in understanding of the relationships between regular schooling and the supplementary tutoring.

UNESCO (2015) has published a sequel to its 1996 Delors Report which proposed four pillars for education, namely: learning to know, learning to do, learning to be, and learning to live together (Delors 1996). The sequel, entitled *Rethinking Education: Towards a Global Common Good?*, includes focus on private supplementary tutoring in conjunction with a chapter entitled 'Education Policy-Making in a Complex World' (UNESCO 2015, p.74). Certainly the expansion and global spread of the phenomenon has introduced new complexities for policy-makers, practitioners and families. These complexities need much careful analysis resulting not only from expanded volume of research but also from improved quality.

To assist in developing tools for this work, the present book has presented experiences and insights from a range of locations and cultures. Many of the tools and approaches resemble those in other parts of the field of educational studies and indeed the social sciences more broadly. Nevertheless, clusters of factors deserve particular attention when researching private supplementary tutoring and especially when conducting research across cultures. They include definitions of the topic and approaches to data collection and interpretation.

Governments have been slow to assess the scale and implications of private supplementary tutoring, in part because they commonly consider it beyond their remit and zone of control. They may also prefer to downplay the phenomenon on the grounds that the existence of shadow education could be considered in some respects a critique of the regular schools for which they are responsible.

Nevertheless, governments are beginning to take the phenomenon more seriously, influenced to some extent by international agencies. One of the editors of this book has played a role in this matter. For example the lead document for the 2015 triennial Conference of Commonwealth Education Ministers (CCEM), which focused on quality education for equitable development, included shadow education among the 'report cards' for the 53 Commonwealth countries, highlighting data gaps as well as data availability (Menefee & Bray 2015). Related works have been published by UNESCO (e.g. Bray 2009; Bray & Kwo 2014), the European Union (e.g. Bray 2011), and the Asian Development Bank (e.g. Bray & Lykins 2012). Other contributions have been made by the Open Society Foundations, including through the book edited by Jokić (2013) and the website of the Privatization of Education Research Initiative (PERI).

Similar remarks about the slow start in attention but the gathering speed apply to the academic world. Faculties of Education in universities have commonly considered their main responsibilities to be training of teachers and other professionals for mainstream schooling, and have tended to ignore the parallel sector. Shadow education may also be difficult to research because the actors involved may be unwilling to expose their roles in arrangements that might be viewed with some suspicion and disapproval. Nevertheless, academic research on the theme has gathered speed This is reflected not only theses, articles and books but also in special issues of journals including the *Asia Pacific Education Review* (Vol.11, No.1, 2010), the *Journal for Educational Research Online* (Vol.6, No.1, 2014) and the *Asia Pacific Journal of Education* (Vol. 34, No.4, 2014).

The University of Hong Kong has taken a lead in the field not only through the work of its own professoriate and students but also through various partnerships. As explained in the Introduction, the origins of this book lay in a 2014 Colloquium hosted by HKU's Comparative Education Research Centre (CERC) with funding from the Prestigious Fellowship Scheme of the Humanities and Social Sciences Panel (HSSP) of Hong Kong's Research Grants Council (RGC). This book showcases the work of some of the PhD and Master's students, and others include Yip (2014), Zhoulin Zhang (2014), Ahmadova (2015) and Brehm (2015). New generations are following, and CERC is glad both to host visitors working on the theme and to organise panels at international conferences.

This book should be viewed as a step on the road for greater volume and improved quality of research on the topic. The authors have reflected on the many and varied methodological issues that arose in their research and have discussed ways in which they have tackled themes at various stages. The book shows that sharing of ways to undertake research and overcome barriers is essential in shadow education as in all other specialisations.

References

Addi-Raccah, Audrey & Dana, Oshra (2015): 'Private Tutoring Intensity in Schools: A Comparison between High and Low Socio-Economic Schools'. *International Studies in Sociology of Education.* DOI 10.1080/09620214.2015.1069719.

Ahmadova, Mehpara (2015): *Regulating Private Tutoring in Azerbaijan: Challenges and Possible Responses.* MEd dissertation, The University of Hong Kong.

Bray, Mark (2009): *Confronting the Shadow Education System: What Government Policies for What Private Tutoring?*. Paris: UNESCO International Institute for Educational Planning (IIEP).

Bray, Mark (2011): *The Challenge of Shadow Education: Private Tutoring and its Implications for Policy Makers in the European Union*. Brussels: European Commission.

Bray, Mark & Kobakhidze, Magda Nutsa (2014): 'Measurement Issues in Research on Shadow Education: Challenges and Pitfalls Encountered in TIMSS and PISA'. *Comparative Education Review*, Vol.58, No.4, pp.590-620.

Bray, Mark & Kwo, Ora (2014): *Regulating Private Tutoring for Public Good: Policy Options for Supplementary Education in Asia*. Hong Kong: Comparative Education Research Centre, The University of Hong Kong, and Bangkok: UNESCO, 98pp.

Bray, Mark & Lykins, Chad (2012): *Shadow Education: Private Supplementary Tutoring and Its Implications for Policy Makers in Asia*. Hong Kong: Comparative Education Research Centre, The University of Hong Kong, and Mandaluyong City: Asian Development Bank.

Brehm, William (2015): *Enacting Educational Spaces: A Landscape Portrait of Privatization in Cambodia*. PhD thesis, The University of Hong Kong.

Chan, Claudia & Bray, Mark (2014): 'Marketized Private Tutoring as a Supplement to Regular Schooling: Liberal Studies and the Shadow Sector in Hong Kong Secondary Education'. *Journal of Curriculum Studies*, Vol.46, No.3, pp.361-388.

Cohn, Elchanan & Geske, Terry G. (1990): *Economics of Education*. 3rd edition, Oxford: Pergamon Press.

Creswell, John W. (2014): *Research Design: Qualitative, Quantitative, and Mixed Methods Approaches*. 4th edition, Thousand Oaks: Sage.

Dang, Hai-Anh (2007): 'The Determinants and Impact of Private Tutoring Classes in Vietnam'. *Economics of Education Review*, Vol.26, No.6, pp.648-699.

Davis, Jenny (2013): *Educational Legitimation and Parental Aspiration: Private Tutoring in Perth, Western Australia*. PhD thesis, The University of Western Australia.

della Porta, Donatella (2008): 'Comparative Analysis: Case-oriented versus Variable-oriented Research', in della Porta, Donatella & Keating, Michael (eds.), *Approaches and Methodologies in the Social Sciences*. Cambridge: Cambridge University Press, pp.198-222.

della Porta, Donatella & Keating, Michael (eds.) (2008): *Approaches and Methodologies in the Social Sciences*. Cambridge: Cambridge University Press.

Delors, Jacques (Chairman) (1996): *Learning: The Treasure Within*. Paris: UNESCO.

Gorard, Stephen & Taylor, Chris (2004): *Combining Methods in Educational and Social Research*. Maidenhead: Open University Press.

Guill, Karin & Bos, Wilfried (2014): 'Effectiveness of Private Tutoring in Mathematics with Regard to Subjective and Objective Indicators of Academic

Achievement: Evidence from a German Secondary School Sample'. *Journal for Educational Research Online*, Vol.6, No.1, pp.34-67.

Guillemin, Marilys & Gillam, Lynn (2004): 'Ethics, Reflexivity, and "Ethically Important Moments" in Research'. *Qualitative Inquiry*, Vol.10, No.2, pp.261-280.

Gunasekara, P.D.J. (2009): 'A Study of the Attendance Patterns of G.C.E. (A/L) Student at School.' *Sri Lankan Journal of Educational Research*, Vol.11, pp.56-89.

Ha, Tran Thu & Harpham, Trudy (2005): 'Primary Education in Vietnam: Extra Classes and Outcomes'. *International Education Journal*, Vol.6, No.5, pp.626-634.

Holliday, Adrian (2013): 'The Politics of Ethics in Diverse Cultural Settings: Colonising the Centre Stage'. *Compare: A Journal of Compara- tive and International Education*, Vol.43, No.4, pp.537-544.

Jelani, Juliana & Tan, Andrew K.G. (2012): 'Determinants of Participation and Expenditure Patterns of Private Tuition Received by Primary School Students in Penang, Malaysia: An Exploratory Study'. *Asia Pacific Journal of Education*, Vol.32, No.1, pp.19-35.

Johnson, Burke & Christensen, Larry (2012): *Educational Research: Quantitative, Qualitative, and Mixed Approaches*. Los Angeles: Sage.

Johnson, Eric M. (2008). *Out of Control? Patterns of Teacher Corruption in Kyrgyzstan and their Implications for the Study of Street-level Corruption Control*. PhD dissertation, Graduate School of Arts and Sciences, Columbia University.

Jokić, Boris (ed.) (2013): *Emerging from the Shadow: A Comparative Qualitative Exploration of Private Tutoring in Eurasia*. Zagreb: Network of Education Policy Centers.

Kobakhidze, Magda Nutsa (2014): 'Corruption Risks of Private Tutoring: Case of Georgia'. *Asia Pacific Education Review*, Vol.34, No.4, pp.455-475.

Kodakos, Anastassios & Kalavasis, Fragiskos (eds.) (2005): *Shadow Education System: Border Management Models of the School with the Structures of Education Market*. Athens: Diadrasi. [partially in Greek]

Koh, Aaron (2014): 'The "Magic" of Tutorial Centres in Hong Kong: An Analysis of Media Marketing and Pedagogy in a Tutorial Centre'. *International Review of Education*, Vol.60, No.6, pp.803-819.

KOSIS [Korean Statistical Information Service] (2015): 'Private Education Participation Rate by School Level'. http://kosis.kr/eng/statisticsList/statisticsList_01List.jsp?vwcd=MT_ETITLE&parentId=C#SubCont, accessed 30 May 2015.

Lee, Chong Jae & Jang, Hyo-Min (2010): 'The History of Policy Responses to Shadow Education in Korea: Implications for the Next Cycle of Policy Responses', in Lee, Chong Jae; Kim, Seong-yul & Adams, Don (eds.), *Sixty Years of Korean Education*. Seoul: Seoul National University Press, pp.512-545.

Manzon, Maria & Areepattamannil, Shaljan (2014): 'Shadow Educations: Mapping the Global Discourse'. *Asia Pacific Journal of Education*, Vol.34, No.4, pp.389-412.

Mariya, Maryam (2012): *I Don't Learn at School, so I take Tuition: An Ethnographic Study of Classroom Practices and Private Tuition Settings in the Maldives*. PhD

thesis, Massey University.
Menefee, Trey & Bray, Mark (2015): *Education in the Commonwealth: Quality Education for Equitable Development*. Report commissioned for the 19th Conference of Commonwealth Education Ministers, The Bahamas, 22-26 June 2015. London: Commonwealth Secretariat.
Merriam, Sharan B. (2009). *Qualitative Research: A Guide to Design and Implementation*. San Francisco : Jossey-Bass.
Mischo, Christoph & Haag, Ludwig (2002): 'Expansion and Effectiveness of Private Tutoring'. *European Journal of Psychology of Education*, Vol.XVII, No.3, pp.263-273.
Moosa, Dheeba (2013): 'Challenges to Anonymity and Representation in Educational Qualitative Research in a Small Community: A Reflection on my Research Journey'. *Compare: A Journal of Comparative and International Education*, Vol.43, No.4, pp.483-495.
Nazeer, Abdulla (2006): *Teaching Economics at Secondary School Level in the Maldives: A Cooperative Learning Model*. PhD thesis, University of Waikato.
Pallegedara, Asankha (2012): 'Demand for Private Tutoring in a Free Education Country: The Case of Sri Lanka'. *International Journal of Education Economics and Development*, Vol.3, No. 4, pp.375-393.
Paviot, Laura Ciero (2015): *Private Tuition in Kenya and Mauritius: Policies, Practices and Parents' Perceptions Examined from an Ecological Systems Perspective*. EdD thesis, University College London (UCL) Institute of Education.
Robinson-Pant, Anna & Singal, Nidhi (2013): 'Research Ethics in Comparative and International Education: Reflections from Anthropology and Health'. *Compare: A Journal of Comparative and International Education*, Vol.43, No.4, pp.443-463.
Seth, Michael J. (2002): *Education Fever: Society, Politics, and the Pursuit of Schooling in South Korea*. Honolulu: University of Hawai'i Press.
Silova, Iveta; Būdienė, Virginija & Bray, Mark (eds.) (2006): *Education in a Hidden Marketplace: Monitoring of Private Tutoring*. New York: Open Society Institute.
Smith, Linda Tuhiwai (1999): *Decolonizing Methodologies: Research and Indigenous Peoples*. London: Zed Books.
Song, K.O.; Park, H.J. & Sang, K.A. (2013): 'A Cross-national Analysis of the Student- and School-level Factors Affecting the Demand for Private Tutoring'. *Asia Pacific Education Review*, Vol.14, No.2, pp.125-139.
Southgate, Darby E. (2009): *Determinants of Shadow Education: A Cross- national Analysis*. PhD dissertation, The Ohio State University.
Spencer-Rowe, Joan (2000): *An Investigation of the Practice of Extra Lessons in Schools at the Primary Level of the Jamaican Education System: A Report*. Kingston: Planning Institute of Jamaica/Ministry of Education and Culture.
Spindler, George & Spindler, Louise (1982): 'Roger Harker and Schönhausen: From Familiar to Strange and Back Again', in Spindler, George (ed.), *Doing the Ethnography of Schooling: Educational Anthropology in Action*. New York: Holt,

Rinehart & Winston, pp.20-46.
Spivak, Gayatri Chakravorty (1988): 'Can the Subaltern Speak?', in Nelson, Cary & Grossberg, Lawrence (eds.), *Marxism and the Interpretation of Culture*. Basingstoke: Macmillan, pp.271-313.
Stewart, Saran (2013): *Everything in di Dark Muss Come to Light: A Postcolonial Examination of the Practice of Extra Lessons at the Secondary Level in Jamaica's Education System*. PhD Dissertation, University of Denver.
Tuitt, Frank (2003): 'Afterword: Realizing a More Inclusive Pedagogy', in Howell, Annie & Tuitt, Frank (eds.), *Race and Higher Education: Rethinking Pedagogy in Diverse College Classrooms*. Cambridge: Harvard Educational Review Reprint Series, pp.243-268.
UNESCO (2015): *Rethinking Education: Towards a Global Common Good?*. Paris: UNESCO.
Watkins, David A. & Biggs, John B. (eds.) (1996): *The Chinese Learner: Cultural, Psychological, and Contextual Influences*. Hong Kong: Comparative Education Research Centre, The University of Hong Kong, and Melbourne: Australian Council for Educational Research.
Wattar, Dania (2014): *Globalization, Curriculum Reform and Teacher Professional Development in Syria*. PhD thesis, University of Alberta.
White, J. & Fitzgerald, T. (2010): 'Researcher Tales and Research Ethics: The Spaces in which We Find Ourselves'. *International Journal of Research and Method in Education*, Vol.33, No.3, pp.273-285.
Wolcott, H.F. (1994): *Transforming Qualitative Data: Description, Analysis, and Interpretation*. Thousand Oaks: Sage.
Wiseman, Alexander W. (2013): 'Foreword', in Aurini, Janice; Davies, Scott & Dierkes, Julian (eds.), *Out of the Shadows: The Global Intensification of Supplementary Education*. Bingley: Emerald, pp.xi-xiii.
Yip, Kam Yuen William (2014): *Shadow Education in Hong Kong: Typology and Educational Functions of Private Supplementary Tutoring*. MEd dissertation, The University of Hong Kong.
Yu, Hongxia & Ding, Xiaoghao (2011): 'How to Get Out of the Prisoners' Dilemma: Educational Resource Allocation and Private Tutoring'. *Frontiers of Education in China*, Vol.6, No.2, pp.279-292.
Zhang, Yu (2011): *The Determinants of National College Entrance Exam Performance in China – with an Analysis of Private Tutoring*. PhD dissertation, Columbia University.
Zhang, Wei (2013): *Private Supplementary Tutoring Received by Grade 9 Students in Chongqing, China: Determinants of Demand, and Policy Implications*. PhD thesis, The University of Hong Kong.
Zhang, Wei & Bray, Mark (2013): 'Researching Supplementary Education: Plans, Realities, and Lessons from Fieldwork in China', in Aurini, Janice; Davies, Scott & Dierkes, Julian (eds.), *Out of the Shadows: The Global Intensification of Supplementary Education*. Bingley: Emerald, pp.67-94.

Zhang, Zhoulin (2014): *Positioning and Roles of English Tutoring Centers in Hangzhou, China: Perceptions and Strategies of Administrators in Six Enterprises*. MEd dissertation, The University of Hong Kong.

Zhou, Min & Kim, Susan S. (2008): 'Community Forces, Social Capital, and Educational Achievement: The Case of Supplementary Education in the Chinese and Korean Immigrant Communities'. *Harvard Educational Review*, Vol.76, No.1, pp.1-29.

Notes on the Authors

Mark BRAY is UNESCO Chair Professor in Comparative Education and Director of the Comparative Education Research Centre at the University of Hong Kong. He has taught at that University since 1986. Between 2006 and 2010 he took leave to work in Paris as Director of UNESCO's International Institute for Educational Planning (IIEP). He previously taught in secondary schools in Kenya and Nigeria, and at the Universities of Edinburgh, Papua New Guinea and London. *Correspondence*: Comparative Education Research Centre, Faculty of Education, The University of Hong Kong, Pokfulam Road, Hong Kong, China. E-mail: mbray@hku.hk.

Boris JOKIĆ is a Scientific Associate in the Centre for Educational Research and Development at the Institute for Social Research in Zagreb, Croatia. His work on private tutoring includes management of a five-country project funded by the Open Society Foundations and published in 2013 under the title *Emerging from the Shadow: A Comparative Qualitative Exploration of Private Tutoring in Eurasia*. He has also spearheaded major curriculum reform in Croatia. *Correspondence*: Amruševa 11/II 10000 Zagreb, Croatia. E-mail: boris@idi.hr.

Husaina Banu KENAYATHULLA is a Senior Lecturer in the Department of Education Management, Planning & Policy, University of Malaya. She graduated from Indiana University, USA, and her research interests include economics of education, education finance, education policy analysis and comparative & international education. Her research includes econometric analysis on private tutoring in Malaysia. *Correspondence*: Department of Education Management, Planning & Policy, University of Malaya, 50603 Kuala Lumpur, Malaysia. E-mail: husaina@um.edu.my

Magda Nutsa KOBAKHIDZE is a doctoral candidate in the Faculty of Education at the University of Hong Kong. Her research interests include private supplementary tutoring in a cross-national perspective and teacher professionalism. She has extensive working experience with the Ministry of Education of Georgia, international organisations and universities. She holds a Master's degree in international education policy from the International Educational Development Program at Teachers College, Columbia University, USA. *Correspondence*: Comparative Education Research Centre, Faculty of Education, The University of Hong Kong, Pokfulam Road, Hong Kong, China. E-mail: nkobakhidze@gmail.com.

Ora KWO is an associate professor at the University of Hong Kong. She has taught at that University since 1981, and has also undertaken numerous consultancies for UNESCO and other agencies. She has conducted empirical work on shadow education in Hong Kong, and is co-author with Mark Bray of a 2014 book entitled *Regulating Private Tutoring for Public Good: Policy Options for Supplementary Education in Asia*. She has also undertaken analyses of the work of teachers, and is editor of the 2010 book *Teachers as Learners: Critical Discourse on Challenges and Opportunities*. *Correspondence*: Faculty of Education, The University of Hong Kong, Pokfulam Road, Hong Kong, China. E-mail: wykwo@ hku.hk.

LIU Junyan is a PhD student at the University of Hong Kong (HKU) with a special interest in shadow education in China. She graduated with a Bachelor's and Master's degree from Peking University. Before moving to studying in HKU, she worked in the Beijing Academy of Educational Sciences, focusing on studies of education policy and planning in Beijing. *Correspondence*: Comparative Education Research Centre, Faculty of Education, The University of Hong Kong, Pokfulam Road, Hong Kong, China. E-mail: liujy211@hku.hk.

Abbas MADANDAR ARANI is an assistant professor at Lorestan University, Iran. He graduated from Mysore University in India, and has extensive international experience. During 2014/15 he was a post-doctoral fellow in the Comparative Education Research Centre at the University of Hong Kong. He is playing a leadership role in the Comparative Education Society of Iran. *Correspondence*: Department of Education, Lorestan University, Khorammabad, Iran. E-mail: rie2000@gmail.com.

Sulata MAHESHWARI studied at the postgraduate level in education at the University of Hong Kong and in business management at the Indian Institute of Management, Bangalore, India. She worked for international companies in India and Japan before moving to Hong Kong, and now lives in Singapore. *Correspondence*: 02-09, Lobby H,

Pebble Bay, 132 Tanjong Rhu Road, Singapore 436919. E-mail: sulata_maiti@yahoo.com

Maryam MARIYA is a Language and Learning Development Tutor at the University of Waikato, New Zealand. She initially graduated from the University of Canberra, Australia, following which she completed a PhD at Massey University, New Zealand, concentrating on classroom practices and private tuition settings in the Maldives. *Correspondence*: Language and Learning Development Unit, Waikato Management School, University of Waikato, New Zealand. Email: maryam@waikato.ac.nz

Saran STEWART is a Lecturer in Comparative Higher Education in the Faculty of Humanities and Education at the University of the West Indies, Mona Campus. She is also a Research Specialist in the Research and Grants Unit in the School of Education. Dr Stewart earned her PhD in Higher Education at the University of Denver, USA. The focus of her research is on access and equity in education, and on teaching and learning in developing country contexts, utilising postcolonial theories and critical pedagogical frameworks. *Correspondence*: School of Education, Faculty of Humanities and Education, University of the West Indies, Mona Campus, Kingston, Jamaica. E-mail: saran.stewart@uwimona.edu.jm.

Kevin W.H. YUNG teaches English for Academic and Specific Purposes at the Centre for Applied English Studies in the University of Hong Kong. He is researching in the field of English teaching and learning in private supplementary tutoring at the Faculty of Education of the same university. His research interests include shadow education, English learning motivation, autonomy in language learning and learner narratives. *Correspondence*: Centre for Applied English Studies, The University of Hong Kong, Pokfulam Road, Hong Kong, China. E-mail: wyunghku@hku.hk.

ZHANG Yu is an assistant professor of economics and education at the Institute of Education, Tsinghua University. She graduated from Columbia University, USA, and her major research interests include education policy evaluation, education equity, and education innovation. Her research includes empirical analyses of both short and long term effects of private tutoring in K-12 education in China. *Correspondence*: Institute of Education, Tsinghua University, Beijing, China. E-mail: zhangyu2011@tsinghua.edu.cn.

ZHANG Wei is a postdoctoral fellow and Secretary of the Comparative Education Research Centre at the University of Hong Kong. She graduated in Russian at Peking University, following which she studied for an MPhil degree at the University of Oslo and then a PhD at the University of Hong Kong focusing on shadow education in Chongqing, China. She has also worked for UNESCO in Bangkok. *Correspondence*: Comparative Education Research Centre, Faculty of Education, The University of Hong Kong, Pokfulam Road, Hong Kong, China. E-mail: weizh@hku.hk.

CERC Studies in Comparative Education (ctd)

13. Mok Ka-Ho (ed.) (2003): *Centralization and Decentralization: Educational Reforms and Changing Governance in Chinese Societies*. ISBN 978-962-8093-58-8. 230pp. HK$200/US$32.

12. Robert A. LeVine (2003, reprinted 2010): *Childhood Socialization: Comparative Studies of Parenting, Learning and Educational Change*. ISBN 978-962-8093-61-8. 299pp. HK$200/US$32.

11. Ruth Hayhoe & Julia Pan (eds.) (2001): *Knowledge Across Cultures: A Contribution to Dialogue Among Civilizations*. ISBN 978-962-8093-73-1. 391pp. HK$250/US$38. [Out of print]

10. William K. Cummings, Maria Teresa Tatto & John Hawkins (eds.) (2001): *Values Education for Dynamic Societies: Individualism or Collectivism*. ISBN 978-962-8093-71-7. 312pp. HK$200/US$32.

9. Gu Mingyuan (2001): *Education in China and Abroad: Perspectives from a Lifetime in Comparative Education*. ISBN 978-962-8093-70-0. 260pp. HK$200/US$32.

8. Thomas Clayton (2000): *Education and the Politics of Language: Hegemony and Pragmatism in Cambodia, 1979-1989*. ISBN 978-962-8093-83-0. 243pp. HK$200/US$32.

7. Mark Bray & Ramsey Koo (eds.) (2004): *Education and Society in Hong Kong and Macao: Comparative Perspectives on Continuity and Change*. Second edition. ISBN 978-962-8093-34-2. 323pp. HK$200/US$32.

6. T. Neville Postlethwaite (1999): *International Studies of Educational Achievement: Methodological Issues*. ISBN 978-962-8093-86-1. 86pp. HK$100/US$20.

5. Harold Noah & Max A. Eckstein (1998): *Doing Comparative Education: Three Decades of Collaboration*. ISBN 978-962-8093-87-8. 356pp. HK$250/US$38.

4. Zhang Weiyuan (1998): *Young People and Careers: A Comparative Study of Careers Guidance in Hong Kong, Shanghai and Edinburgh*. ISBN 978-962-8093-89-2. 160pp. HK$180/US$30.

3. Philip G. Altbach (1998): *Comparative Higher Education: Knowledge, the University, and Development*. ISBN 978-962-8093-88-5. 312pp. HK$180/US$30.

2. Mark Bray & W.O. Lee (eds.) (1997): *Education and Political Transition: Implications of Hong Kong's Change of Sovereignty*. ISBN 978-962-8093-90-8. 169pp. [Out of print]

1. Mark Bray & W.O. Lee (eds.) (2001): *Education and Political Transition: Themes and Experiences in East Asia*. Second edition. ISBN 978-962-8093-84-7. 228pp. HK$200/US$32.

CERC Monograph Series in Comparative and International Education and Development

12. Raymond E. Wanner (2015): *UNESCO's Origins, Achievements, Problems and Promises: An Inside/Outside Perspectives from the US*. ISBN 978-988-14241-2-9. 84pp. HK$100/US$16.

11. Maria Manson (ed.) (2015): *Changing Times, Changing Territories: Reflections on CERC and the field of Comparative Education*. ISBN 978-988-17852-0-6. 105pp. HK$100/US$16.

10. Mark Bray & Ora Kwo (2014): *Regulating Private Tutoring for Public Good: Policy Options for Supplementary Education in Asia*. ISBN 978-988-17852-9-9. 93pp. HK$100/US$16. [Also available in Chinese]

9. Mark Bray & Chad Lykins (2012): *Shadow Education: Private Supplementary Tutoring and Its Implications for Policy Makers in Asia*. ISBN 978-92-9092-658-0. (Print). ISBN 978-92-9092-659-7. (PDF). 100pp. HK$100/US$16.

8. Nirmala Rao & Jin Sun (2010): *Early Childhood Care and Education in the Asia Pacific Region: Moving Towards Goal 1*. ISBN 978-988-17852-5-1. 97pp. HK$100/US$16.

7. Nina Ye. Borevskaya, V.P. Borisenkov & Xiaoman Zhu (eds.) (2010): *Educational Reforms in Russia and China at the Turn of the 21st Century: A Comparative Analysis*. ISBN 978-988-17852-4-4. 115pp. HK$100/US$16.

6. Eduardo Andere (2008): *The Lending Power of PISA: League Tables and Best Practice in International Education*. ISBN 978-988-17852-1-3. 138pp. HK$100/US$16.

5. Linda Chisholm, Graeme Bloch & Brahm Fleisch (eds.) (2008): *Education, Growth, Aid and Development: Towards Education for All*. ISBN 978-962-8093-99-1. 116pp. HK$100/US$16.

4. Mark Bray & Seng Bunly (2005): *Balancing the Books: Household Financing of Basic Education in Cambodia*. ISBN 978-962-8093-39-7. 113pp. HK$100/US$16.

3. Maria Manzon (2004): *Building Alliances: Schools, Parents and Communities in Hong Kong and Singapore*. ISBN 978-962-8093-36-6. 117pp. HK$100/US$16.

2. Mark Bray, Ding Xiaohao & Huang Ping (2004): *Reducing the Burden on the Poor: Household Costs of Basic Education in Gansu, China*. ISBN 978-962-8093-32-8. 67pp. HK$50/US$10. [Also available in Chinese]

1. Yoko Yamato (2003): *Education in the Market Place: Hong Kong's International Schools and their Mode of Operation*. ISBN 978-962-8093-57-1. 117pp. HK$100/US$16.

Order through bookstores or from:

Comparative Education Research Centre
Faculty of Education,
The University of Hong Kong
Pokfulam Road. Hong Kong, China.

Fax: (852) 3917 4737
E-mail: cerc@hku.hk
Website: http://cerc.edu.hku.hk

The list prices above are applicable for order from CERC, and include sea mail postage. For air mail postage, please add US$10 for 1 copy, US$18 for 2-3 copies, US$40 for 4-8 copies. For more than 8 copies, please contact us direct. For titles of CERC/Springer Series No.24 and 30, air mail postage is US$15 per copy.

CERC Studies in Comparative Education 19

Comparative Education Research *second edition*
Approaches and Methods

Edited by
Mark Bray, Bob Adamson and Mark Mason

Publishers:
Comparative Education Research Centre and Springer
ISBN 978-988-17852-8-2
2014; 453 pages
HKD250/USD38

Approaches and methods in comparative education are of obvious importance, but do not always receive adequate attention. This second edition of a well-received book, containing thoroughly updated and additional material, contributes new insights within the long-standing traditions of the field.

A particular feature is the focus on different units of analysis. Individual chapters compare places, systems, times, cultures, values, policies, curricula and other units. These chapters are contextualised within broader analytical frameworks which identify the purposes and strengths of the field. The book includes a focus on intra-national as well as cross-national comparisons, and highlights the value of approaching themes from different angles. As already demonstrated by the first edition of the book, the work will be of great value not only to producers of comparative education re-search but also to users who wish to understand more thoroughly the parameters and value of the field.

The editors: Mark Bray is UNESCO Chair Professor of Comparative Education at the University of Hong Kong. Bob Adamson is Professor and Head of the Department of International Education and Lifelong Learning at the Hong Kong Institute of Education; and Mark Mason is Professor at the Hong Kong Institute of Education and a Senior Programme Specialist at the UNESCO International Bureau of Education (IBE) in Geneva.

This book is also available in Chinese, Farsi, French, Italian, Japanese, Portuguese, Russian and Spanish.
Website: http://cerc.edu.hku.hk

CERC Studies in Comparative Education 29

Comparative Education: The Construction of a Field

Maria Manzon

Publishers: Comparative Education Research Centre and Springer

ISBN 978-988-17852-6-8
2011; 295 pages
Price: HK$200 / US$32

This book is a remarkable feat of scholarship — so remarkable in fact that I put it in the same league as the great classics of the field that had so much to do with setting the direction of Comparative Education. Indeed, this volume goes further than earlier classics to reveal, through textual analysis and interviews with key figures, how the epistemological foundations of the field and crucial professional developments combined to, as the title indicates, construct Comparative Education.

Manzon's work is indispensable — a word I do not use lightly — for scholars who seek a genuine grasp of the field: how it was formed and by whom, its major theoreticians, its professional foundations, and so on. Clearly too, this book marks the rise of a young star, Maria Manzon, who shows promise of joining the ranks of our field's most illustrious thinkers.

Erwin H. Epstein
Director, Center for Comparative Education
Loyola University, Chicago, USA

Maria Manzon is a Research Associate of the Comparative Education Research Centre (CERC) at the University of Hong Kong. She was Editor of CIEclopedia in 2009 and 2010, and Assistant Secretary General of the World Council of Comparative Education Societies (WCCES) in 2005.

More details:
http://cerc.edu.hku.hk/product/comparative-education-the-construction-of-a-field/

CERC Monograph Series in Comparative and International Education and Development No.9

Shadow Education:
Private Supplementary Tutoring and Its Implications for Policy Makers in Asia

Mark Bray and Chad Lykins

Publishers:
Comparative Education Research Centre (CERC) in collaboration with Asian Development Bank (ADB)

ISBN 978-92-9092-658-0 (Print)
ISBN 978-92-9092-659-7 (PDF)
2012; 100 pages
This book is downloadable for free

In all parts of Asia, households devote considerable expenditures to private supplementary tutoring. This tutoring may contribute to students' achievement, but it also maintains and exacerbates social inequalities, diverts resources from other uses, and can contribute to inefficiencies in education systems.

Such tutoring is widely called shadow education, because it mimics school systems. As the curriculum in the school system changes, so does the shadow.

This study documents the scale and nature of shadow education in different parts of the region. For many decades, shadow education has been a major phenomenon in East Asia. Now it has spread throughout the region, and it has far-reaching economic and social implications.

This book is also available in Chinese, Russian and Vietnamese.

Website: http://cerc.edu.hku.hk

CERC Monograph Series in Comparative and International Education and Development No.10

Regulating Private Tutoring for Public Good
Policy Options for Supplementary Education in Asia

Mark Bray and Ora Kwo

Publishers:
Comparative Education Research Centre (CERC) in collaboration with United Nations Educational, Scientific and Cultural Organization (UNESCO)

ISBN 978-988-17852-9-9
2014; 93 pages
US$16/HK$100

Recent years have brought global expansion of private supplementary tutoring alongside regular school systems. This expansion has far-reaching implications for the nurturing of new generations, for social and economic development, and for the operation of school systems. Some dimensions are positive while other dimensions are problematic.

Supplementary tutoring is especially visible in Asia. The formats of tutoring range from one-to-one provision to large classes. Some tutoring is provided by teachers and by specialist companies, while other tutoring is provided informally by university students and others.

Using a comparative lens, this book examines possible government responses to the expansion of private supplementary tutoring. In general, the book suggests, the sector should be given more attention. The work shows wide diversity in the regulations introduced by governments in the Asian region. It notes not only that these governments can learn much from each other, but also that policy makers in other parts of the world can usefully look at patterns in Asia. The book also stresses the value of partnerships between governments, tutoring providers, schools, teachers' unions, and other bodies.

Mark BRAY is UNESCO Chair Professor in Comparative Education at the University of Hong Kong, and is a former Director of UNESCO's International Institute for Educational Planning.

Ora KWO is an Associate Professor and a member of the Comparative Education Research Centre in the Faculty of Education at the University of Hong Kong.

This book is also available in Chinese and Korean.
Website: http://cerc.edu.hku.hk